Vladimir Nabokov's *Lolita*

A CASEBOOK

CASEBOOKS IN CRITICISM

General Editor, William L. Andrews

Gabriel García Márquez's
*One Hundred Years of Solitude*: A Casebook
edited by Gene H. Bell-Villada

Leslie Marmon Silko's
*Ceremony*: A Casebook
edited by Allan Chavkin

Ernest Hemingway's
*The Sun Also Rises*: A Casebook
edited by Linda Wagner-Martin

# VLADIMIR NABOKOV'S

## *Lolita*

◆  ◆  ◆

## A CASEBOOK

Edited by
Ellen Pifer

**OXFORD**
UNIVERSITY PRESS

2003

# OXFORD
## UNIVERSITY PRESS

Oxford   New York

Auckland   Bangkok   Buenos Aires   Cape Town   Chennai
Dar es Salaam   Delhi   Hong Kong   Istanbul   Karachi   Kolkata
Kuala Lumpur   Madrid   Melbourne   Mexico City   Mumbai   Nairobi
São Paulo   Shanghai   Taipei   Tokyo   Toronto

Copyright © 2003 by Oxford University Press, Inc.

Published by Oxford University Press, Inc.
198 Madison Avenue, New York, New York 10016

www.oup.com

Oxford is a registered trademark of Oxford University Press

Library of Congress Cataloging-in-Publication Data
Vladimir Nabokov's Lolita : a casebook / edited by Ellen Pifer.
p. cm. — (Casebooks in criticism)
Includes bibliographical references.
ISBN 0-19-515032-5; 0-19-515033-3 (pbk.)
1. Nabokov, Vladimir Vladimirovich, 1899–1977. Lolita.   I. Pifer, Ellen.   II. Series.
PS3527.A15 L638   2003
813'.54—dc21        2002066796

1  3  5  7  9  8  6  4  2

Printed in the United States of America
on acid-free paper

# Credits

*or Doll: Images of the Child in Contemporary Writing and Culture* (Charlottesville: University Press of Virginia, 2000), 65–88, 245–48. Reprinted with permission of the University Press of Virginia.

Jenefer Shute, "'So Nakedly Dressed': The Text of the Female Body in Nabokov's Novels," *Amerikastudien/American Studies* 30, no. 4 (1985): 537–45. Copyright Jenefer Shute. Reprinted by permission of the author.

Susan Elizabeth Sweeney, "'Ballet Attitudes': Nabokov's *Lolita* and Petipa's *The Sleeping Beauty*," in *Nabokov at the Limits: Redrawing the Critical Boundaries,* ed. Lisa Zunshine (New York: Garland, 1999), 111–26. Copyright 1999 Lisa Zunshine. Reprinted by permission of Routledge, Inc., part of the Taylor and Francis Group.

Nomi Tamir-Ghez, "The Art of Persuasion in Nabokov's *Lolita*," *Poetics Today* 1, no. 1 (1979): 65–83. Copyright 1979, Porter Institute for Poetics and Semiotics. All rights reserved. Reprinted by permission of Duke University Press.

Michael Wood, "Revisiting *Lolita*," *New York Review of Books*, 26 Mar. 1998, 9–13. Copyright 1998 NYREV, Inc. Reprinted with permission from *New York Review of Books*.

# Contents

Vladimir Nabokov's *Lolita*

A CASEBOOK

# Introduction

ELLEN PIFER

✦   ✦   ✦

MIDWAY THROUGH THE TWENTIETH CENTURY, *Lolita* burst on the literary scene, a Russian exile's extraordinary gift to American letters and the New World. Before Vladimir Nabokov's adopted country could accept that gift, however, his novel was rejected by five American publishers. Those not put off by the novel's stylistic complexity were convinced that its scandalous subject—the sexual passion of a middle-aged European for a twelve-year-old American girl—would undoubtedly lead to prosecution on charges of obscenity (see Boyd, *American Years,* 264). *Lolita*'s inauspicious debut thus took place in Paris, where it appeared in 1955 under the imprint of the Olympia Press, known for the frank sexual content of its publications. As Andrew Field ironically observes, *Lolita* was "probably the most chaste book ever printed by Olympia," whose list sported such titles as *White Thighs* and *The Sexual Life of Robinson Crusoe* (Field 336). The prominent British novelist Graham Greene first drew public attention to *Lolita*'s artistic merit by naming it, in the London *Sunday Times,* one of the best books of 1955 (Clegg 8). Almost immediately, Nabokov's third novel in English became the focus of debate, both literary and legal. The controversy concerning *Lolita*'s status as art or pornography soon caught the attention of American critics and writers, many of whom read the book and championed its cause in this country. Not until 1958, however, did Nabokov's "poor little girl," as he liked to put it, officially cross the Atlantic and appear between the covers of the novel's first American edition (Nabokov, *Strong Opinions,* 94).

While the scandal and controversy sparked by *Lolita*'s provocative subject has never fully abated, the critical acclaim it received during the 1960s and 1970s served to dampen, if not quell, the outrage expressed by some readers (and nonreaders) of the novel. By 1970, a mere dozen years after its American debut, Alfred Appel, Jr., published a hefty scholarly edition, *The Annotated Lolita,* adding to the novel's three hundred pages of text nearly as many pages of scholarly notes and commentary. Something of a landmark in publishing history, Appel's "is the first annotated edition of a modern novel to be published in the lifetime of its author" (Clegg 66). As the popularity of this annotated edition, revised and updated in 1991, suggests, *Lolita*'s current readers are more likely to be interested in good books than in reading matter secreted between plain covers. Certainly most scholars and critics today would join Appel in lauding the achievement of the Russian-born émigré who in *Lolita* "re-created America so brilliantly" and in the process became "an American writer" (Appel, *Annotated Lolita,* xl). Even now, nearly a half century after the novel's publication, *Lolita*'s rapid ascent from suspect immigrant to respectable classic seems charged with the magic of a dream—the American dream—come true. For Nabokov, who had spent most of his adult life trying to balance the exigencies of a writing career with those of earning a living, *Lolita*'s success was liberating. Having taught literature first at Wellesley College and then at Cornell University, he was finally free to devote himself full time to writing.

Born in 1899 into a privileged world of landed wealth and social prominence, Nabokov was forced, like so many other Russians of his class and culture, to flee the Bolshevik Revolution, which stripped his family of its property and wealth. After graduating from Cambridge University in England, the aspiring writer took up residence in the Russian émigré community of Berlin, later moving briefly to Paris, and supplemented his meager earnings as a writer by giving tennis and English lessons. By the time that a new set of political crises was about to dismantle Europe's émigré communities—and much else on the Continent—Nabokov had published nine novels in Russian and established his reputation among émigré readers, critics, and literary scholars as the leading writer of his generation. By the late 1930s, as Europe was preparing for war and the prospect of a return to his native Russia had disappeared, Nabokov realized that he and his Jewish wife, Véra, and their six-year-old son, Dmitri, would have to flee Europe. Fluent in English and French since childhood, he made the decision—"one of the most difficult he had ever made"—to become an English writer (Boyd, *Russian Years,* 494–95). In December 1938, he began work on his first English novel, *The Real Life of Sebastian Knight.* In the spring of 1940, as Hitler's armies advanced into Holland, Belgium, and France, the Nabokovs boarded a ship chartered for refugees and sailed from St. Nazaire, Brittany, to New York harbor. Twenty years later, as a result of the fame and financial independence that *Lolita* unexpectedly brought him, Nabokov, by now the author of a dozen books in English, resigned his professorship at Cornell and moved back to Europe with his wife. The couple settled in Montreux, Switzerland, where Nabokov's prolific career as a novelist—and his half-century-long marriage to Véra—was interrupted only by his death in 1977.

Another lifetime pursuit of Nabokov's, the study of lepidoptera, has only recently received full attention, as evidence of his pioneering contributions to the field—particularly his discoveries relating to a group of butterflies known as "Blues"—has been substantiated. From 1941 to 1948, his demanding schedule notwithstanding, Nabokov managed to find time, sometimes "as much as fourteen hours a day," to conduct research at Harvard's Museum of Comparative Zoology, where he held a part-time fellowship. As Kurt Johnson and Steve Coates point out in their highly informative book, *Nabokov's Blues: The Scientific Odyssey of a Literary Genius,* even after *Lolita* made Nabokov "an international superstar of literature, he ranked lepidoptery as one of his three professions, along with teaching and literature." He came, moreover, "to regard himself as a sort of public ambassador of lepidoptery" and endeavored to gain wider public appreciation for this branch of scientific study (8–9, 6–7). The relationship between Nabokov's two lifelong passions—literature and lepidoptery—should be approached cautiously, however. Developing an analogy between Humbert's pursuit of Lolita and Nabokov's hunt "for the female of *Lycaeides sublivens,*" one critic drew these comments from the novelist: "[Diana Butler's] essay might have been amusing had she known something about Lepidoptera. Alas, she revealed complete ignorance and the muddle of terms she employed proved to be only jarring and absurd" (cited in Johnson and Coates 298). As Dieter Zimmer notes in the privately published and exquisitely illustrated *Guide to Nabokov's Butterflies and Moths,* Nabokov was still more outspoken in a letter he wrote to Page Stegner on 14 October 1966: "Mrs. Butler's article is pretentious nonsense from beginning to end." By equating, in Zimmer's words, "Humbert Humbert's passion for nymphets with Nabokov's passion for butterflies, and Lolita with what Butler wrongly assumed to be 'the most important butterfly of Nabokov's life,'" the critic proved both philosophically and scientifically naive (Zimmer 374). Unlike Nabokov, moreover, Humbert is "notoriously ignorant and dismissive of nature. He can't distinguish a butterfly from a moth, or a hawkmoth from a hummingbird" (Johnson and Coates 310). The most important influence that Nabokov's interest in butterflies had on the novel's composition springs not from any alleged identification between the author and his protagonist but from the cross-country trips that Nabokov and his wife took during the summer months to collect butterfly specimens. As they traveled from one promising site to another, Véra would take charge of the driving as Vladimir jotted down notes and observations on the people and places they encountered. Familiarity with the motels, restaurants, gas stations, and other roadside attractions of America's highways and byways proved indispensable to the author of *Lolita*, as did the series of local bus rides he took to record teenage jargon and "schoolgirl slang" (Boyd, *American Years*, 211). As Nabokov puts it in his afterword to *Lolita*, "It had taken me some forty years to invent Russia and Western Europe, and now I was faced with the task of inventing America" (*Lolita* 312).

Although Nabokov spent the last two decades of his life in Europe, he did not relinquish his U.S. citizenship or his claim to being an American writer. As he told an interviewer in 1964:

> I came to America in 1940 and decided to become an American citizen, and make America my home. It so happened that I was immediately exposed to the very best in America, to its rich intellectual life and to its easygoing, good-natured atmosphere. I immersed myself in its great libraries and its Grand Canyon. I worked in the laboratories of zoological museums. I acquired more friends than I ever had in Europe. My books—old books and some new ones—found some admirable readers. I became stout as Cortez—mainly because I quit smoking and started to munch molasses candy instead, with the result that my weight went up from my usual 140 to a monumental and cheerful 200. In consequence, I am one-third American—good American flesh keeping me warm and safe. (Nabokov, *Strong Opinions*, 26–27)

Nabokov's pride in having transformed himself into an American writer helps to explain the indignation he felt when some readers, shifting their attention from the sexual to the satiric elements of *Lolita*—the fun it makes of American manners, mores, and materialism—concluded that the novel was "anti-American." Their assumption that Nabokov set out to ridicule the nation that had welcomed him to its shores proved even more offensive to the author than the charge of obscenity. The charge that "*Lolita* is anti-American," Nabokov states in the afterword to his novel, "pains me considerably more than the idiotic accusation of immorality." He continues, "Nothing is more exhilarating than philistine vulgarity," but no nation, culture, or class has a monopoly on that. Any "proletarian from Chicago," Nabokov says with a flourish, "can be as bourgeois (in the Flaubertian sense) as a duke." In *Lolita,* "I chose [to depict] American motels instead of Swiss hotels or English inns only because I am trying to be an American writer and claim only the same rights that other American writers enjoy. On the other hand, my creature Humbert is a foreigner and an anarchist, and there are many things, besides nymphets, in which I disagree with him" (*Lolita* 315). That Nabokov sought to distance himself from Humbert's sexual proclivities is hardly surprising. More noteworthy is the way that he delays this point until the end of his statement, as though it were of secondary importance, a mere afterthought to his main concern: to emphasize to readers that he—unlike Humbert, a "foreigner" and "anarchist"—is a patriotic American.

If pride in his acquired identity as an American was more than a pose on Nabokov's part, why did he leave the United States as soon as he was financially able? Part of the reason, as he himself explained, was his and Véra's desire to live closer to their son, Dmitri, who at the time was studying and performing opera in Europe. But Nabokov also offered his readers another, more provocative explanation. From his perch overlooking Lake Geneva, he said, "I think I am trying to develop, in this rosy exile, the same fertile nostalgia in regard to America, my new country, as I evolved for Russia, my old one, in the first post-revolution years of West-European expatriation" (*Strong Opinions* 49). Here Nabokov suggests that, for him, exile had become a fertile condition, cultivated for his own artistic purposes. As he told an interviewer in 1971, even as a boy "during trips with my family to Western Europe, I imagined in bedtime reveries what it would be like to become an exile who longed for a remote, sad, and . . . unquenchable Russia" (*Strong Opinions* 178). In his autobiography he similarly states, "homesickness has been with me a sensuous and particular matter" (*Speak, Memory* 250).

Displacement from familiar surroundings and estrangement from habit proved liberating for Nabokov, fueling the intensity of awareness necessary for artistic perception and creation. To be homesick means, among other things, to be aware of existing at a remove from one's origins, from that elusive "reality" that one's imagination and memory strive to possess. "You can get nearer and nearer . . . to reality," he said, "but you never get near enough because reality is an infinite succession of steps, levels of perception, false bottoms, and hence unquenchable, unattainable. You can know more and more about one thing but you can never know everything about one thing" (*Strong Opinions* 11). To exist at an extreme remove from one's home or origins is what the exile literally experiences, but it is also the quintessential condition of human consciousness. Each of us lives estranged from the mysterious origins of existence; we may struggle to know or comprehend ultimate "reality," but we can never, metaphysically speaking, arrive home. As Van Veen says in Nabokov's *Ada,* we are all "visitors and investigators in a strange universe, indeed, indeed" (107). Van's words take on added suggestiveness when we consider the presence of an otherworld in Nabokov's fiction, to which his widow drew attention in 1979. In her introduction to a volume of her husband's Russian poems, Véra Nabokov announced the "principal theme" of Nabokov's work to be the "hereafter"; since then, a number of critics have traced the influence of this "otherworld" on the lives of his characters (Véra Nabokov 3; see also Alexandrov; Boyd, *Pale Fire*; Pifer). If Nabokov's own characters tend to miss, or misconstrue, the influence of otherworldly ghosts or shades on their existence, it is hardly surprising. Unlike the ghosts peopling the landscapes of fairy tales or horror stories, Nabokov's shades do not participate directly in the world of the living. Their influence is always oblique; creating sudden shifts in the atmosphere, they encode phenomena with cryptic signs and messages. In Nabokov's late novel *Transparent Things,* for example, the voice of dead Mr. R. describes the way in which he and the novel's other shades tend to operate: "Direct interference in a person's life," he says, "does not enter our scope of activity, nor, on the other . . . hand, is [that person's] destiny a chain of predeterminate links. . . . The most we can do . . . is to act as a breath of wind and to apply the lightest, the most indirect pressure" (141–42).

Whether or not readers are prepared to acknowledge such intimations of immortality in Nabokov's universe, most will discern in his account of deceptive "reality"—as an infinite succession of steps, grades, and levels of perception—an apt description of his fictional landscapes. As we embark on a reading of *Lolita,* for example, we encounter layer after tantalizing layer of images, shapes and grades of associations and connections that create alluring patterns of meaning and significance. As we strive to get to the bottom of things, however, we are likely to find that what seemed like firm ground becomes, in Nabokov's phrase, one more "false bottom," a trap door that springs open to reveal yet another quandary, a further conundrum. In this sense, all the self-conscious devices in the author's cunningly wrought fiction, all the puns and parodies, allusions and alliterations that declare the novel's status as a work of art, faithfully reflect his vision of reality. In Nabokov's view, the world we perceive and call "reality" is known to us only through subjective awareness or perception. The word itself, he liked to point out, means "nothing without quotes": "whatever the mind grasps, it does so with the assistance of creative fancy" (afterword to *Lolita* 312; *Strong Opinions* 154). As individual consciousness registers phenomena, each of us creates out of the raw data of experience the shape and meaning—the distinctive "reality"—of the world(s) we inhabit.

*Lolita* offers readers, among other things, a fascinating demonstration of the way that Humbert Humbert's own "creative fancy"—what we may more bluntly call his obsessed imagination—transforms the twelve-year-old American kid, Dolores Haze, into the bewitching nymphet. The word *nymphet,* which Nabokov was proud of contributing to the English language, hints at the dire consequences this imaginative transformation has for the child. Beyond its many associations with myth, particularly the wood or water sprites of Greek mythology and religion, a *nymph* designates, in entomological terms, "an immature stage of a hemimetabolic insect," which, unlike a butterfly, "does not undergo complete metamorphosis" (Johnson and Coates 36). Visiting his fantasy of the nymphet—a fairytale "girl-child" who must "never grow up"—on an immature child who has every right to do so, Humbert not only violates Dolly Haze's body but stunts her growth. As he finally comes to admit, "something within her [was] broken by me" (*Lolita* 19, 21, 232). While Humbert makes every effort to deny, twist, or elude this fact, he ultimately acknowledges the consequences of his conduct. The remorse he expresses near the end of his story is only the belated articulation of a theme—the haunting threnody of a child's thwarted life and broken future—that sounds throughout the novel.

Remarkably, in the decade following *Lolita*'s publication—once the first charges of obscenity had been roundly quashed by widespread critical acclaim for the novel's literary value—commentators were eager to brush aside the shocking nature of Humbert's sexual conduct and his crime against the child. They preferred to concentrate, instead, on solving the novel's linguistic puzzles or tracing the contours of its cunning design. Thus Appel, in his preface to *The Annotated Lolita,* could quip, "Many readers are more troubled by Humbert Humbert's use of language and lore than by his abuse of Lolita and the law." He adds, "Their sense of intimidation is not unwarranted; *Lolita* is surely the most allusive and linguistically playful novel in English since *Ulysses* (1922) and *Finnegans Wake* (1939)" (xi). The best studies, however—including Appel's own groundbreaking 1967 essay, "Nabokov's Puppet Show"—reveal that close examination of the novel's narrative structure does not exclude but rather invites consideration or the moral and psychological dimensions of Nabokov's art. Over the last two decades of the twentieth century, moreover, with increasing public attention focused on child abuse, new questions have been raised about *Lolita* and its depiction of the victimized child. Given the complexity of the novel's intricate style and structure, such questions are not easily resolved. Just as "reality," in Nabokov's words, comprises an "infinite succession of steps" or "levels of perception," so the "reality" that *Lolita* evokes is not fixed or stable; its shape and effects are subject to the reader's own efforts, insights, and levels of perception. As Gabriel Josipovici observes, this novel "does not reveal its secret once and for all; the imaginative effort must be renewed each time it is reread. Ultimately the theme is the imaginative effort itself" (220). In the decades since that statement was made, more than a few commentators have proved themselves unequal to the task of reading Nabokov wisely or well. Failing to grasp the shifting tones and devious rhetorical strategies of the novel's scurrilous narrator, they rush to condemn a chimera: *Lolita*'s alleged tolerance for—or, worse yet, promotion of—the child's sexual exploitation by an adult.

The best available criticism on *Lolita* avoids such pitfalls by negotiating, rather than neglecting, the complex relationship between the novel's outrageous subject and its cunningly wrought design. Unless one pays scrupulous attention to the latter, no reading of the novel will be worth the paper on which it is printed. Each of the essays selected to appear in this volume—despite their notable differences in argument and approach—participates in that crucial act of critical negotiation. Shrewdly attentive to the complex relationship that exists, in all of Nabokov's fiction, between word and world, each makes a convincing and unique case for reading *Lolita.* This volume concludes with a lively interview with *Lolita*'s author by the American novelist Herbert Gold, conducted after the Nabokovs had moved to the Montreux-Palace Hotel. Leading up to the interview are nine critical essays, which follow a general progression: focusing first on textual and thematic features of the novel and then proceeding to broader issues and cultural implications, including *Lolita*'s relation to other works of literature and art and to its film adaptations. Within this overall design, the essays—some well known, others less accessible to contemporary readers—are arranged roughly (but only roughly) in chronological order.

The outrage expressed by many of *Lolita*'s readers over the past fifty years may be due, at least in part, to the discomfort they feel at finding themselves taken in by the narrator's rhetoric, at realizing that they have unwittingly accepted—and even identified with—Humbert's perverse desire. In a valuable essay, "The Art of Persuasion in Nabokov's *Lolita*," Nomi Tamir-Ghez carefully examines the novel's major rhetorical devices to reveal what such readers have overlooked in the text. Informed by careful analysis of narrative theorists from Gérard Genette to Mikhail Bakhtin, Tamir-Ghez's article effectively demonstrates that the arguments Humbert uses to excuse his deeds are the very means by which the author exposes his narrator's culpability. This detailed analysis provides an excellent starting point for approaching the intricacies of *Lolita*; and because the "unreliable narrator" is so common a feature of Nabokov's fiction, it draws attention to rhetorical devices, or speech events, to be found in his other novels as well.

Permeating the text of *Lolita*, parody is another narrative method at work throughout Nabokov's oeuvre. In the process of parodying or mimicking other styles or works of art, Humbert (and behind him, his author) creates what Appel calls "a verbal vaudeville, a series of literary impersonations," whose effect is often hilarious (*Annotated Lolita* xxvii). At the same time, however, Nabokov employs parody to create effects that rise above the merely comic or burlesque. Like his invented novelist, Sebastian Knight, he "uses parody as a kind of springboard for leaping into the highest region of serious emotion" (Nabokov, *Sebastian Knight,* 91). This "springboard," Appel observes, is also "the major means by which Nabokov breaks the circuit of reader-character identification that one associates with the conventional novel" ("Springboard" 215). Thomas R. Frosch's contribution to this volume, "Parody and Authenticity in *Lolita*," builds on Appel's observation, showing how parody "breaks the circuit" not only of the reader's identification with the protagonist but of Humbert's identification with the romantic tradition from Rousseau to Proust. Ultimately, Frosch points out, such parody acts in a proleptic, or anticipatory, way. Exposing all that is objectionable in Humbert's romantic worship of the nymphet, it paradoxically renews the possibilities for enchantment. In *Lolita*, parody both critiques and reinvents the romantic.

As admiration, and even awe, for the complex artistry of Nabokov's fiction has grown among those who study it, so has a tendency to regard the master as infallible. Brian Boyd, author of the definitive two-volume biography of Nabokov, lays siege to this assumption in his carefully structured essay, " 'Even Homais Nods': Nabokov's Fallibility; or, How to Revise *Lolita*." Thoroughly acquainted with the novelist's insistence on precision and attention to detail, Nabokov's biographer nonetheless reminds us that this writer, like other mortals, was perfectly capable of making mistakes.

Among other insights, Boyd calls attention to twenty-one demonstrable errors in the author's autobiography, *Speak, Memory,* most of them involving calendar dates. Citing crucial instances of Nabokov's tendency to muddle dates and numbers in his novels, despite his repeated efforts to eliminate inconsistencies, Boyd forcefully challenges a line of argument developed by a number of critics from the 1970s through the 1990s, each of whom bases a radically revised interpretation of *Lolita* on a discrepancy found in its calendar. Despite the fact that this discrepancy hinges on a single typographical character—the number 6 in place of (an easily reversible) 9—these critics arrive at similar conclusions. Major scenes in the novel, including Humbert's final meeting with Lolita in Coalmont and his murder of Quilty, do not take place within the novel's depicted "reality" but only in Humbert's deluded imagination. Boyd's essay is particularly valuable because, in mounting his detailed refutation of these critics' claims, he addresses specific aspects of each of the arguments. References to these works are cited in full, so that readers provoked by the debate may search out the other essays and draw their own conclusions.

In "Nabokov's Novel Offspring: Lolita and Her Kin," a chapter culled from my recent book on the child's image in contemporary writing and culture, I treat as crucial some basic issues that many readers, dazzled by the novel's aesthetic playfulness, have tended to dismiss as irrelevant. Central to my argument is the frequently blurred distinction between "the North American girl-child," Dolores Haze, and Humbert's fantasized image of Lolita. Through the haze of his solipsistic desire for the nymphet, Humbert rarely pays attention to the child he holds captive. Yet it is to the child, whose claims to innocence and freedom Humbert egregiously ignores, that the novel pays enduring tribute. My discussion of some early works by Nabokov alongside novels by Charles Dickens and Mary Shelley provides a useful context for revealing Nabokov's abiding faith in the Rousseauean idyll of childhood innocence and his depiction of the child's tragic betrayal by a world of adults. Focusing on the child's image from another vantage, Jenefer Shute's brief but provocative essay, " 'So Nakedly Dressed': The Text of the Female Body in Nabokov's Novels," analyzes the rhetorical devices by which Nabokov syntactically "paints" the image of the female child's body as an object of art. Drawing on the aesthetic theories of John Berger and Roland Barthes, her close reading of passages from Nabokov's *Ada* sheds further light on Humbert's consuming passion for the nymphet.

Although *Lolita* is now considered an American classic, what Nabokov observed in his afterword to the novel still holds true: "every appraisal" of

*Lolita* that is made "on the strength of my English" novels alone "is bound to be out of focus," because it leaves out "my Russian books" (*Lolita* 316). Susan Elizabeth's Sweeney's essay, "'Ballet Attitudes': Nabokov's *Lolita* and Petipa's *The Sleeping Beauty,*" helps to adjust and clarify that focus. Paying close attention to one set of the novel's intertextual allusions, Sweeney demonstrates how intimately tied to Nabokov's Russian background and influences is his most American novel. Embedded in *Lolita* are myriad allusions both to Russian works of ballet and music and to the European fairy tales on which they draw. By showing how profoundly *Lolita*'s verbal and visual images recall the story of a prince held captive by his vision of a sleeping princess, moreover, Sweeney underscores the powerful spell that imagination exerts over Humbert, holding both him and his nymphet in thrall.

Acknowledging Nabokov's Russian background from another perspective, John Haegert reads *Lolita* as the work of an émigré writer laying claim to a new American identity. His essay, "Artist in Exile: The Americanization of Humbert Humbert," examines the way in which Nabokov imbues his tale of a wayward European and would-be artist with an abiding theme of American literature and myth: the conflict between New World possibilities and Old World sensibilities. Humbert's initial preference for Old World stereotypes, which he imposes on the confusing plenitude of American life, gives way in the last third of the novel, Haegert argues, to the émigré's quest for a more authentic vision of his adopted land. Not coincidentally, Haegert suggests, Humbert's newly awakened appreciation for the American landscape occurs at the same time that he begins to acknowledge the child's autonomous identity. In this volume's subsequent essay, "*Lolita* and the Poetry of Advertising," Rachel Bowlby also examines the relationship of the New World to the Old, but she does so as part of her broader challenge to the polarities in which the novel tends to be discussed. These clear-cut oppositions—between innocence and experience, high culture and mass culture, art and advertising, aestheticism and consumerism—are, Bowlby argues, more apparent than viable in *Lolita* where, in contrast to Humbert's polemical rhetoric, they are undermined and complicated. Employing psychoanalytic, feminist, and cultural approaches to criticism, Bowlby offers a revisionist reading of the role that mass culture and consumerism play in the text.

By now, of course, *Lolita* has played as prominent a role in American mass culture as the latter occupies in the novel. As Michael Wood points out in the final essay of this volume, Lolita-the-girl has become part of our cultural imagery, just as the word *nymphet* is a permanent word in our dictionaries. (In sad testimony to the power of Humbert's rhetoric, how-ever—or to the moral lethargy of Nabokov's readers—our cultural for-mulations about the nymphet often leave out what the novel poignantly evokes: the plight of the victimized child.) Having sold more than fifty million copies around the world and having been translated into some twenty languages, *Lolita* has also inspired two Hollywood movies. In "Re-vising *Lolita*," Wood compares the two cinematic adaptations of the novel with an eye to both the novel's text and the evolution of American cul-tural attitudes. He notes the shaping influence these attitudes have had on the production and reception of Stanley Kubrick's 1962 film (for which Nabokov wrote a screenplay, which was barely used by Kubrick but was published in 1974) and Adrian Lyne's 1997 version. In 1998, when Wood's essay was first published, Lyne's version of *Lolita* was still awaiting American distribution, although it had already been released in Italy, Germany, and France (Wood saw the film in Paris) and was about to appear in Britain. After prolonged delay, the film was screened not in movie houses throughout the United States but on Showtime, a cable television channel. Until its airing in August 1998, Lyne's film was, as Stephen Schiff says in his introduction to the published version of the screenplay he wrote for Lyne, "the most talked-about, the most written-about, the most notorious movie no one had ever seen" (x). After so much public anticipation, protest, and debate, the television debut proved anticlimactic; audience re-sponse was, at best, lackluster. If Kubrick's film can be faulted for its comic excesses, Lyne's is devoid of humor to a remarkable degree. The novel's peculiar magic—spinning comedy out of despair, tragedy out of farce—has, not surprisingly, eluded all attempts (including Nabokov's own) to translate it to the silver screen.

Herbert Gold opens his 1967 interview with Nabokov by asking him about the morality of *Lolita* and proceeds to range over numerous related topics, some of which have been touched on in this introduction. They in-clude, for example, Nabokov's view of "reality" as subjectively constructed, the screenplay he wrote for Kubrick's film adaptation of the novel, his 1967 translation of *Lolita* into Russian, his claim to being an American writer, his method of composing a novel, his passion for lepidoptery, his famous definition of *poshlost,* and his provocative comments on other writers. Nabokov's characteristic wit is evident in his closing statement, in which he insists that he is not famous but rather "an obscure, doubly obscure, nov-elist with an unpronounceable name."

A decade before his interview with Gold, Nabokov wrote to thank Gra-ham Greene for his "kindness" in publicly recommending *Lolita* to readers

(Dmitri Nabokov and Matthew Bruccoli, *Selected Letters,* 197–98). Having rescued the novel from its obscure debut with the Olympia Press, Greene's admiring appraisal of *Lolita* soon landed it at the center of a controversy that would make both the novel and, contrary to Nabokov's modest demurral, its author famous. The cultural distance that *Lolita* has traveled since then, not only in America but throughout the world, is remarked in a tribute paid it, forty years later, by yet another prominent British novelist, Martin Amis. Saluting Nabokov's disturbing but "irresistible" novel, Amis calls it a "tale of chronic molestation" that is at once "tragic" and "embarrassingly funny," "perhaps the funniest novel in the language" ("*Lolita* Reconsidered" 109–10, 113, 119). Such praise from one of the leading writers of his generation appears to confirm that *Lolita* is no longer under threat. There is no danger of its disappearing from public view and, therefore, no further need for rescue. Or is there? Fame, Amis points out, incurs its own dangers and distortions, and *Lolita,* he contends, "has been partly isolated and distorted by its celebrity" (109–10). Setting the record straight in his own way, Amis brilliantly demonstrates that the case for reading—and rereading— *Lolita* remains stronger than ever. The process, he concludes, is ongoing:

> I have read *Lolita* eight or nine times, and not always in the same edition; but the margins of my staple hardback bear a Pompeiian litter of ticks, queries, exclamation marks, and lines straight and squiggly and doubled and tripled. My penciled comments, I realize, form a kind of surrealistic summary of the whole. . . . Clearly, these are not a scholar's notes, and they move toward no edifice of understanding or completion. They are gasps of continually renewed surprise. I expect to read the novel many more times. And I am running out of white space. (120)

## Works Cited

Alexandrov, Vladimir E. *Nabokov's Otherworld.* Princeton, N.J.: Princeton University Press, 1991.

Amis, Martin. "*Lolita* Reconsidered," *Atlantic Monthly,* Sept. 1992, 109–20.

Appel, Alfred, Jr., ed. *The Annotated Lolita.* Rev. ed. New York: Vintage, 1991.

———. "*Lolita*: The Springboard of Parody." *Wisconsin Studies in Contemporary Literature* 2 (Spring 1967): 204–41.

———. "Nabokov's Puppet Show," *New Republic,* 14 Jan. 1967, 27–30; 21 Jan. 1967, 25–32.

Boyd, Brian. *Nabokov's "Pale Fire."* Princeton, N.J.: Princeton University Press, 1999.

————. *Vladimir Nabokov: The American Years.* Princeton, N.J.: Princeton University Press, 1991.

————. *Vladimir Nabokov: The Russian Years.* Princeton, N.J.: Princeton University Press, 1990.

Butler, Diana. "Lolita Lepidoptera." *New World Writing* 16 (1960): 58–84.

Clegg, Christine, ed. *Vladimir Nabokov, "Lolita": A Reader's Guide to Essential Criticism.* Cambridge: Icon, 2000.

Field, Andrew. *Nabokov: His Life in Art.* Boston: Little, Brown, 1967.

Johnson, Kurt, and Steve Coates. *Nabokov's Blues: The Scientific Odyssey of a Literary Genius.* Cambridge, Mass.: Zoland, 1999.

Josipovici, Gabriel. "*Lolita*: Parody and the Pursuit of Beauty." In Josipovici, *The World and the Book: A Study of Modern Fiction,* 201–20. London: Macmillan, 1971.

Nabokov, Dmitri, and Matthew J. Bruccoli, eds. *Vladimir Nabokov: Selected Letters, 1940–1977.* New York: Harcourt Brace, 1989.

Nabokov, Véra. "Predislovie." In Vladimir Nabokov, *Stikhi,* 3–4. Ann Arbor, Mich.: Ardis, 1979.

Nabokov, Vladimir. *Ada, or Ardor: A Family Chronicle.* New York: McGraw-Hill, 1969.

————. *Lolita.* New York: Vintage, 1989.

————. *The Real Life of Sebastian Knight.* Norfolk, Conn.: New Directions, 1941.

————. *Speak, Memory: An Autobiography Revisited.* New York: Putnam, 1966.

————. *Strong Opinions.* New York: McGraw-Hill, 1973.

————. *Transparent Things.* Greenwich, Conn.: Fawcett, 1972.

Pifer, Ellen. "Shades of Love: Nabokov's Intimations of Immortality." *Kenyon Review,* 11, no. 2 (Spring 1989): 75–86.

Schiff, Stephen. *Lolita: The Book of the Film.* New York: Applause, 1998.

Zimmer, Dieter E. *A Guide to Nabokov's Butterflies and Moths 2001.* Hamburg, Germany: n.p., 2001.

# The Art of Persuasion in Nabokov's *Lolita*

NOMI TAMIR-GHEZ

◆　◆　◆

THE PUBLICATION OF *Lolita* in America in 1958 caused a considerable stir. Most reviews of the novel dealt with the narrow issue of its alleged obscenity.[1] Indeed, the novel was published three years earlier in France, since Nabokov could not find an American publisher ready to risk publishing it. After the initial shock subsided, the attention of literary critics was drawn to the text itself, with its frequent literary allusions, multilingual vocabulary, and network of parodic structures, puzzles, word games, and so on. (See especially Proffer, and Appel, *Annotated Lolita.*) Nevertheless, the novel's morality remained a central issue. What enraged or at least disquieted most readers and critics was the fact that they found themselves unwittingly accepting, even sharing, the feelings of Humbert Humbert, the novel's narrator and protagonist, the "maniac," the "nympholept," the "shining example of moral leprosy," in the words of John Ray, Jr., the fictive editor of Humbert's manuscript (7).[2] Instead of passing moral judgment on this man, who violated a deep-rooted sexual and social taboo, readers caught themselves identifying with him. Many literary critics have pointed out this strange effect that the novel has on the reader. Miller claims that "*Lolita . . .* can be quite simply described as an assault on the reader," who "softened by the power of appeal is . . . ready to forgive all" (188, 198). Lionel

Trilling, who describes the dynamics of the reader's reaction to the novel, contends:

> We find ourselves the more shocked when we realise that, in the course of reading the novel, we have come virtually to condone the violation it presents . . . we have been seduced into conniving in the violation, because we have permitted our fantasies to accept what we know to be revolting. (14)

Booth discusses *Lolita* as an example of a novel in which a "vicious center of consciousness" (Humbert) with "full and unlimited control of the rhetorical resources" (390) almost makes a case for himself. Appel suggests that the novel actually represents a contest between the author and the reader:

> What is extraordinary about *Lolita* is . . . the way in which Nabokov enlists us, against our will, on Humbert's side. . . . Humbert has figuratively made the reader his accomplice in both statutory rape and murder. (224)

The purposes of the present essay are, first, to give a more detailed (though by no means exhaustive) description of the major rhetorical devices that Nabokov uses while practicing his art of persuasion in *Lolita*. In spite of the fact that many critics have felt the strong effect that the novel's rhetoric has on the reader, the specific devices employed to achieve it have not been described. Second, I will argue that the narrator does not, in effect, have unlimited control over the rhetorical resources.

It is Nabokov who controls the rhetorical effects in *Lolita*, and he does it most subtly and skillfully. He allows the narrator's blandishments to affect us just as much as is needed for the novel's total effect. Far from losing hold of the narrator (as Booth's discussion suggests), the author is always there, behind the scene, pulling the strings. He ensures that Humbert's arguments are not airtight and that enough incriminating information leaks out. Nabokov does intend us to identify with the protagonist to a certain degree, to accept him as a human being, while at the same time strongly to condemn his deeds. Throughout the novel, while Humbert does his best to justify himself the reader is made aware of his rhetoric, and this awareness counteracts any feelings of empathy that might have developed. Only at the end, when he leaves behind all pretense of self-justification and turns instead to self-castigation, does Humbert win over the reader and close the distance between them. While all the efforts of the narrator to win over the reader fail, the author finally wins us over, using as his strongest weapon the protagonist's own realization of his guilt. Thus, the novel demonstrates how perfectly a skilled author can control his narrative, even when he imposes upon himself the most restrictive rules (for example, giving an unreliable narrator full control over the whole discourse). In *Lolita* we witness the subtle art of an author playing chess against himself, as it were. In *Speak, Memory,* Nabokov compares the composition of a chess problem to "the writing of one of those incredible novels where the author, in a fit of lucid madness, has set himself certain unique rules that he observes, certain nightmare obstacles that he surmounts, with the zest of a deity building a live world from the most unlikely ingredients" (quoted by Appel in Nabokov x1).

From all that has been said up to now it should be clear how important it is not to confuse the rhetorical purposes of the narrator with those of the author, nor the devices each of them use to attain his goal. As will be shown later, the same arguments that are used by Humbert to justify himself are often used (indirectly) by Nabokov to expose his narrator's guilt. In short, the narrator is but a pawn in the author's general scheme.

BEFORE ANALYZING THE SPECIFIC rhetorical devices used in *Lolita*, a few remarks about the possibilities of rhetorical manipulation in narrative in general are necessary.

Any aspect of the narrative text—not only direct statements of the characters or the narrator—can be manipulated for rhetorical purposes. Hrushovski considers that the literary text can be described by a three-dimensional model containing (1) a complex of speech events; (2) a semantic complex of meanings and references embodying a "world" with people, objects, places, and so on; and (3) an aesthetically organized structure, for the organization of which some aspects of 1 and 2—as well as other devices—are used.

The text is in the first place a complex linguistic structure, which is presented to the reader as a multilevel embedding of speech events (*énonciations* in the French terminology). The text as a whole represents a discourse of the author, directed at his potential readers. The author presents a narrator or speaker, who in turn presents the characters. As a result, we are usually faced with a basic three-level structure of addressers and addressees, which can be schematically described as follows:[3]

$$A \; [S \, (c \longleftrightarrow c) \; Ad] \; R$$

(A = author, S = speaker, c = character, Ad = addressee, R = reader, [ ], ( ) = embedding)

Only the italicized part represents the verbal material of the text, though the only act of communication taking place in reality is between the two extreme elements of the model: the author, whose intentions are reconstructed by the reader on the basis of material given in the text (cf. Bakhtin 179), and the reader. The rest is part of the fictional world, which means that it consists of imitations of speech acts, which have no performative force in the real world (cf. Ohmann).

The narrator may be just a "voice," an almost transparent and hardly felt subject of the speech events (in which case I prefer to call him "speaker" or "subject of enunciation"). But he may also be a well-identified person, who is an active agent of the fictional world. This is the case of the so-called first-person narration (or "personal narration"; see Tamir 1976). In personal narratives such as *Lolita*, where the narrator tells us about himself, the identity of the different subjects of enunciation may be represented as follows:

$$A \neq (S = c)$$

The author is different from the speaker, who is identical with the main character.[4]

Often, when the text presents us with a well-identified narrator, there is also an explicit addressee (or "narratee") who is the immediate target of the speaker's speech act. This fictional addressee should not be confused with the reader, just as the author should not be confused with the speaker of the literary discourse  (see Prince 1971, 1973). This principle holds true even when the narratee is referred to as "my dear reader" and the like, since he is always part of the fictional world and is often endowed with qualities that suit the rhetorical purposes of the speaker and/or author. The addressee, just like the narrator, may be only implied by the text or may be a fully realized persona, with a profession, a name, and other identifying qualities. How the addressee can be manipulated for rhetorical purposes will be shown later.

Every subject of enunciation in the above-mentioned hierarchical model of speech events governs the speech event(s) embedded in his own (and reported by him) and can manipulate them directly or indirectly and drive home certain values and attitudes. The subject of the embedded speech normally does not have access to the higher-level discourse. The subject can "infiltrate" the higher speech in the form of the so-called free indirect speech but cannot use it for his own rhetorical purposes. The author, being the highest frame of all the other speech instances, the one in which all the others are embedded, is the highest authority and the one responsible for the whole verbal structure and its total message.

There are three main strategies for manipulating others' speech: (1) *Selection*—a narrator cannot report everything that might have been said by all of the characters of the fictional world (the narration being necessarily limited in scope). He therefore has to select material that is reported either directly (as direct speech or quotation) or indirectly. The quoted or reported speech is then at the mercy of the higher-level speaker, who can decide whom, and how much, to quote. (2) *Interpretation*—the higher subject of enunciation can always add his own commentary to the speech quoted, thus attributing to it false intentions and meanings, changing emphases, or inserting it in the wrong context. (3) *Alteration*—or misrepresentation—of others' speech, which happens when the narrator is extremely "unreliable." This can occur even when the embedded speech event is in the form of a direct speech or a document, such as a letter or a diary. Humbert resorts to this maneuver more than once. For example, that is how he "quotes" a hotel manager who was trying to persuade him that the hotel beds were big enough: "'One crowded night we had three ladies and a child like yours sleep together. I believe one of the ladies was a disguised man (my static)'" (120). Obviously, this method is effective only if the reader is somehow informed that the quoted speech was actually misquoted (here by the insertion of "my static"), otherwise he accepts it at face value, according to the convention that whatever is in quotation marks is a direct and accurate quote.

Similar procedures can be applied to the world that the speech events embody. The different speakers can omit relevant information about characters, events, atmosphere, or ideas, and they can distort, misinterpret, or misrepresent them. Their freedom to do so depends, though, on their respective location in the speech hierarchy. It is only the author who can create the fictive world and do so in a way that is most suitable for his rhetorical purposes. All other speakers are limited to the reality of the fictive world, and their statements about it can typically be verified by checking them against other statements in the same work, which refer to this "internal field of reference" (to use Hrushovski's terminology).

The organization of the text and of each of the speech events can be turned into a most powerful rhetorical device. The order in which information is disclosed—by the author and/or by the fictive speakers—is must crucial for the general effect of any narrative. The sequential unfolding of information can be manipulated in a variety of ways, such as delayed communication of favorable (or unfavorable) facts, disclosure of charged materials at strategic points, and so on.[5] Moreover, the material can be organized in such a way as subtly to imply a network of negative and positive analogies among characters, events, and actions.

Again, it is ultimately the author who is responsible for the choice of speakers, for the details of the fictional world, and for the overall organization of the text, and if he is successful, they are all used to convey his message.

IN ORDER TO CREATE the desired delicate balance between the reader's feelings of identification with and rejection of Humbert, Nabokov makes some initial decisions of overall strategy, which have crucial consequences for the rhetorical structure of the novel. Since Humbert has so much working against him (the reader knows from the outset that he is a criminal and a murderer, though the specifics of the crimes are not yet disclosed), the author's first moves are aimed at investing the character with some special advantages to offset the negative balance. (1) *Choice of point of view* from which the narrative is told—Nabokov decides to unfold the story from the criminal's point of view. We can easily imagine how different the book would have been had it been narrated from the perspective of an uninvolved witness or (so much the worse for Humbert) from Lolita's point of view. When we are given a glimpse into Lolita's feelings (always through a Humbertian filter and mainly toward the end of the novel), we get an idea what such a story would have been like:

> In her washed-out gray eyes  . . .  our poor romance was for a moment reflected, pondered upon, and dismissed like a dull party, like a rainy picnic to which only the dullest bores had come: like a humdrum exercise, like a bit of dry mud caking her childhood. (274)

> I was to her not a boy friend, not a glamour man, not a pal, not even a person at all, but just two eyes and a foot of engorged brawn—to mention only mentionable matters. (285)

Notice that, due to the fact that they are introduced from Humbert's point of view, even such paragraphs, which point quite strongly at his guilt, still make the reader sympathize with him. The context is always Humbert's emotional world, and in this context what is communicated to us is *his* pain as he realizes how meaningless he was for Lolita. (2) *Choice of voice*—not only is the narrative told from Humbert's point of view, but he is the one who tells it, in his own words, using his own rhetoric (the novel could be told from his point of view but by an impersonal narrator, for example).[6] Hence it is a personal (or first-person) narration and as such one of the best devices to induce the reader's identification with the hero (or anti-hero, if you wish). It is not surprising that personal narration with an inside view of the narrator's emotional world is used in many modern narratives (for example, Mailer's *An American Dream*) that portray criminal or otherwise immoral or reprehensible behavior and where the author wishes the reader to sympathize (at least partially or temporarily) with the hero. (3) *Choice of character*—in order further to secure our empathy for the criminal-speaker, Nabokov presents us with an intelligent, well-educated, middle-class man with good manners and a sharp tongue, a man with whom the average reader can easily identify. Moreover, he is a sophisticated rhetorician, who is able to present his case in a most skillful manner (whence Booth's complaint about "the reader's inability to dissociate himself from a vicious center of consciousness presented to him with all of the seductive self-justification of skillful rhetoric" [390]). (4) *A decision to give Humbert full control over the discourse*—in many personal narratives the author introduces some independent speech events in the form of letters, diaries, or reliable quotations of characters other than the main narrator. This enables the reader to check, verify, and put the narrator's speech into perspective. Thus, for example, Faulkner's *The Sound and the Fury* is composed of three independent, personal speech events (or monologues) and one impersonal section, which helps us to further check off the subjective interpretation of events of the three other sections. In *Lolita,* Nabokov refrains from using this device. All we have to rely on (with the exception of the tongue-in-cheek "preface" by John Ray, Jr., and a few quotations of Lolita's) is Humbert's continuous dicourse.

Before proceeding to describe the rhetorical devices used by Humbert once he is given formal control over the discourse, it should be emphasized once again that his control is only apparent, that everything he does and says is ultimately manipulated by the author.

THE TEXT OF *Lolita* is supposedly written by Humbert as a defense speech, which he intends to read during his trial. This is the realistic motivation for the highly argumentative and rhetorical style that he uses. My discussion will necessarily be limited only to the major devices to which Humbert resorts. I will start with a description of the general strategies used by the narrator to unfold his story, will then discuss direct arguments of self-justification, and finally will point to some of the more subtle and indirect rhetorical devices.

As mentioned above, the entire narrative is composed of Humbert's continuous discourse. All other speech events are embedded in his and are therefore at his mercy. He takes advantage of this by exercising his privilege of selection. Thus, one of the major strategies he employs for self-justification is simply not to allow his potential accuser, Lolita, to voice her complaints. There are very few direct quotations of her speech in the novel and not many indirect presentations or summaries of it either. Her direct speech is conspicuously absent, especially through the crucial chapters 1–29 of part 2, which describe the relationship between Humbert and Lolita during their "cohabitation." Typically, when Humbert recounts a heated argument between them during that period—an occasion on which Lolita apparently dared remonstrate with him—he omits most of her accusations with the pretext that "she said unprintable things" (207). What he does allow, though, is reported in indirect speech, to which he adds a description that makes her look almost comic: "She said she loathed me. She made monstrous faces at me, inflating her cheeks and producing a diabolic plopping sound" (207).

Not only is Lolita's voice almost silenced, her point of view, the way she sees the situation and feels about it, is rarely mentioned and can be only surmised by the reader. Again, the realistic justification is quite simple: since it is Humbert who tells the story, it seems natural that he should emphasize his own emotions. The result is that throughout most of the novel the reader is absorbed in Humbert's feelings of fear, desire, suffering, and so on, and tends to forget Lolita's side of the story.

What seems like an innocent preoccupation with himself is soon revealed to be a deliberate suppression of important information on the part of the narrator. For many long pages, while trying to build up his defense and prove to his "judges" that, in his words, "I did everything in my power to give my Lolita a really good time" (165), there is no mention of Lolita's feelings or even of facts that could suggest how she felt. But, as argued above, the author does not wish the reader to be completely taken in by Humbert. Constantly striving to create the desired balance, Nabokov makes his narrator disclose some of the suppressed information and in strategically foregrounded points. These are, for example, the concluding sentences of the first part of the novel, while describing the night after Humbert first makes love to Lolita, after their first "quarrel," and after she finds out that her mother is dead:

> At the hotel we had separate rooms, but in the middle of the night she
> came sobbing into mine, and we made it up very gently. You see, she had ab-
> solutely nowhere else to go. (144)

Later on, half-disguised by the catalog of items that precedes it, the truth
of her suffering again emerges for a short moment, only to disappear again
in Humbert's flow of rhetoric:

> Our long journey . . . in retrospect, was no more to us than a collection
> of dog-eared maps, ruined books, old tires, and her sobs in the night—every
> night, every night—the moment I feigned sleep. (178)

Evidently she cries every night, and he has known it for quite some time
but mentions it here for the first (and only) time.

Such revealing passages are, however, rare. Only at the end of the story,
in one of the last chapters of the book (chap. 32), is the truth fully admit-
ted, the crime against the lonely, helpless, and desperate child fully acknowledged.[7] This brings us to the general question of the distribution of
information in the novel and its motivation.

The fictive preface of Dr. John Ray, Jr., informs the reader that Humbert wrote his narrative in prison while awaiting his trial. This means that
when Humbert began writing the story, he already knew its end and
everything leading to it. Moreover, Humbert as narrator (the "narrating
I") has learned a few things about himself that, as an "experiencing I," he
did not yet realize,[8] mainly the fact that he was, and still is, truly in love
with Lolita. Still, he (and the author) chooses to unfold events in their
chronological order, limiting himself (and the reader) most of the time to
his past perspective and knowledge.[9]

Humbert's expressed motivation for choosing his past perspective as a
principle of disclosure and distribution of information is his devotion to
"retrospective verisimilitude" (73). "I am only a conscientious recorder,"
he announces innocently (74). The question is: what are the rhetorical advantages  and disadvantages  of this choice both for the narrator and for
the author?

Telling his story in chronological order and limiting himself to his past
perspective enable Humbert to take advantage of the characteristics of two
distinct types of personal narration—the *diary* and the *memoir*.[10] The main
characteristic of the diary is the minimal distance between the narrator's
"epic situation" (that is, the situation of telling the story) and the events
described. As a result, the narrator's experiences are conveyed most vividly,

with the immediacy of an experience just gone through. Humbert uses this technique to dramatize the past, to evoke in great detail past events and emotions, and thus to induce the reader to share his feelings (cf. Trilling 14). The more scenic and dramatized the narration, the more closely is the reader brought into contact with the material, identifies with it, and accepts it as human and understandable.

However, since the story is, after all, a memoir, written some years after the initial events took place, Humbert can allow himself to intervene from time to time from the vantage point of his "reformed" and remorse-ful narrating self. Thus he can remind us at a delicate point—when de-scribing how he was waiting in the hotel lobby for Lolita to fall asleep after administering to her a dose of sleeping pills—that he now regrets it all (125).

Humbert pays dearly, though, for the advantages gained. Most of the time the reader is confronted with the cruel, cynical, unfeeling, egotistic self of his past, obsessed with the nymphet in Lolita and totally disregard-ing her feelings ("it was always my habit and method to ignore Lolita's states of mind while comforting my own base self" [289], he admits at the end of the novel). On the whole, unfolding the story from the point of view of the experiencing self is more damaging for Humbert than ad-vantageous. So much so, that one might wonder how come a clever rhetorician like Humbert did not realize these consequences of his choice. Had he started the story with some of the later expressions of true love for Lolita ("how much I loved my Lolita, *this* Lolita, pale and polluted, and big with another's child" [280]), had he taken upon himself the full blame from the outset ("Unless it can be proven to me—to me as I am now, today, . . .—that in the infinite run it does not matter a jot that a North American girl-child named Dolores Haze had been deprived of her child-hood by a maniac, unless this can be proven (and if it can, then life is a joke), I see nothing for the treatment of my misery" [285])—he would have had the reader's sympathy on his side all along. But that is precisely what Nabokov wants to prevent.

It is Nabokov, of course, who makes Humbert choose the less advanta-geous way. While the chosen narrative perspective, as far as the *narrator* is concerned, works both to his advantage and to his disadvantage, in the hands of the *author* it is an ideal tool for properly balancing the reader's re-action to Humbert.

Nabokov has also an aesthetic motivation for preferring this narrative perspective, namely, to create his own version of a suspense story and to play with the reader's expectations. In *Lolita* we know from the beginning that Humbert is imprisoned for having committed a crime, probably murder. We do not know the exact nature of the crime, and if it were murder, who was the victim. This question is a source of great suspense in the novel, especially since the narrator (who is a true representative of the author's intentions in this respect) constantly teases the reader and leads him to form false hypotheses. Thus, in contrast to the conventional "whodonit," here the central questions are rather "what was done?" and "who was done in?" Humbert could have been arrested for rape of a minor or for transporting a minor across states lines (violating the Mann Act). If the crime were murder, there are a few possible victims. The first is Charlotte, Lolita's mother. After a number of hints that something terrible will happen to her ("a bad accident is to happen soon" [81]) and dreams about her death ("her mother is messily but instantly and permanently annihilated" [55]), he actually plans to kill her and keeps the reader on edge for a few pages before admitting, "I just could not make myself do it" (89). Another candidate is Lolita herself, whom he could have murdered out of anger, fear, or, at the end, jealousy and revenge (although the preface informs us that "Mrs. 'Richard F. Schiller' died in childbed" [6], we discover only at the end of the novel that this is Lolita's married name). He misleads us to think of such a possibility when he quotes a song about Carmen (he often calls Lolita "Carmen")—"And the gun I killed you with, O my Carmen, The gun I am holding now" (64)—and again at the end, when he goes to meet Lolita (now Mrs. Schiller) for the last time, his gun in his pocket ("'Husband at home?' I croaked, fist in pocket. I could not kill *her*, of course, as some have thought" [272]). Lolita's husband is another possible victim ("I rehearsed Mr. Richard F. Schiller's violent death" [269]). However, the real victim—as we find out only in chapter 35—is Quilty, the debauched playwright and Humbert's double (cf. Gezari 104–7).

TYPICALLY, HUMBERT'S DISCOURSE (with the exception of the last chapters) is a mixture of self-accusation and self-justification. He often calls himself "maniac," "hound," and other derogatory names, but he usually gives the impression that he is half jesting, that the self-accusation is only lip service, part of his rhetorical schemes. He is evidently trying the best he can to explain himself to his judges and to prove that he is not really guilty of any crime. There are numerous overt statements to that effect in the novel (for example, "I insist upon proving that I am not, and never was, and never could be, a brutal scoundrel" [133]). They are easy to detect and require no special comment. I would like to mention only a few arguments of self-justification to which Humbert resorts quite often when overtly defending himself.

The first argument that Humbert employs as a justification of his crime is a psychological one:[11] childhood fixation, the cause of which is an unconsummated childhood love for a young girl during a summer vacation in a resort hotel on the beach. The girl died shortly afterward:

> There might have been no Lolita at all had I not loved, one summer, a certain initial girl-child. In a princedom by the sea. (11)

> All I want to stress is that my discovery of her [Lolita] was a fatal consequence of that "princedom by the sea" in my tortured past. (42; cf. 17, 41)

With the passage of time the need to redeem the past, to "break the spell," to close the circle, turns into a disease, almost madness (Humbert was hospitalized a few times in mental institutions), hence the term *nympholepsy,* which Humbert uses to refer to his "condition," suggesting a mental disorder (*lepsy* = seizure, as in "epilepsy"; cf. Appel's annotation in Nabokov 339). Moreover, using this term, he implies that this is a known and recognized disease and that he is not the only case (for example, "nympholepts" [19]). A sick man cannot be considered responsible for his actions, and Humbert does his best to emphasize this argument.

Another line of self-justification, different from the above-mentioned one, rests on detailed and learned accounts, spread throughout the book, of cases that supposedly prove that moral rules and taboos have only relative value, since they differ from country to country and from period to period:

> Marriage and cohabitation before puberty are still not uncommon in certain East Indian provinces. Lepcha old men of eighty copulate with girls of eight, and nobody minds. After all, Dante fell madly in love with his Beatrice when she was nine. . . . And when Petrarch fell madly in love with his Laureen, she was a fair-haired nymphet of twelve. (21)

According to this line of reasoning, Humbert is neither a sick pervert nor a criminal ("I have but followed nature," he claims elsewhere [137]). He is only an unfortunate victim of an arbitrary social convention: "I found myself maturing amid a civilization which allows a man of twenty-five to court a girl of sixteen but not a girl of twelve" (20). The argument conceals a misleading analogy, though: he is not twenty-five but probably about thirty-five, and he does not *court* Lolita but forces her into a relationship that she detests.

Blaming Lolita for the past is another convenient excuse. Humbert tries hard to prove that despite the uncontrollable urge to satisfy his sexual needs and despite the fact that after her mother's death Lolita was completely at his mercy, "I was firmly resolved to pursue my policy of sparing her purity by operating only in the stealth of the night, only upon a completely anesthetized little nude" (126). It was Lolita who seduced him, he claims, and he was not even her first lover (134–37). He depicts himself as a naive lover, confused and nervous ("What a comic, clumsy, wavering Prince Charming I was!" [111]), while she is a corrupt, experienced, vulgar little girl, who knows no shame. Humbert might be faithfully reporting the situation when he says that "not a trace of modesty did I perceive in this beautiful hardly formed young girl, whom modern co-education, juvenile mores, the campfire racket and so forth had utterly and hopelessly depraved" (135). We also have no reason to disbelieve him when he claims that he was not the one who deflowered Lolita. He would like us to think that these are the strongest accusations against him, that this is the worst he could possibly have done to her. The point is that these arguments have little to do with his culpability. They serve only to divert the reader's attention from Humbert's real crimes (see also n. 7). He himself knows (and admits) that her earlier sexual experiences were but part of a common, "tough kid" game: "While eager to impress me with the world of tough kids, she was not quite prepared for certain discrepancies between a kid's life and mind. Pride alone prevented her from giving up" (136).

Yet another strategy Humbert uses for exonerating himself is claiming that Lolita is a "nymphet." Being a nymphet, she is not, according to his learned theories, a normal child anyway, but a demon disguised as a child. Listen to this "scientific" lecture-for-beginners on nymphets, nympholepts, and nympholepsy and notice the charm of the poetic language and the rhetoric it hides:

> Between the age of nine and fourteen there occur maidens who, to certain *bewitched travelers,* twice or many times older than they, reveal *their true nature which is not human, but nymphic (that is demonic).* You have to be an *artist* and a *madman,* a creature of infinite melancholy, with a bubble of hot poison in your loins and a super-voluptuous flame permanently aglow in your subtle spine . . . , in order to discern at once, by ineffable signs . . . the little deadly demon among the wholesome children. (18–19, my emphasis)

Thus, while seemingly describing objective facts, Humbert transforms the pervert into a "bewitched traveler" haunted by the deadly nymphet. Notice the plural ("travelers") and the second person ("you")—he is not alone in this plight! It is his special sensitivity ("you have to be an artist and a madman") that makes him vulnerable to the magical power of the "demons." After making love to Lolita for the first time, Humbert describes her body as "the body of some immortal daemon disguised as a child" (141), and one of the many (often contradictory) reasons he gives for writing the story is the need "to fix once and for all the perilous magic of nymphets" (136). You see, it is they who are dangerous, not he. He treats Lolita accordingly, as a bewitching, adorable nymphet—but not as the human, lonely child she really is.

As can be seen from the examples quoted here and from many others in the novel, Humbert's overt rhetoric is made transparent without too much difficulty. The indirect devices he uses are much more difficult to detect and therefore easier to succumb to.

IN STANDARD LANGUAGE, the speech situation is consistent and the first and second person refer uniquely. In Banfield's words: "For every expression (E), there is a unique referent of *I* (the speaker) and a unique referent of *you* (the addressee)" (20). In other words, the speaker and the addressee remain the same throughout a given speech unit. Most narratives respect this rule and present a consistent speech situation. Not so in *Lolita*. Humbert sometimes addresses his words to a jury or to a judge and sometimes to a reader. He thereby implies the coexistence of two different and inconsistent speech situations: that of a defendant in court (who is also his own defense lawyer), with the jury as audience ($Ad_1$), and that of an author in prison, writing a manuscript to be published as a book and read by readers ($Ad_2$). The real reader (we as readers, R) is encouraged to visualize at times the first situation, at other times the second, according to details mentioned by the speaker, which imply one or the other. Compare, for example, the two following groups of utterances:

I. "Ladies and gentlemen of the jury, exhibit number one is . . ." (11). "I am going to pass around in a minute some . . . picture-postcards" (11). "Exhibit number two is a pocket diary" (12). "Ladies and gentlemen of the jury, I wept" (105).

II. "I want my learned readers to participate in the scene" (59). "However, I shall not bore my learned readers with a detailed account" (135). "The reader (ah, if I could visualize him as a blond-bearded scholar with rosy lips sucking la pomme de sa canne as he quaffs my manuscript!)" (228).

The incongruity of the implied speech situations becomes especially evident when Humbert changes addresses in the middle of recounting one scene (see 59, 63). This incongruity receives a somewhat forced explanation at the end of the novel, when Humbert explains that he first meant this memoir to be his defense speech at his trial but later decided that the facts should not be made known as long as Lolita lives and that the document should instead be published as a book after her death (310). However, this fails to account for the fact that the apostrophe to the reader appears for the first time early in the novel, and that the jury is still addressed toward the end. The truth is that Humbert needs both addresses for building up his defense, and he shrewdly plays one (the reader) against the other.

The main strategy employed in the discourse addressed to $Ad_1$ is reasoning. Using some of the arguments mentioned above, as well as many others, Humbert tries to prove to the "ladies and gentlemen of the jury" that he is actually innocent of any crime ("Ladies and gentlemen of the jury, the majority of sex offenders . . . are innocuous, inadequate, passive, timid strangers who merely ask the community to allow them to pursue their practically harmless, so-called aberrant behavior, . . . without the police and society cracking down upon them. We are not sex fiends! We do not rape as good soldiers do" [89–90]). Slowly, his tone changes when he addresses them and turns into sarcasm, directed mainly at the women among them: "Gentlewomen of the jury! Bear with me! Allow me to take just a tiny bit of your precious time!" (125). Eventually, it turns into an implicit accusation of the jury, suggesting that they have no right to judge him, that they represent conventionality and are therefore unable to understand the "artist" and "madman": "Frigid gentlewomen of the jury! . . . I am going to tell you something very strange" (134). Of course, by ridiculing $Ad_1$, Humbert subtly courts $Ad_2$—the reader—suggesting that *he* is neither frigid (or impotent) nor conventional in his way of thinking and therefore is able to understand.

This attack on the jury is intensified when Humbert addresses it with what at first seems to be a peculiar adjective: "Oh, *winged* gentlemen of the jury" (127; cf. 232). On the one hand, Humbert might be implying that he actually addresses his defense not to the jury of flesh and blood but to a higher authority ("I thought I would use these notes in toto in my trial, to save not my head, but *my soul*" [310], he states at the end of the novel; my emphasis). On the other hand, if we turn to Edgar Allan Poe's poem "Annabel Lee," we shall discover that this adjective cleverly conceals an accusation against the jury. Poe's poem plays an important role in *Lolita* (see Appel's comments in Nabokov 330). Humbert's childhood love story is a reenactment of the love described in the poem:

> She was a child and I was a child
>> in this kingdom by the sea,
> But we loved with a love that was more than love—
>> I and my Annabel Lee—
> With a love that the *winged seraphs* of Heaven
>> Coveted her and me. (my emphasis)

It is the jealousy of the "winged seraphs" that brings about the death of both Poe's and Humbert's Annabel, and when Humbert opens the story of his childhood love he echoes Poe's lines: "Ladies and gentlemen of the jury, exhibit number one is what the seraphs, the misinformed, simple, *noble-winged* seraphs, envied" (11; my emphasis). Referring to the jurors as "winged gentlemen" means, therefore, accusing them of being envious (and maybe also simple or misinformed) of his love for Lolita.

The strategy toward Ad$_2$ is different: "the reader" is addressed mostly as a friend and equal, and he is called upon to participate in the events and emphasize with the speaker ("I want my learned reader to participate in the scene" [59]). As Humbert's attitude toward Ad$_1$ becomes more critical and cynical, his tone when addressing Ad$_2$ becomes gradually warmer and warmer. The increased number of exclamations, such as "*my* Reader" (76). "O, Reader, my Reader!" (205) can testify to that. Moreover, the capital *R* used here and on other occasions is intended to create the impression that the unknown addressee is actually a familiar person, whose given name is simply "Reader." Eventually, the reader is addressed as "comrade" (169) and "Bruder" (brother, 264), echoing the famous lines of Baudelaire's *Les fleurs du mal* and implying a shared guilt ("Hypocrite lecteur,—mon semblable,—mon frère").

An interesting device used for manipulating Ad$_2$ ("Reader") and, through him, R (the actual reader) is what Bakhtin calls "the internal polemic," a discourse that is aware of another (often antagonistic) discourse and reacts to it either by replying to it or by anticipating it. Humbert's speech acts are often a reaction to an assumed or anticipated comment of his addressee. But the supposed reaction of the addressee, which can be reconstructed from Humbert's words, is not the reader's most likely reaction but rather what Humbert would have wished it to be. What actually happens is that Humbert tries to dictate an attitude to the reader, by formulating his attitude for him. Here is an example. The relations between Humbert and Lolita have reached the stage where she (hoping to free herself of him) takes advantage of his lust to extort money from him. Clearly, it is he who prostituted her in the first place, paying her from the beginning a weekly allowance "under condition she fulfilled her basic obligations" (185) and demanding to be sexually compensated for fulfilling any of her wishes. Now he complains about the "drop in Lolita's morals" and asks the reader not to laugh at him: "O Reader! Laugh not, as you imagine me, on the very rack of joy, noisily emitting dimes and quarters" (186). But does the reader really feel like laughing? The situation is more tragic than comic (tragic mainly when considered from Lolita's point of view). Using the internal polemic technique, Humbert tries to force a certain position on the reader and to make him consider the situation from his, rather than Lolita's, perspective.

The same technique is used in the novel's most delicate situation, which requires Humbert's most powerful rhetoric—the first time he makes love to Lolita. He gives her sleeping pills and waits for her to fall asleep. They are both in bed, but he is afraid that she is not yet fast asleep and delays his planned action. Describing these moments, he addresses the reader as follows: "Please, reader: no matter your exasperation with the tenderhearted, morbidly sensitive, infinitely circumspect hero of my book, do not skip these essential pages!" (131). Not only does Humbert ascribe here to the reader a rather positive judgment of himself (tenderhearted, sensitive, and so on), but he actually implies that the reader is impatient to see the deed done and would have liked Humbert to be more resolute in the execution of his design to rape the twelve-year-old girl.

The duality of the addressee finds its counterpart in a duality of the speaker himself. As previously mentioned, there is a narratively inevitable duality in the protagonist, who is both the narrating I of the present and the experiencing I of the past. Furthermore, while according to the norms of standard language, a speaker refers to himself using the first-person pronoun. Humbert often does so in the third person, thus suggesting a split between the "I" and the "not I" (cf. Laferrière): "there must have been times, if I know my Humbert—when . . ." (72); "so Humbert the Cubus schemed and dreamed" (73); "oh miserly Hamburg! Was he not a very Enchanted Hunter as he deliberated with himself" (111); and so on.

This duality, or split, in the personality of the speaker is further underlined by Humbert's utilization of his favorite figure of speech: the synecdoche. Trying to create the impression that it was not he, but the "other" in him who stealthily fondled Lolita, who plotted the crime, he often resorts to statements such as the following (with my emphasis): "*my glance* slithered over the kneeling child . . . the vacuum of my soul managed to suck in every detail of her bright beauty" (41); "Humbert the Hoarse put his arm around her" (50); "*my hand* swept over her agile giggling legs"

(57); "my knuckles lay against the child's blue jeans" (53); and "my tentacles moved towards her" (132). The split is between body and mind, and the body is presented as acting on its own, against the inclinations of the soul, or, as he himself summarizes it: "While my body knew what it craved for, my mind rejected my body's every plea" (20).

IN SPITE OF THE FACT that the author hands the narrative over to Humbert, in spite of the fact that everything is seen through Humbertian eyes, in spite of Humbert's cajolery and argumentation, his cruelty toward Lolita, the harm done her, cannot be smoothed over. The reader need not be "most skillful and mature" (Booth 390) to realize that Lolita complies out of fear and despair. Enough details indicating her condition are spread throughout the story. We are told that she has nowhere else to go (144), that she cries every night (178), that Humbert terrorizes her in different ways to keep her submissive (150–53). He isolates her from other children, bribes her with money, which he later steals from her (186), and with promises, which he later retracts (171). He imposes his sexual demands upon her even when she is sick and feverish (200) and resorts to force when necessary ("thrusting my fatherly fingers deep into Lo's hair from behind, and then gently but firmly clasping them around the nape of her neck, I would lead my reluctant pet to our small home for a quick connection before dinner" [166]).

That Lolita does not enjoy the whole thing (to put it mildly) is clear, and Humbert himself admits it at quite an early stage:

> She had entered my world, umber and black Humberland, with rash curiosity. She surveyed it with a shrug of amused distaste; and it seemed to me now that she was ready to turn away from it with something akin to plain repulsion. (168)

All this taken into account, it is hard to agree with Trilling that the novel (i.e., Nabokov) brings us "to condone the violation it presents" (14). The reader is made to see the violation all along and must condemn it, especially at the end, when Humbert himself explains the full damage he has inflicted upon Lolita ("oh, my poor, bruised child" [286]).

Paradoxically, the fullest disclosure of Humbert's guilt triggers the reader's strongest feelings of sympathy for him (though not for his deeds!). It is his self-castigation, his readiness to face and admit his guilt, and his suffering at the realization of the truth that make us accept him. At the end of the narrative he at last gives up the cynicism underlying his rhetoric, and his tone becomes more sincere. For the first time he is now able to transcend his self-centered passions and think of Lolita as a human being:

> What I heard was but the melody of children at play, . . . and then I knew
> that the hopelessly poignant thing was not Lolita's absence from my side,
> but the absence of her voice from that concord. (310)

Moreover, only at the end does he (and therefore the reader) understand that he actually loves Lolita, not the nymphet in her. When he first meets her and announces, "I knew I had fallen in love with Lolita forever," his love is actually directed at "the eternal Lolita as reflected in my blood" (67). The thought that often haunts him during their trip is that "around 1950 I would have to get rid somehow of a difficult adolescent whose magic nymphage had evaporated" (176). But after confronting the "grown-up," pregnant Lolita, "hopelessly worn at seventeen" (279), he understands himself and his love: "I looked and looked at her, and knew as clearly as I know that I am to die, that I loved her more than anything I had ever seen or imagined on earth, or hoped for anywhere else" (279).

Seen that way for the first time—without his jesting pose, suffering for the pain he had inflicted on the girl, and realizing that his love transcends his passion—Humbert at last wins us over, just as the author intends.

## Notes

An earlier version of this essay was presented at the Conference on Culture and Communication, Temple University, Philadelphia, March 1977.

1. For a bibliography of these early reviews see Bryer, 335–40.

2. All references are to the annotated edition (Nabokov 1970), edited by Alfred Appel, Jr.

3. An earlier version of this scheme, which took into account only the speech situation of personal (first-person) narratives, was presented in Tamir (423). That early version did not yet locate the addressee in the speech situation. The scheme suggested here was developed and formalized in collaboration with Benjamin Hrushovski. It is presented and discussed at length in Tamir-Ghez and Hrushovski.

4. By "identical," I mean simply that the speaker and the main character appear as the same person in the fictional world.

5. This aspect was developed theoretically and demonstrated in detail by M. Perry (see esp. his research on Bialik, Mendele, Faulkner). For a publication devoted to this subject, see Sternberg.

6. On the distinction between voice and vocalization, see Genette (203) and Tamir (417–19).

7. One of the twists of the novel is that Humbert's crime against Lolita is neither rape (she complies) nor defloration (she was not a virgin) but having destroyed her childhood, her life, and her spirit.

8. On the distinction between the *erzählendes Ich* and the *erlebendes Ich,* see Spitzer.

9. This is a different case from the one discussed above. Here we are dealing with temporarily withheld information, with realistic justification, while before we discussed important information that was suppressed in spite of the fact that it was already known to the experiencing self.

10. For a discussion of these (and other) types of personal narrative, see Romberg, esp. III:3.

11. In *Lolita*, Nabokov parodies (among many other things) psychologists and psychotherapy.

### Works Cited

Appel, Alfred, Jr. "*Lolita:* The Springboard of Parody." *Wisconsin Studies in Contemporary Literature* 8 (1967): 204–24.

Banfield, Ann. "Narrative Style and the Grammar of Direct and Indirect Speech." *Foundations of Language* 10 (1973): 1–39.

Bakhtin, Mikhail. "Discourse Typology in Prose." In *Readings in Russian Poetics,* ed. L. Matejka and K. Pomorska. Cambridge, Mass.: MIT Press, 1971.

Booth, Wayne C. *The Rhetoric of Fiction.* Chicago: University of Chicago Press, 1961.

Bryer, Jackson R. "Vladimir Nabokov's Critical Reputation in English: A Note and a Checklist." *Wisconsin Studies in Contemporary Literature* 8 (1967): 335–40.

Genette, Gerard. *Figures III.* Paris: Seuill, 1972.

Gezari, Janet K. "Roman et problème chez Nabokov." *Poétique* 17 (1974): 96–113.

Hrushovski, Benjamin. "Segmentation and Motivation in the Text Continuum of Literary Prose: The First Episode of *War and Peace.*" In *Russian Poetics: Proceedings of the International Colloquium at UCLA, September 22–26, 1975,* ed. Thomas Eekman and S. Worth-Dean. Columbus, Ohio: Slavica, 1982. 117–46.

———. "A Three-Dimensional Model of Semiotic Objects." Paper presented at the International Conference on the Semiotics of Art, Ann Arbor, Mich., May 1978.

Laferrière, Daniel. "The Subject and Discrepant Use of the Category of Person." Paper presented at the First Congress of the International Association for Semiotic Studies, Milan, Italy, June 1974.

Miller, Norman. "The Self-Conscious Narrator-Protagonist in American Fiction since World War II. Ph.D. diss. University of Wisconsin, 1972.

Nabokov, Vladimir. *The Annotated Lolita.* Ed. A. Appel. New York: McGraw-Hill: 1970.

Ohmann, Richard. "Speech Acts and the Definition of Literature." *Philosophy and Rhetoric* 4 (1971): 1–19.

Prince, Gerald. "Notes towards a Categorization of Fictional 'Narrattees.' " *Genre* 4 (1971): 100–106.

————. "Introduction à l'étude du narrataire." *Poétique* 14 (1973): 178–96.

Proffer, Carl R. *Keys to Lolita.* Bloomington: Indiana University Press, 1968.

Romberg, Bertil. *Studies in the Narrative Technique of the First Person Novel.* Stockholm, Sweden: Almquist & Wiksell, 1962.

Spitzer, Leo. "Zum stil Marcel Proust." In Spitzer, *Stilstudien 2,* 365–497. Munich, Germany: N. Neuber, 1928.

Sternberg, Meir. *Expositional Modes and Temporal Ordering in Fiction.* Baltimore, Md.: Johns Hopkins University Press, 1978.

Tamir, Nomi. "Personal Narrative and Its Linguistic Foundations." *PTL: A Journal for Descriptive Poetics and Theory* 1 (1976): 403–29.

Tamir-Ghez, Nomi, and Benjamin Hrushovski. "Speech and Position in Literature: A General Model." *Poetics Today.*

Trilling, Lionel. "The Last Lover—Vladimir Nabokov's *Lolita."* *Encounter* 11, no. 4 (1958): 9–19.

# Parody and Authenticity in *Lolita*

## THOMAS R. FROSCH

◆　◆　◆

I T  H A S  B E E N  S A I D  that *Lolita* is simultaneously "a love story and a parody of love stories" and that its parody and its pathos are "always congruent."[1] In this article I wish to explore what such a condition—that of being both parodic and authentic at the same time—may mean.

First, however, I suggest that we best describe *Lolita* generically not as a love story or a novel of pathos but as a romance. The plot itself is composed of a series of typical romance structures, each one a version of the quest or hunt and each one an embodiment of a specific type of suspense or anxiety. We begin with the pursuit of Lolita and the anxiety of overcoming sexual obstacles. Next, once Humbert and Lolita are lovers, we have a story of jealousy and possessiveness, as Humbert is beset by fears of rivals and by Lolita's own resistance. Finally, in Humbert's dealings with Quilty, we have a third and fourth type, each with its attendant style and anxiety: the double story and the revenge story. Furthermore, these plot structures are infused with the demonic (that is, a quality of uncanny power possessed originally by beings, whether good or evil, midway between gods and people), which is a primary characteristic of romance as a literary mode. Lolita is an inherently unpossessable object; her appeal consists partly in her transience—she will only be a nymphet for a brief time—and partly in her status as a demonic visitor to the common world. The quest is thus an impossible one from the outset; it is variously presented as a quest for Arcadia, for the past, for the unattainable itself, it is nympholepsy. Even in the rare moments when Humbert is free from his typical anxieties, he is not totally satisfied; he wants to "turn my Lolita inside out and apply voracious lips to her young matrix, her unknown heart, her nacreous liver, the sea-grapes of her lungs, her comely twin kidneys" (167). Humbert is a believer in the enchanted and the marvelous. Like Spenser's Red Cross Knight, he rides forth on his quest adorned by the image of his guiding principle, in his case a blue cornflower on the back of his pajamas—the blue cornflower being Novalis's symbol of infinite desire. *Lolita* contains numerous parodic allusions to other literary works, especially to Mérimée's *Carmen* and Poe's "Annabel Lee," but the real antitext implied by the allusions and parodies together is the romantic sensibility in general from Rousseau to Proust.

But exactly how seriously are we meant to take Humbert and his quest? The book's complexity of tone and the question of Humbert's reliability as a narrator are the first issues in an investigation of the relationship between the parodic and the authentic.

Nabokov takes great delight in rapid and unpredictable changes in tone; we are never permitted to rest for long in the pathetic, the farcical, the rapturous, or the mocking. One of the clearest examples of tonal complexity is the novel's primal scene, the seaside love scene with Annabel Leigh. After a buildup of high erotic suspense during which the two children are repeatedly frustrated in their sexual attempts, the famous episode concludes as follows: "I was on my knees, and on the point of possessing my darling, when two bearded bathers, the old man of the sea and his brother, came out of the sea with exclamations of ribald encouragement, and four months later she died of typhus in Corfu" (15). We misread this little roller-coaster ride from the impassioned to the hilarious to the poignant if we take any one of its tonalities as definitive. Certainly this is not simply a satire of the romantic; its effect comes rather from the coexistence of its three tonalities in a single moment. In such a passage, we might expect the romantic to go under, partly because of its inherent vulnerability and partly because, as the dominant tone of the long buildup, it is apparently punctured by the intrusion of the burlesque. Yet the paragraphs that follow return to a tone of erotic rapture in a scene that is chronologically earlier than the seaside scene. The second scene, describing another frustrated tryst, concludes: "That mimosa grove—the haze of stars, the tingle, the flame, the honeydew, and the ache remained with me, and that little girl with her seaside limbs and ardent tongue haunted me ever since—until at last, twenty-four years later, I broke her spell by incarnating her in another" (17). If Nabokov had intended to puncture Humbert's rhapsody, it would have been more appropriate for him to arrange the two scenes chronologically so that the ribald bathers would appear at the end of the entire sequence, instead of in the middle. As it is, nothing is punctured; if anything, the romantic has found a new energy after the interruption. It is as if, in the following paragraphs, the romantic has been given the bolstering it needs to be able to hold its own with the jocular.

The novel's narrative point of view is as elusive as its tone. Clearly, when Humbert tells us, as he does repeatedly, that he has an essentially gentle nature and that "poets never kill" (90), he is belied by the destruction he wreaks on Charlotte, Quilty, and Lolita. And when Humbert accuses Lolita of "a childish lack of sympathy for other people's whims," because she complains about being forced to caress him while he is spying on schoolchildren, Nabokov is being sarcastic (163). Humbert also fails to see things that the reader can pick up; for example, he misses the name Quilty ("Qu'il t'y") concealed in a friend's letter to Lolita (225). Just as clearly, though, Humbert is sometimes Nabokov's champion as, for example, in Humbert's satirical comments about psychoanalysis and progressive education. At other points, Nabokov's attitude toward his persona is quite intricate: Humbert says of his relationship with Annabel that "the spiritual and the physical had been blended in us with a perfection that must remain incomprehensible to the matter-of-fact, crude, standard-brained youngsters of today" (16); and Humbert does serve as a serious critic of modern love from the standpoint of a romantic exuberance of feeling, even if his criticism is undercut by his own divided love, in which what he calls his "tenderness" is always being sabotaged by what he calls his "lust" (287).

But if we compare Humbert to another demented storyteller in Nabokov, Hermann in *Despair*, we see how Nabokov operates when he really wants to make a dupe out of his narrator. *Despair* is a take-off on the doppelgänger theme, in which the hero, Hermann, takes out an insurance policy on himself and then murders his double in order to collect; it doesn't work, however, because he's the only one who sees the resemblance. Hermann is among other things a Marxist, a sure sign that Nabokov is using him ironically, and Nabokov puts into his mouth frequent and obvious reminders of his unreliability. "I do not trust anything or anyone," he tells us.[2] His wife's hero worship of him is one of his constant themes, and yet his self-satisfaction and blindness are such that he can find her undressed in the apartment of a man who is her constant companion and not experience a moment's doubt of her fidelity. Nabokov himself, calling both Humbert and Hermann "neurotic scoundrels," does make an important distinction between them, when he writes, "There is a green lane in Paradise where Humbert is permitted to wander at dusk once a year, but Hell shall never parole Hermann."[3]

Even Hermann, however, at times seems a stand-in for Nabokov as, for instance, whenever he speaks of outwitting or playing games with the reader. Much has been written of Nabokov's fondness for game playing, such as the use of the *Carmen* parallel in *Lolita* to tease the reader into believing that Humbert will kill his nymphet.[4] In fact, it is difficult to find a Nabokov hero or narrator, however antipathetic, who does not at times sound like the author in his nonfiction. Even John Ray, the fool who introduces *Lolita,* asserts a prime Nabokovian theme when he says that every great work of art is original and "should come as a more or less shocking surprise" (7). And many readers have noticed the relationship between the desperate nostalgia of Humbert or that of the crazed Kinbote in *Pale Fire* and Nabokov's own commitment to the theme of remembrance. Conversely, Van Veen in *Ada*—who is the liberated Byronic Hero, among other things, as Humbert is the Enchanted Quester and Hermann the Metaphysical Criminal—although he has been taken as almost a mouthpiece for Nabokov himself, has been condemned by his creator as a horrible creature.[5] The fact seems to be that Nabokov in his fictional and nonfictional utterances has created a composite literary persona, just as Norman Mailer has. His heroes, like Mailer's D. J. and Rojack, tend to be more or less perverse or absurd inflections of his own voice. In two of Nabokov's favorite works, *Don Juan* and *Eugene Onegin,* we have narrators who keep intruding on their heroes to deliver speeches and who also are at pains to differentiate themselves from those heroes. Nabokov behaves similarly, except that he does so within the range of the single voice. As in the case of tone, we discover an interplay of engagement and detachment, an interplay that is most active and subtle in the most memorable of the characters, like Humbert and Kinbote.

With this general sense of the status of tone and narrator in *Lolita,* we can turn now to consider what Humbert actually says. Humbert subtitles his story a confession. More accurately, it is a defense. Portraying himself as a man on trial, Humbert repeatedly refers to his readers as his jury. "Oh, winged gentlemen of the jury!" he cries, or "Frigid gentlewomen of the jury!" (127, 134). But he also frequently addresses us directly as readers; in the middle of a torrid sequence he speculates that the eyebrows of his "learned reader  . . .  have by now traveled all the way to the back of his bald head" (50). Late in the book, in a parody of Baudelaire's "Au lecteur," he addresses the reader as his double: "Reader! *Bruder!"* (264). The reader is sitting in judgment of Humbert; the purpose of his story is to defend what he calls his "inner essential innocence" (302); and the rhetoric of the book as a whole, its strategy of defense, is proleptic, an answering of objections in advance. Humbert's self-mockery, for example, has to be understood as a proleptic device, and, indeed, to follow the style of *Lolita* is to track the adventures of a voice as it attempts to clear itself of certain potential charges. As we will see, in many ways the defense is Nabokov's, even more than Humbert's.

At the end of the novel, Humbert sums up his defense by passing judgment on himself; he would give himself "at least thirty-five years for rape" and dismiss the other charges, meaning chiefly the murder of Quilty (310). But there are further accusations that the novel strives to evade. As a whole, the book defends itself against a utilitarian concept of art. This charge is rather easily evaded by the use of John Ray, who introduces the novel as an object lesson in the necessity of moral watchfulness on the part of "parents, social workers, educators" (8). Nabokov's obvious satire here is intended to remove the allegation of his having a conventional moral purpose. Other accusations are handled within the text itself. In addition to conventional moralists, Nabokov detests psychiatrists and literary critics, and it is against these types of readers—or these metaphors for the Reader—that Humbert wages constant war. Anti-Freudianism is one of Nabokov's pet themes, and Humbert is a man who, in his periodic vacations in insane asylums, loves nothing more than to take on a psychiatrist in a battle of wits. His chief defense against a psychoanalytic interpretation of *Lolita* is to admit it readily and dismiss it as trite and unhelpful. When he describes his gun, he says, "We must remember that a pistol is the Freudian symbol of the Urfather's central forelimb" (218); Humbert beats the analysts to the draw and says, in effect, "So what?" At another point, he anticipates a Freudian prediction that he will try to complete his fantasy by having intercourse with Lolita on a beach. Of course he tried, Humbert says. In fact, he went out of his way to look for a suitable beach, not in the grip of unconscious forces but in "rational pursuit of a purely theoretical thrill," and when he found his beach, it was so damp, stony, and uncomfortable that "for the first time in my life I had as little desire for her as for a manatee" (169).

Ultimately, we have to understand Nabokov's anti-Freudianism in the context of a hatred for allegory and symbolism in general. In *Ada,* Van Veen says of two objects that both "are real, they are not interchangeable, not tokens of something else."[6] Nabokov is against interpretation; an image has no depth, nothing beneath or behind or beyond; it is itself. Discussing Hieronymus Bosch, Van tells us, "I mean I don't give a hoot for the esoteric meaning, for the myth behind the moth, for the masterpiece-baiter who makes Bosch express some bosh of his time, I'm allergic to allegory and am quite sure he was just enjoying himself by crossbreeding casual fancies just for the fun of the contour and color" (437). Another of Nabokov's heroes, Cincinnatus in *Invitation to a Beheading,* is a man whose mortal crime is to be opaque, or inexplicable, while everyone else is transparent. To be inexplicable is to be unrelatable to anything else; Humbert refers to the "standardized symbols" of psychoanalysis (287), and Hermann, a bad literary critic, points out a resemblance that nobody else can see. Nabokov's hero-villains are often allegorists like Humbert, who imposes his fantasy of Annabel Leigh on Lolita and turns her into a symbol of his monomania.

Allegory, as Angus Fletcher has shown, is demonic and compulsive; it is a spell, enchanted discourse.[7] Nabokov, on the contrary, tries to create structures that defy interpretation and transcend the reader's allegorism, Freudian or otherwise. Like Mallarmé, he dreams of a literature that will be allegorical only of itself. Thus, Humbert evades our attempts to explain him according to prior codes or assumptions. First of all, he insists that women find his "gloomy good looks" irresistible (106), therefore, we cannot pigeonhole him as someone forced into perversion by his inability to attract adult women. Then, too, Lolita is not "the fragile child of a feminine novel" (46) but a child vamp, who, furthermore, is not a virgin and who, even further, Humbert claims, actually seduces him—a claim that is at least arguable. Finally, when we are forced to compare Humbert to Quilty, a sick, decadent, and cynical man, a man who is immune to enchantment, it becomes impossible simply to categorize Humbert as a pervert like all others. In all these ways, Humbert is not only made to look better than he otherwise would; he is also made difficult to explain and classify, and his uniqueness is a crucial theme of his defense. In *Ada,* Van Veen acclaims the "individual vagaries" without which "no art and no genius would exist" (237). In *Despair*, Hermann the Marxist longs for the "ideal sameness" of a classless society, where one person is replaceable by another, while his rival, the artist Ardalion believes that "every face is unique" (168–69, 50). Ultimately, even Hermann admits that his double resembles him only in sleep or death; vitality is individuation. It is a favorite theme of Nabokov. We are told in *Pnin* that schools of art do not count and that "genius is non-conformity."[8] The author himself always hates being compared to other writers: "Spiritual affinities have no place in my concept of literary criticism," he has said.[9] In light of this, it is worth noting that the alienation and linguistic eccentricity of a character like Pnin are, in addition to being poignant and comical, valuable signs of his singularity. Whatever else they are, heroes like Pnin, Humbert, and Kinbote are recognizable; they are rare birds. Humbert tells us that he is even singular physiologically in that he has the faculty of shedding tears during orgasm.

Humbert's chief line of defense is that he is no "brutal scoundrel" but a poet (133). Nympholepsy is aesthetic as well as sexual; the nymphet in the child is perceived by the mind. Humbert does not wish merely to tell us about sex, which anyone can do; he wants "to fix once for all the perilous magic of nymphets" (136); he wants to fix the borderline between "the beastly and beautiful" in nymphet love (137). He calls himself "an artist and a madman, a creature of infinite melancholy" (19); he is an explorer of that special romantic domain of sensation, the feeling of being in paradise and hell simultaneously; and he is a sentimentalist who revokes the antiromantic bias of modernism in a sentimental parody of Eliot's "Ash Wednesday." The problem is that in portraying himself as a romantic dreamer and enchanted poet, rather than as a brutal scoundrel, he leaves himself open to another charge: literary banality. He recognizes his position as a spokesman for values that no one takes seriously any more and says that his judges will regard his lyrical outbursts and rhapsodic interpretations as "mummery," so much hot air to glorify his perversion (42). His nymphet, on the other hand, is at best bored by his mummery, and the two often operate as a vaudeville team, in which he is the alazon and she the eiron:

> "Some day, Lo, you will understand many emotions and situations, such as for example the harmony, the beauty of spiritual relationship."
> "Bah!" said the cynical nymphet. (114)

Humbert fears Lolita's "accusation of mawkishness" (202), and his madcap and mocking humor defends him against any such accusation by the reader. So too does the presence of Charlotte, a trite sentimentalist whose mode of expression he mocks and against which his own appears unimpeachable. Yet he says, "Oh, let me be mawkish for the nonce. I am so tired of being cynical" (111).

If the book's central rhetorical figure is prolepsis, its central structural figure is displacement, or incongruity. Often cultural or geographical, incongruity appears in such local details as Charlotte's calling her patio a "piazza" and speaking French with an American accent; but more generally it appears in Humbert's Old World, European manner—aristocratic,

starchy, and genteel—set in a brassy America of motels and movie magazines and in his formal, elegant style of speaking posed against Lolita's
slang. But Humbert is not only out of place, he is also out of time, since he
is still pursuing the ghost of that long-lost summer with Annabel Leigh.
The incongruity is also erotic, in the sexual pairing of a child and an adult,
and, in the application of romantic rhetoric to child molesting, it appears
as a problematic relation between word and deed. The geographical, linguistic, and temporal aspects of Humbert's dislocation are often related to
Nabokov's own exile, but I wish to emphasize here another primal displacement: Humbert's status as a nineteenth-century hero out of his age.
In this literary dislocation, a romantic style is placed in a setting in which it
must appear alien and incongruous. Humbert's problem is to defend his
romanticism in a de-idealizing, debunking, demythologizing time.

In *Eugene Onegin,* Tatiana wonders if Onegin is a mere copy of a Byronic
hero:

> who's he then? Can it be—an imitation,
> an insignificant phantasm, or else
> a Muscovite in Harold's mantle,
> a glossary of other people's megrims,
> a complete lexicon of words in vogue? . . .
> Might he not be, in fact, a parody?[10]

Humbert, in his displaced and belated romanticism, must prove that he is
not an imitation. Nabokov's use throughout his work of various doubles,
mirrors, antiworlds, and reflections has been much documented and explored. His heroes are typically set in a matrix of doubleness: the condemned man Cincinnatus in *Invitation to a Beheading,* for example, is doubled
both by his secret inner self—his freedom or his imagination—and by his
executioner. Among its many functions, the double serves as a second-
order reality, or parody The double Quilty parodies Humbert who parodies
Edgar Allan Poe. Humbert is referred to many times as an ape, and an ape
is not only a beast but an imitator.[11] Nabokov has written that the inspiration for *Lolita* was a story of an ape who, when taught to draw, produced a
picture of the bars of this cage.[12] So Humbert, the ape, the parody, gives us
a picture of his emotional and moral imprisonment and enchantment. To
be free is to be original, not to be a parody.

"I am writing under observation," says the jailed Humbert (12). Once
upon a time, observers walked out of the sea to destroy the best moment
of his life, before their arrival, he and Annabel had "somebody's lost pair of
sunglasses for only witness" (15). Fear of discovery is Humbert's constant

anxiety; he feels that he lives in a "lighted house of glass" (182). The observer, the jury, and the brother in the mirror represent the reader and also the self-consciousness of the writer. Robert Alter has pointed out in his excellent study *Partial Magic* that an entire tradition of the "self-conscious novel," stemming from *Don Quixote*, employs a "proliferation of doubles" and mirror images to present a fiction's awareness of itself as fiction and to speculate on the relation between fiction and reality.[13] *Lolita* certainly participates in this tradition, but the sense of time expressed by its displacements and its literary allusions suggests that we understand its self-consciousness as specifically historical, as in the theories of Walter Jackson Bate and Harold Bloom. Humbert's jury is the literary past, which sits in judgment of his story. Humbert is both a mad criminal and a gentleman with an "inherent sense of the *comme il faut*" (249); self-consciousness figures here as the gentleman in the artist, his taste or critical faculty, his estimation of what he can get away with without being condemned as an imitator, a sentimentalist, or an absurdly displaced romantic.

What is on trial, then, is Humbert's uniqueness and originality, his success in an imaginative enterprise. To what judgment of him does the book force us? Quilty is the embodiment of his limitations and his final failure. He first appears to Humbert in the hotel where the affair is consummated. Thus, as soon as the affair begins in actuality, Humbert splits in two, and later, practicing to kill Quilty, he uses his own sweater for target practice. Described as the American Maeterlinck, Quilty is a fin-de-siècle decadent and thus the final, weak form of Humbert's romanticism; his plays reduce the themes of the novel to the sentimental and the banal; the message of one of them is that "mirage and reality merge in love" (203). Quilty, who is worshiped by Lolita and who could not care less about her, incarnates the ironies of Humbert's quest: to possess is to be possessed; to hunt is to be hunted. In addition, to be a parody, as Humbert is of a romantic quester, is to be defeated by doubleness: Quilty is an ape who calls Humbert an ape.[14]

In relation to Lolita, Humbert accepts complete guilt. The end of the book is filled with outbursts against himself for depriving her of her childhood. A poet and a lover of beauty, he finishes as a destroyer of beauty. At one point, learning how to shoot, Humbert admires the marksmanship of John Farlow, who hits a hummingbird, although "not much of it could be retrieved for proof—only a little iridescent fluff" (218); the incident aptly characterizes Humbert's actual relationship to his own ideal. At the end, he recognizes that "even the most miserable of family lives was better than the parody of incest, which, in the long run, was the best I could offer the waif" (289). All he can achieve is parody. When he calls himself a poet, the point is not that he's shamming but that he fails. Authenticity eludes him, and he loses out to history. What he accomplishes is solipsism, a destructive caricature of uniqueness and originality, and he succeeds in creating only a renewed sense of loss wherever he turns. Of his first voyage across America with Lolita, he says: "We had been everywhere. We had really seen nothing. And I catch myself thinking today that our long journey had only defiled with a sinuous trail of slime the lovely, trustful, dreamy, enormous country" (177–78).

Humbert is finally apprehended driving down the wrong side of the road, "that queer mirror side" (308). This is his last dislocation and is symbolic of all of them. We can now address one further form of displacement in Humbert's quest: the displacement of the imagination into reality. The mirror side of the road is fantasy, and Humbert has crossed over. Lolita was a mental image, which Humbert translated into actuality and in so doing destroyed her life and his, but his guilt is to know that she has a reality apart from his fantasy. The narrator of Nabokov's story "That in Aleppo Once . . . ," measuring himself against Pushkin, describes himself as indulging in "that kind of retrospective romanticism which finds pleasure in imitating the destiny of a unique genius . . . even if one cannot imitate his verse."[15] So Humbert is proud to inform us that Dante and Poe loved little girls. Hermann, in *Despair*, treats the artist and the criminal as parallels in that both strive to create masterpieces of deception that will outwit observers and pursuers; it is Hermann's failure not only to be found out but to be told that his crime, an insurance caper, was hopelessly hackneyed. Kinbote too confuses imagination and reality in *Pale Fire*, for he thinks he has written a critique and a factual autobiography, whereas he has really produced a poem of his own.[16] Crime and mythomania are parodies of art; Humbert parodies the novelist who attempts to displace the imagination into actuality, and this would seem to be the judgment of him handed down by the novel itself. Note, however, that this is the way romantic heroes—for example, Raskolnikov, Frankenstein, Ahab—typically fail. Perhaps it is Humbert's deeper failure to think, not that he could succeed, but that he could achieve the same kind of high romantic failure as those heroes of a lost age.

In any case, at the end, Humbert—who was a failed artist early in his career, who tried to translate art into life and again failed, and who then turned a third time to art, now as a refuge, a sad compensation, and a "very local palliative" (285)—sees art as a way to "the only immortality" he and Lolita may share (311). Having in effect destroyed her, he now wants to make her "live in the minds of later generations" (311). A new idea of art does begin for him in his own imaginative failures. Then, too, he now claims to love Lolita just as she is, no longer a nymphet and now possessing an identity, dim and gray as it may be, that is separate from his private mythology. Thus, unlike Hermann, who will never be paroled from Hell, Humbert is finally able to see beyond the prison of his solipsism.

AT THIS POINT I WISH to turn from Humbert's engagement with the parodic and the romantic to Nabokov's, and I will begin with several points about parody in general.[17] Parody is representation of representation, a confrontation with a prior text or type of text. The mood of the confrontation varies with the instance. We can have parody for its own sake; for example, in *TLS* (21 Jan. 1977), Gawain Ewart translated an obscene limerick into two prose passages, one in the style of the *Oxford English Dictionary,* the second in the style of Dr. Johnson's dictionary. Then we can have parody for the purpose of critique, satirical parody, such as J. K. Stephen's famous take-off on Wordsworth and his "two voices": "one is of the deep . . . And one is of an old half-witted sheep." *Lolita* includes examples of both types, for instance, the roster of Lolita's class with its delightful names (Stella Fantazia, Vivian McCrystal, Oleg Sherva, Edgar Talbot, Edwin Talbot [54]) and the Beardsley headmistress's spiel about her progressive school ("We stress the four D's: Dramatics, Dance, Debating and Dating" [179]). But as a whole, the novel participates in a third type, parody that seeks its own originality, what Robert Alter would call metaparody: parody that moves through and beyond parody.[18]

When Alter calls parody "the literary mode that fuses creation with critique," he is saying something that is strictly true only of satirical parody.[19] What is common to all three types is that they fuse creation with differentiation. Parodists use a voice different from their own in such a way as to call attention to themselves. Parody is at once an impersonation and an affirmation of identity, both an identification with and a detachment from the Other. This sense of displaced recognition, this incongruous simultaneity of closeness and distance, is a primary source of the delight and humor of parody, although it should be noted that parody is not inevitably comic, as in the case of John Fowles's *The French Lieutenant's Woman,* for example. Some parody, such as Stephen's, emphasizes the distance, but we also need to remember John Ashbery's idea of parody to "revitalize some way of expression that might have fallen into disrepute."[20] It may be true that some aggression is inherent in all parody, no matter how loving, but it is an aggression that is more primal than intellectual critique; it is the kind of aggression that says, "This is me. This is mine."

Page Stegner has said that Nabokov uses parody to get rid of the stock and conventional,[21] and Alfred Appel, Jr., that he uses parody and self-parody to exorcise the trite and "to re-investigate the fundamental problems of his art."[22] I think it is finally more accurate to say that he uses parody to evade the accusation of triteness and to elude the literary past in the hope of achieving singularity. Nabokov's parodism is an attempt to control literary relations, a way of telling his jury that he already knows how his book is related to prior work. More than that, it is a way of taking possession of the literary past, of internalizing it. Nabokov has repeatedly noted, and critics—most vividly, George Steiner[23]—have often stressed the idea that he writes in a borrowed language. But in his difficult condition of personal and linguistic exile, Nabokov also points to another, more general kind of displacement. Irving Massey has suggested that many works of literature deal with the problem that "*parole* is never ours," that we all speak a borrowed idiom in expressing ourselves in the public medium of language.[24] It is also relevant that a writer inevitably speaks in the borrowed language of literary convention. Like so many other writers of the nineteenth and twentieth centuries, Nabokov dreams of detaching his representation from the history of representations, of creating a *parole* that transcends *langue.*

In relation to romance, parody acts in *Lolita* in a defensive and proleptic way. It does not criticize the romance mode, although it criticizes Humbert; it renders romance acceptable by anticipating our mockery and beating us to the draw. It is what Empsom calls "pseudo-parody to disarm criticism."[25] I am suggesting, then, that *Lolita* can only be a love story through being a parody of love stories. The most valuable insight about *Lolita* that I know is John Hollander's idea of the book as a "record of Mr. Nabokov's love-affair with the romantic novel, a today-unattainable literary object as short-lived of beauty as it is long of memory."[26] I would add that parody is Nabokov's way of getting as close to the romantic novel as possible and, more, that he actually does succeed in recreating it in a new form, one that is contemporary and original, not anachronistic and imitative. Further, it is the book's triumph that it avoids simply recreating the romantic novel in its old form; for Nabokov to do so would be to lose his own personal, twentieth-century identity.[27]

Nabokov has tried to refine Hollander's "elegant formula" by applying it to his love affair with the English langauge.[28] His displacement of the formula from the literary to the linguistic is instructive. Indeed, both in theory and practice, he is always moving the linguistic, the stylistic, and the artificial to center stage. "Originality of literary style . . . constitutes the only real honesty of a writer," says Van Veen, who characterizes his own literary activities as "buoyant and bellicose exercises in literary style" (471, 578).

Language that calls attention to itself relates to romance in one of two ways. Either it becomes, as in Spenser or Keats, a magical way of intensifying the romance atmosphere or, as in Byron with his comical rhymes and his farcical self-consciousness, it demystifies that atmosphere. As in *Don Juan*, language in *Lolita* is used to empty out myth and romance. The novel opens with Humbert trilling Lolita's name for a paragraph in a parody of incantatory or enchanted romance language and proceeds through a dazzling panorama of wordplay, usually more Byronic than Joycean: zeugmas, like "burning with desire and dyspepsia" (132); puns, such as "we'll grill the soda jerk" (227); alliterations, such as "a pinkish cozy, coyly covering the toilet lid" (40); unexpected and inappropriate condensations, such as the parenthetical comment "(picnic, lightning)" following Humbert's first mention of his mother's death (12); instances of language breaking loose and running on mechanically by itself, as in "drumlins, and gremlins, and kremlins" (35–36); and monomaniacal distortions of diction: "adults one dollar, pubescents sixty cents" (157).

Certainly, verbal playfulness for its own sake is an important feature of Nabokov's art; certainly, too, we ought not underestimate the way in which Nabokov's linguistic exile has contributed to his sense of language as an objective presence, not merely as a vehicle. It may also be that wordplay is used to overcome language: in *Despair*, Hermann says that he likes "to make words look self-conscious and foolish, to bind them by the mock marriage of a pun, to turn them inside out, to come upon them unawares" (56). But I would suggest that language is finally a false clue in Nabokov's work unless we see that his centering of language and style chiefly has the value of a poetic myth. A literature of pure language and convention is a dream, congruent with the dream of a literature beyond interpretation; it is a dream of literature as a word game with no depth, a manipulation of conventions, a kind of super-Scrabble. The function of this poetic myth, or "bellicose exercise," is here proleptic; it detaches the writer from the romantic so that he may then gain for the romantic an ultimate acceptability.

This is also true of the idea of games in Nabokov and of all the devices of self-consciousness that Alfred Appel, Jr., has valuably described, such as the kind of coincidental patterning that runs the number 342 into the novel in different contexts to emphasize the artificiality of the fiction.[29]

Humbert and Quilty share with their creator a love for the magic of games, as do so many other of Nabokov's characters, and sometimes that magic can assume diabolical form, as it does in the case of Axel, a forger of paintings and checks in *Laughter in the Dark*. The vicious Axel completely identifies creativity with game playing; for him, "everything that had ever been created in the domain of art, science or sentiment, was only a more or less clever trick."[30] Parody, Nabokov has said, is a game, while satire is a lesson.[31] A game is a matter of manipulating conventions; it is also a matter of play, a little Arcadia; and it is also a matter of competition. We can look at the idea of the game as a trope, a clinamen in Harold Bloom's sense, by which Nabokov swerves from the dead seriousness of typical romance. But I see it ultimately, like parody and the centering of style, as an enabling poetic myth, the I-was-only-looking that permits us to get away with shocking utterances, like romantic rhapsodies in the mouth of an urbane, sophisticated, literate person like Humbert. It is the fiction that permits fiction to occur.

We might say that Nabokov must kill off a bad romantic and a bad artist in Humbert in order for his own brand of enchantment to exist. Nabokov's recurrent fascinations are romantic ones, he writes about passion, Arcadia, memory, individualism, the ephemeral, the enchanted, imagination, and the power of art. Indeed, his problem in *Lolita* is essentially the same as Humbert's: first, to be a romantic and still be original, and, second, to get away with being a romantic. *Lolita* has been taken as a critique of romanticism, and I am not arguing that it should be read as a romantic work. Rather, in its final form, it is a work of complex relationship to romanticism, a dialectic of identification and differentiation. Like Byron in *Don Juan,* Nabokov in *Lolita* is divided against himself, although in a different way. Byron is a poet struggling against his own romantic temperament, while in Nabokov we see a romantic temperament trying to achieve a perilous balance in an unfriendly setting. But the results do illuminate each other. In *Don Juan* a romantic lyricism and melancholy are achieved through mocking parody and farce; in somewhat similar fashion, Nabokov uses the energies of his style—its parody, its centering of language, its flamboyant self-consciousness—first against the spirit of romance and then in behalf of it. This, then, is the status of style in *Lolita*, and this is why style is elevated to such prominence. Perhaps this is even why it must be a comic style: it functions as a defensive strategy both against the romanticism of the material and against the antiromanticism of the "jury."

Indeed, the tradition of romance continues most interestingly and convincingly in writers, such as Thomas Pynchon and John Fowles, who are ambivalent about it and who often present it negatively. In such teasing and parodic works as *V.* and *The Magus* we see an attempt to gain the literary power of romance without falling under its spell. These are romances for a demythologizing age. The phenomenon of the romantic antiromance is hardly new: *Don Quixote, The Odyssey,* and *Huckleberry Finn,* in addition to *Don Juan,* are works of enchantment that simultaneously reject enchantment. All of them create a language that, in Marthe Robert's description of *Don Quixote,* is both "invocation and critique"—indeed, Alter applies this phrase to the self-conscious novel as a tradition.[32] What may be new, however, is the anxiety created by novels like *V.* and *The Magus* in their skeptical and modernistic perspectives on the demonic. That anxiety—our uncertainty about how we are meant to take the demonic—is the source of the suspense in such works. In *Lolita,* the comedy considerably mitigates this anxiety; it is, however, produced to an extent by the dizzying narcissism of Kinbote in *Pale Fire* and, even more, by the celebratory tone of *Ada,* that incestuous love story with a happy ending.

Writing of Spenser, Harry Berger, Jr., has said that advertised artificiality in Renaissance art functioned to mark off an area in which artist and audience could legitimately indulge their imaginations.[33] Today similar techniques of self-consciousness serve to keep our imaginations in check by telling us that what we are offered is only a fiction, merely a myth. Yet these cautionary measures, even when—as in *V.*—they seem to constitute the major theme of the work, may, once again, serve chiefly to allow us to enter a demonic universe with a minimum of guilt and embarrassment. In sophisticated art, we can consent to romance only after it has been debunked for us.

In *the Magus,* Fowles tells a fable of a young man who learns that the only way to avoid being victimized by magical illusions is to be a magician himself. This is also true of Nabokov. In *Invitation to a Beheading,* everyone in Cincinnatus's totalitarian society appears to him to be a parody, a shadow of a reality, a copy. To be a parodist is one way of not being a parody. In *Despair,* Hermann, who seeks originality and hates and shuns mirrors, falls prey to a fake doubleness, Kinbote and Humbert are also trapped by reflections and doubles. But uniqueness resides in being able to manipulate doubleness; the inability to do this seems to be one of Nabokov's central criticisms of his failed artists. As for *Lolita* itself, it does beyond a doubt achieve singularity; however, singularity is not, as Nabokov would have it, to transcend literary relations but to be able to hold one's own among them.

Appel points out that Jakob Gradus, the assassin of *Pale Fire,* is an anagrammatic mirror reversal of another character in that novel, Sudarg of

Bokay, described as a "mirror-maker of genius," or artist.[34] Both death and the artist create doubles of life, and each struggles against the other. For the writer, the assassin comes from many directions: previous literature, current critical standards, the expectations of the audience, the resistance of language, the writer's own self-consciousness. Nabokov has spoken of the artist as an illusionist trying to "transcend the heritage" with his bag of tricks.[35] This is the magic of sleight of hand, and Nabokov is referring to matters of style, technique, and language. But we are really dealing in works such as *Lolita* with the magic of the shaman, and, in this case, parody—together with the other features of a proleptic comic style—is perhaps his most powerful spell.

### Notes

1. Alfred Appel, Jr., introduction and notes, *The Annotated Lolita* (New York: McGraw-Hill, 1970), 35, liv (same pagination as the 1958 Putnam edition). Hereafter cited in text.

2. Nabokov, *Despair* (New York: Putnam, 1966), 113.

3. Nabokov, *Despair*, 9.

4. Carl R. Proffer, *Keys to "Lolita"* (Bloomington: Indiana University Press, 1968), 45–53.

5. Alfred Appel, Jr., "*Ada* Described," in *Nabokov: Criticism, Reminiscences, Translations, Tributes,* ed. Appel and Charles Newman (Evanston, Ill.: Northwestern University Press, 1970), 182.

6. Nabokov, *Ada or Ardor: A Family Chronicle* (New York: McGraw-Hill, 1969), 363. Hereafter cited in text.

7. Angus Fletcher, *Allegory: The Theory of a Symbolic Mode* (Ithaca, N.Y.: Cornell University Press, 1964).

8. Nabokov, *Pnin* (New York: Doubleday, 1957), 96, 89.

9. Nabokov, *Invitation to a Beheading* (New York: Putnam, 1959), 6.

10. Aleksandr Pushkin, *Eugene Onegin: A Novel in Verse,* trans. with commentary by Vladimir Nabokov, rev. ed., 2 vols. (Princeton, N.J.: Princeton University Press, 1975), 1:262 (ellipses in original).

11. Appel notes that the ape metaphor is common in double stories; *Annotated Lolita,* lxiv.

12. Nabokov, "On a Book Entitled *Lolita*," in *Annotated Lolita,* 313.

13. Robert Alter, *Partial Magic: The Novel as a Self-Conscious Genre* (Berkeley: University of California Press, 1975), 21.

14. Appel, *Annotated Lolita,* lxiv.

15. Nabokov, *The Portable Nabokov,* ed. Page Stegner (New York: Viking, 1971), 146.

16. See Alter's fine discussion of *Pale Fire* in *Partial Magic*, 180–217. See also G. D. Josipovici's discussion of the confusion of imagination and reality in *Lolita* and in Nabokov's other works, "*Lolita*: Parody and the Pursuit of Beauty," *Critical Quarterly* 6 (1964): 35–48.

17. Some of the points in this section are discussed in greater detail in Thomas R. Frosch, "Parody and the Contemporary Imagination," *Soundings* 56 (1973): 371–92.

18. Alter, *Partial Magic*, 215.

19. Alter, *Partial Magic*, 25.

20. Anon., "Craft interview with John Ashbery," *New York Quarterly* 9 (1972): 30.

21. Stegner, *The Portable Nabokov*, xix–xxi.

22. Appel, "*Ada* Described," 174, 171.

23. George Steiner, "Extraterritorial," in *Nabokov*, ed. Appel and Newman, 119–27.

24. Irving Massey, *The Gaping Pig: Literature and Metamorphosis* (Berkeley: University of California Press, 1976), 30.

25. William Empson, *Some Versions of Pastoral* (Harmondsworth, England: Penguin, 1966), 52.

26. John Hollander, "The Perilous Magic of Nymphets," in *On Contemporary Literature* ed. Richard Kostelanetz (New York: Avon, 1964), 480.

27. Both Lionel Trilling and G. D. Josipovici have approached the same general understanding of the book as a serious engagement with the romantic, although in ways different from my own. Trilling sees Humbert as the last exponent of "passion-love," which, although traditionally finding its setting in the story of adultery, now requires a more extreme vehicle, like child molesting, for adequate shock value. Trilling calls *Lolita* a "regressive book": "although it strikes all the approved modern postures and attitudes, it is concerned to restore a foregone mode of feeling" ("The Last Lover—Vladimir Nabokov's *Lolita*," *Encounter* 11 [1958]: 9–19). For Josipovici, in "*Lolita*: Parody and the Pursuit of Beauty," Humbert fails to capture Lolita in life, but he does capture her in his memoir, that is, in and as language. His ability to do so depends upon his learning to distinguish reality from imagination and understanding words as arbitrary signs, not objects. Parody, as the mode that treats convention as convention rather than as reality, becomes the medium through which Humbert can successfully conduct his quest for beauty, which is otherwise unattainable. Trilling and Josipovici are far more accurate guides to the novel than those who read it as a satire, but neither accounts for the interplay of the romantic and the comical, which constitutes the book's special impact.

28. Nabokov, "On a Book Entitled *Lolita*," in *Annotated Lolita*, 318.

29. Appel, *Annotated Lolita*, esp. xxvii–xxxi, lviii–lxxi.

30. Nabokov, *Laughter in the Dark* (New York: Bobbs-Merrill, 1938), 182.

31. Nabokov, *Strong Opinions* (New York: McGraw-Hill, 1973), 11.

32. Alter, *Partial Magic*, 11.

33. Harry Berger, Jr., *Spenser: A Collection of Critical Essays, Twentieth-Century Views* (Englewood Cliffs, N.J.: Prentice Hall, 1968), 3–5.

34. Alfred Appel, Jr., "*Lolita:* The Springboard of Parody," in L. S. Dembo, ed., *Nabokov: The Man and His Work* (Madison: University of Wisconsin Press, 1967), 108.

35. Nabokov, "On a Book Entitled *Lolita*," in *Annotated Lolita,* 319.

# "Even Homais Nods"

## Nabokov's Fallibility; or, How to Revise Lolita

BRIAN BOYD

◆　◆　◆

The *New Yorker's* wonderful research department
several times saved Mr. Nabokov—who seems
to combine a good deal of absentmindedness with
his pedantism—from various blunders regarding
names, numbers, book titles and the like.
—Nabokov, pseudoreview of *Conclusive Evidence*

I N *Pnin* Nabokov glances at one of the most famous mistakes in literature, when night after night Victor tries to induce sleep by sinking into
fantasies of himself as a king about to flee, pacing, as he awaits rescue, a
strand on the Bohemian Sea. Ben Jonson was the first to mock Shakespeare for having a ship wrecked on the coast of Bohemia in *The Winter's
Tale*; Samuel Johnson assumes Shakespeare is "little careful of geography";
*Tristram Shandy* turns the point to its own advantage.[1]

But Coleridge more than once talked of having often dismissed as a
fault in Shakespeare what he later saw as a "beauty." Just as Victor knew
what he was doing in choosing this impossible seacoast—and this is probably Nabokov's particular point—so did Shakespeare in stressing the coast
of Bohemia, since it would be hard to find a more landlocked region in Europe.[2] Shakespeare rewrote geography in order to emphasize the fantastic
nature of his plot—as he did in choosing *The Winter's Tale* for a title and in
all the expressions of incredulity at the play's close—just as for instance
he chose to violate history for other ends by fusing classical Rome and Renaissance Italy in *Cymbeline.*

In the twentieth century the professionalization of criticism and the
ever-increasing prestige of Shakespeare have led critic after critic to resur-
rect as virtues in this or that play what had once seemed defects. This has

yielded many valuable insights, but it has also led to a working principle that Shakespeare could not make a mistake. This of course, in the schizoid world of modern criticism, where some blithely combine Freud and Marx, is not incompatible with others insisting that Shakespeare always contradicts himself. But the widespread assumption of Shakespeare's infallibility has often led to absurd consequences.[3]

In Nabokov's case, too, both the professionalization of criticism and the prestige of the author have encouraged critics to adopt as an article of faith that he also soars above error. He does of course let pass far fewer mistakes than Shakespeare. Where Shakespeare paid little if any attention to the publishing of his works other than his poems, Nabokov kept meticulous control over his texts, in all the languages he knew. Aware that he was writing for an audience that would see a play only once, Shakespeare could distort the time scale of his stories to combine a sense of rapid pace with gradual development, since the dual calendar would be noticed only be a careful reader. But that careful reader is precisely Nabokov's ideal audience.

Besides, Nabokov was of a notoriously precise, even pedantic temperament, hard on anyone else's mistakes, exigent about particulars, insistent on an exactitude of detail and a delicacy of interconnections that make it natural to expect him to ensure the accuracy of all his work. Nearly always, the expectation is justified. Line 3 of Humbert's poem "Wanted, wanted, Dolores Haze"—"Age: five thousand three hundred days"[4]—seems only to combine the continuation of the "wanted" poster format, an affectionate approximation, and a rhyme. But after we calculate the gap between Lolita's birth, 1 January 1935, and 5 July 1949, the day Humbert discovers her missing, and find it to be exactly 5,300 days, we will hesitate to attribute any discrepancy in Nabokov's work to oversight.

All the more so when we recall how fascinated he was by deception in nature, especially mimicry, and how much he liked to find in his art equivalents for the sly playfulness he sensed behind things. He even wrote that "in art, as in nature, a glaring disadvantage may turn out to be a subtle protective device."[5] As if this were not enough, he has said, in discussing the editing of *Eugene Onegin:* "Even obvious misprints should be treated gingerly; after all, they may be supposed to have been left uncorrected by the author."[6]

But even Homer nods, and so does Nabokov, and to build wholesale interpretations on details that seem much more explicable as errors is fraught with danger.

I have in mind especially the thesis, first proposed in 1976 by Elizabeth

Bruss,[7] developed in 1979 by Christina Tekiner,[8] in 1989 by Leona Toker,[9] in 1990 by Alexander Dolinin,[10] in 1995 by Julian Connolly,[11] and summarized by Dieter E. Zimmer[12]—and independently by others who have spoken and written to me in the wake of the biography and still others on the Nabokov electronic bulletin board[13]—that a hidden inconsistency in *Lolita*, in Toker's words, "untells Humbert's tale."[14] On the last page of the novel, Humbert says that he started work on his manuscript in captivity fifty-six days ago. In John Ray, Jr.'s foreword, we discover Humbert dies on 16 November 1952. Counting back fifty-six days from there, we reach 22 September, the day Humbert receives the letter from Lolita. But since he is not in prison on that date, since over the next few days he drives first to Lolita in Coalmont, then to Ivor Quilty in Ramsdale, and finally to Clare Quilty at Pavor Manor, he has no time for these visits and for composing the text we are reading. That is Nabokov's hint, say these attentive readers, that Humbert has merely invented the visit to seventeen-year-old Lolita and the murder of Quilty. In the Russian *Lolita*, some of these critics add, Nabokov has placed further stress on these dates.

To refute this reading, I will first show that Nabokov could indeed make mistakes, especially in dating, and that second thoughts often merely compounded the confusion. I will then show how little is required to eliminate the revisionist interpretation of *Lolita* (the emendation of a single typographical character would suffice), and how plainly it contradicts itself and the rest of the text.

FIRST, SOME EXAMPLES of Nabokov's fallibility. One of the reviewers of *Vladimir Nabokov: The American Years* listed as the "most intriguing fact" in the book my claim that Nabokov had committed twenty-one demonstrable errors in his autobiography, most of which I did not have space to list.[15] Let me mention a few here.

Nabokov's map of the Vyra region in the endpapers of the revised *Speak, Memory* is thoroughly muddled.[16] What looks like a small tributary coming past the Batovo estate is in fact the Oredezh itself; the river labeled "Oredezh" running past the Rozhdestveno estate is actually the Gryazno, a very short-lived little stream; and when the Oredezh passes the Vyra estate it does not continue west and away from Siverskaya but turns to flow east toward the town. Other errors in *Speak, Memory* are equally close to home. Nabokov lists his father as the second son of Dmitri and Maria Nabokov, and Sergey as the third, when it was the other way around (59). But most of his autobiography's inaccuracies involve minor details of dating: the birth of his grandfather, his father's graduation, the sale of Batovo, the duration of the German occupation of Yalta, and the like.

Dates are a common source of error in Nabokov, as he confesses in the foreword to *Speak, Memory*: "Among the anomalies of a memory, whose possessor and victim should never have tried to become an autobiographer, the worst is the inclination to equate in retrospect my age with that of the century. . . . Mnemosyne, one must admit, has shown herself to be a very careless girl" (13). Protesting to Katharine White about the *New Yorker*'s wanting to change one of the visual details in *Speak, Memory*'s final chapter, he insisted, "I very seldom err when recalling colors," but only after first making the concession: "As you have probably noticed I often make mistakes when recalling names, titles of books, numbers."[17] Very often Nabokov, like many of us, would date a letter in January to the previous year, but he could do this as late as October.[18] He could be quite wildly wrong about the dates of his works, as when he recorded the date of composition of "The Potato Elf" as 1929[19] rather than the correct April 1924, despite the vast stylistic gap between the stories he wrote in early 1924 and the mastery he had achieved by the time, five years later, that he was writing *The Defense*.

Errors of memory, especially when they involve dates, may, like casual slips of the tongue or the pen, seem of a different order from apparent inconsistencies in fictional worlds whose details Nabokov entirely controlled himself. But even there, although he was meticulous in the extreme in correcting his work for the smallest imprecisions of phrasing or fact, errors still persisted. Véra Nabokov, never one to denigrate her husband, told me he was very "absentminded." When I asked her about resolving editorial problems by consulting the manuscripts, she told me the "manuscripts should not be trusted" as copy texts, since "he would often write one word when he meant another" and "might not catch it until the galleys."[20]

*Pnin* is a novel where mistakes matter: Pnin's garbled English; his endearing errors (like when he discovers, after laboriously returning a bulky library tome he cannot understand anyone else needing , that the person who has recalled it was himself); Cockerell's false version of Pnin's mishap at Cremona; and the discrepancies between Pnin's and the narrator's accounts of Pnin's past. In view of these and other meaningful mistakes, Nabokov ought to have tried harder than ever to eliminate unintended errors. But he still did not succeed.

In February 1953 Pnin teaches elementary Russian to a class that includes Frank Carroll.[21] In September 1954 Pnin invites to his party "old Carrol, the Frieze Hall head janitor, with his son Frank, who had been my friend's only talented student and had written a brilliant doctor's thesis for him on the relationship between Russian, English and German iambics; but Frank was in the army" (147–48). Somehow, in the space of a year and a half, Frank Carroll has advanced from elementary Russian to having completed—some months ago, it seems, given his army service—a Ph.D. that requires a sophisticated command of the language and, presumably, could only have been envisaged by someone with a long-standing interest in Russian verse read in the original. He has also found the time to lose a letter from his surname.

Al Cook (Aleksandr Petrovich Kukolnikov) and his American wife, Susan, have a summer house, "The Pines," to which they invite "every even-year summer, elderly Russians . . . ; on odd-year summers they would have *amerikantsi*" (117). But only three pages later, Varvara Bolotov is said to have visited the Pines for the first time "in 1951" (120) and finds that its birches and bilberries remind her of her "first fifteen summers" near Lake Onega in northern Russia. Are we to deduce that she is an American falsely posing as a Russian, or a Russian whom Al Cook has mistaken for *an amerikanka,* or simply that Nabokov should have written "1950" or "1952"?

Nabokov was pressed for time, distracted by teaching, and publishing chapters serially over several years when he wrote *Pnin.* But there were no such excuses at the time of *Ada.*

Van recalls dining at a restaurant with Ada "on New Year's Eve, 1893,"[22] in other words on 31 December 1893. But according to the novel's very precise calendar, Van and Ada do not meet between 5 February 1893 and 11 October 1905. Now we could deduce from this that Van has either fantasized this dinner with Ada, perhaps in desperate consolation, or that he has deliberately suppressed some of his time with Ada to exaggerate, for effect, the bleakness of their separation. Or we could simply decide that Nabokov made a natural error: he meant the day before New Year's Day 1893 and should have written "on New Year's Eve, 1892."

Another, much more serious error, or rather cluster of errors, was subsequently noticed by Nabokov himself. In part 1, chapter 26, Van describes the codes he and Ada used to correspond in the year between Ardis the First and Ardis the Second. One would expect Van and Nabokov to have been utterly vigilant after a comment like this: "Again, this is a nuisance to explain, and the explanation is fun to read only for the purpose (thwarted, I am afraid) of looking for errors in the examples" (161–62). In fact, the first time the code was used, several pages earlier, Nabokov let slip a misprint ("xlic" [157]), which he corrected in later editions (to "xliC").[23]

But that is not the mistake I mean. Look at this tangle of thorns. In describing the code, Van states: "The entire period of that separation was to span almost four years . . . from September, 1884 to June, 1888, with two brief interludes of intolerable bliss (in August, 1885 and June, 1886) and a couple of chance meetings" (160). The terminal dates are correct, but if the second interlude refers to Van meeting feverish Ada at Forest Fork (178), that occurs on 25 July 1886, not in June. "The entire period of that separation" is also interrupted by the Brownhill visit, not a "chance meeting" but taking place in November or December 1884 (167: "he had not seen his Ada for close to three months"). The rest of the novel, then, implies that Van meets Ada between the summers of 1884 and 1888 only at Brownhill, in late 1884, anything but an "interlude of intolerable bliss," and at Forest Fork, in June 1886. But part 1, chapter 26, implies two trysts, August 1885—never mentioned elsewhere, though Van otherwise assiduously records his meetings with and partings from Ada as milestones and crossroads in his life—and July 1886, and two other "chance" meetings. All four meetings seem either partially or totally incompatible with the rest of the novel.

But this short chapter, a mere two pages of solid text, is incompatible even with itself. Three paragraphs after the first passage, Van explains, "In the second period of separation, beginning in 1886, the code was radically altered" (161). This could be taken as implying that they changed the code at Forest Fork in July, or is it June, 1886, but it ignores the August 1885 interlude, which surely ought to start "the second period of separation." The next paragraph makes matters still worse: "in their third period of separation, from January, 1887, to June, 1888 (after a very long-distance call and a very brief meeting)" (162). The January 1887 meeting is not "chance," and since it marks the third of the three numbered periods in the four-year separation, it is perhaps one of the two "brief interludes of intolerable bliss," except that *they* have been dated 1885 and 1886.

No wonder then that Nabokov, on his own copy of the novel, the one he marked on the recto of the front loose endpaper "author's copy" and "Genial'naia kniga—perl' amerikanskoi literatury" ("a book of genius, the pearl of American literature"), lists on the half-title page thirty-odd corrections to be made and this note: "p. 161 not worth correcting." Ingenious readers who had spotted these contradictions without seeing Nabokov's comment might perhaps have suggested that Van's aversion to the hints of betrayal in Ada's coded correspondence makes him recoil from close attention to codes or dates, or that Ada's Forest Fork fever somehow infects him so that he deliriously confuses this patch of their past. There is no end of possible conjecture, if all we need is an inconsistency as a springboard for fancy. That Nabokov might have become bored with or fatigued by his attempt to outline the codes and simply failed to scrutinize the dates sufficiently would strike some readers as methodologically impermissible, since it moves outside the world of the book, or as just plain heresy.

Nabokov could muddle things further in his attempts to correct real or imagined errors. In part 1, chapter 2, of *Ada*, for instance, Marina's "meeting with Baron O." (12) seems odd, sandwiched as it is between the first and third references to her opposite number in a stage travesty of *Eugene Onegin*: "a local squire, Baron d'O." and "Baron d'O., now in black tails and white gloves." Why, this second time, is he not also "d'O."? Things become no clearer when on the next page Demon, now occupying the role of Marina's real-life opposite, meets an art dealer—and soon, he discovers, her lover—called Baron d'Onsky, who in one of the three references to *his* name becomes (simply?) "d'O." (13). Why the solitary "Baron O." on the previous page? Is it to unsettle the bizarre equation between d'O. and d'Onsky? Does it suggest the theme of transfiguration with which Nabokov is preoccupied in his treatment of the *Eugene Onegin* travesty and even in these semi-interchangeable barons? Or is "O." a mere oversight for "d'O"?

In Nabokov's master copy of *Ada*, he began to answer those questions when he changed the third reference to Marina's opposite, ten lines after the second, from "d'O." to "O."—but he forgot to turn back to the previous page to alter *that* "d'O." to "O." But at least it was clear now what he wanted, that there should be *less* overlap between d'O. and d'Onsky. Accordingly, the three references to Marina's stage partner were changed to "O." in the German edition, which Nabokov checked through for eleven days, in company with the German translators, while leaving the abbreviation of "d'Onsky" to "d'O." untouched."[24]

At last everything was correct. Or so it seemed. For in revising the French translation of *Ada*, which he did at his own pace and over a period of six intense months, Nabokov returned all three references to Marina's opposite to "d'O."[25] And this indeed seems what he originally, and finally, intended. In reading through his master copy, he had noticed the inconsistency on page 12 and made the second instance conform to the first, not realizing that both now differed from the previous occurrence, on page 11. His German translators, presumably, rectified the discrepancy by making the first occurrence conform to the other two, with no objections from Nabokov, who was never at ease with (and almost never subjected himself to) teamwork. Only in rereading even more slowly and in his own time did Nabokov realize what had happened and restored what he had first meant. This, indeed, now seems the "obvious" reading, since it links d'O. not only with d'Onsky but also with "the Don," Ada's opposite in *Don Juan's Last Fling,* pointedly associated with Marina's play as another orgasmically interrupted performance.[26]

One of the many curious features about this sequence of corrections and countercorrections is that it shows Nabokov quite clearly forgetting what he had once meant. That is even more strikingly noticeable in another change in the *Ada* master copy, where he "corrected" the account of a gambling evening during which Van notices Dick Schuler cheating on and winning a fortune off a pair of French twins. In "the unfortunate twins were passing to each other a fountain pen, thumb-pressing and repressing it in disastrous transit as they calculated their losses" (174), Nabokov changed "fountain pen" to "ball pen," which seems like a legitimate correction—we "thumb-press" only ball pens, not fountain pens—but which destroys an incidental joke: that the twins are so drunk ("happily and hopelessly tight" [173]) that they treat the fountain pen as *if* it were a ball pen.

Enough has been shown, surely, to prove that Nabokov not infrequently made mistakes, especially with dates, and that even second thoughts did not necessarily improve matters. Let's now start to move toward *Lolita.*

In Nabokov's published screenplay, act 1 opens: "The words LAST DAY OF SCHOOL are gradually scrawled across the blackboard."[27] Dialogue confirms it as the last day of school for Dolly and her classmates, and consistent time cues move the action forward by degrees to the next day, the day of Humbert's arrival in Ramsdale and his discovery that the McCoo house—in which he had hoped to enjoy Ginny McCoo's proximity—has just burned down. He finds himself steered to the Haze house and is about to reject it when he sees Lolita. While Charlotte happily pays for the taxi and installs his belongings in the house, Humbert chats up Lolita. He eagerly agrees to help her with her homework, but then she shrugs, "Well, there's not much today. Gee, school will be over in three weeks" (43). Shortly, Charlotte returns and calls Lolita to the phone: "It's Kenny. I suspect he wants to escort you to the big dance next month" (45). Two pages later, Nabokov headlines a jump in time: "THREE WEEKS LATER, THE DAY OF THE SCHOOL DANCE" (47). This appears not to be an intertitle, simply an objective indicator for the film's potential director, whether in studio or study. The dance ensues, with a cameo appearance by Clare Quilty.

Two clearly marked sequences, then, reinforce themselves and remain stubbornly incompatible with each other. In one, Humbert arrives at the Haze home on the last day of school. In the other, he has been at the Haze home for three weeks when Lolita's school year ends. In the time problem in the novel, there are almost three hundred pages between the incompatible dates, which involve a single indicator in each case. Here in the screenplay one elaborate series of time markers leads almost immediately into another quite incompatible with it.

Surely, some will chorus, a writer as attentive to detail and as wily as Nabokov could never have left such a glaring inconsistency without meaning it. (As far as I know, the discrepancy has never before been remarked on in print. Inconsistencies tend to become "glaring" only when someone points them out.) Is one of the two time sequences unreal, invented perhaps by Humbert? If so, which one? Or is the whole sequence proof that Humbert *is* Quilty, or that Quilty is *only* Humbert's double, since both arrive on Lolita's (different) last day(s) of school?

It is easy, all too easy, to invent fancy interpretations of this kind. Twentieth-century criticism has become expert, if that is the word, in strategies for retrieving a "higher" consistency from seeming inconsistency—although this often resembles a craft skill, an easily acquired habit, rather than real inquiry after explanation. Readers inclined, in this so-called postmodern era, to suppose a story will slyly undermine itself overlook other problems and possibilities. In the *Lolita* screenplay, the inconsistent time sequences cannot be easily explained as Humbert's invention, since the time indicators are objective, supplied in one case by Lolita's classmates before Humbert arrives in Ramsdale (although of course Humbert might have invented this scene too, to say nothing of Lolita and himself—this road can quickly lead to bog and fog) and in the other case by Nabokov himself in a stage direction.

But the screenplay's incompatible time schemes can easily be explained as a mere mistake. Nabokov composed a long first attempt at a *Lolita* screenplay in the spring and early summer of 1960.[28] It had a prologue, Humbert's killing of Quilty, and three acts, the first of which starts with Lolita on her last day at school, the day Humbert arrives. Nabokov here introduced Quilty to Ramsdale and to Lolita by way of Quilty's uncle, the dentist. But he then had the idea of reinstating a scene he had envisaged when he first composed the novel, of McCoo engaging Humbert in an irrelevant and comically spooky guided tour of the house where he would have had him as a lodger had lightning not just burnt it down.[29] Nabokov therefore wrote an alternative version of act 1 that begins with Humbert's arrival in Ramsdale and the scene at the McCoos'. This version then moves straight to Lawn Street and Humbert's conversation with sunbathing Lolita, who runs off to talk on the phone to Kenny, the boy who will take her in three weeks' time to the end-of-school dance—which in this alternative version Nabokov uses as the means of introducing Quilty in Ramsdale.

Nabokov appears to have allowed Kubrick to decide between the two versions, for he offered both, one paginated normally, the other as "alternative 1," "alternative 2," and so on, together with the rest of the typescript. When Kubrick protested that he needed to cut drastically, Nabokov offered a much shorter and more filmable version, in which act 1 drew entirely on the alternative version.[30] In late 1970, anxious to publish his screenplay before both Alan Jay Lerner's *Lolita* musical and the deadline for his multibook McGraw-Hill contract, Nabokov looked back over his screenplay, which now included *three* versions of act 1, the original, the alternative, and the abbreviated.[31] He decided he needed to introduce Lolita in Ramsdale before Humbert's arrival, so he returned to the original opening of act 1, but eliminated her clumsy encounter in the dentist's chair with Quilty and opted instead for Humbert at the McCoos', on the piazza with Lolita, and at the school dance with Quilty.

Nabokov conflated, for sound enough reasons, what seemed the best bits of each version, but he did so perfunctorily. He left very spare instructions for his secretary, Jacqueline Callier, to amalgamate the blocks as she retyped the manuscript. That he was anything but in command of dates in his own life, let alone in five versions of Humbert's (the novel and then the ancestral, the alternative, the abbreviated, and the amalgamated screenplays), is almost comically indicated in his record at the top of his instructions: "Added from Brown to Blue Oct 1930 Screenplay." The blue folder contained the shortened and revised version of the screenplay, which he had submitted to Kubrick in September, now remembered as "October" 1960, here misrecorded as "1930." Perhaps the "1930" date proves that everything subsequent, including the novel *Lolita* and Nabokov's meeting with Kubrick, was his invention? Or could we accept the simple proposition that he made a mistake here, as in the screenplay itself, and perhaps, in a much smaller way, in the novel?

LET US TURN NOW to *Lolita* itself.

The argument that the final scenes of Humbert's story—his meeting with the married Lolita and his murder of Quilty—are his invention or fantasy depends on a single piece of evidence: that Humbert says on the last page of his book, "When I started, fifty-six days ago, to write *Lolita*, first in the psychopathic ward for observation, then in this well-heated, albeit tombal seclusion, I thought I would use these notes in toto at my trial, to save not my head, of course, but my soul" (310). According to John Ray, Jr.'s foreword, Humbert "died in legal captivity, of coronary thrombosis, on November 16, 1952, a few days before his trial was scheduled to start" (5). Flipping back fifty-six days, we arrive at 22 September, the day Lolita's letter reached Humbert. Since the visit to Lolita, the discovery of the name of her abductor, and the murder of Quilty all take place over the next three days, when Humbert says he has been writing in a psychopathic ward, they are therefore, according to the revisionists, fabrications or delusions of Humbert Humbert.

In view of Nabokov's fallibility, it seems much sounder, let alone much more economical, to call into question a single numeral than to doubt the detailed reality of a whole series of major scenes. It seems especially peculiar to suppose that virtually everything in the last eighth of the novel is fabricated, except for the first nine words of the sentence quoted above: "When I started, fifty-six days ago, to write *Lolita*." Why, if even the trial mentioned in this sentence is Humbert's fiction (as it usually is for the revisionists),[32] if the psychopathic ward too is a fraud (as it is for Dolinin and sometimes for others), is the "fifty-six" swimming in this sea of falsity to be fished out as incontestable fact?

That Nabokov could err in dating his own life and the lives of his characters has been amply demonstrated already. But let us be clear that—as the revisionists know—*Lolita* itself is no zone of immunity. To take the life first: in his November 1956 "On a Book Entitled *Lolita*," Nabokov wrote that he had not "reread *Lolita* since I went through the proofs in the winter of 1954." He altered this to "in the spring of 1955" for *The Annotated Lolita* (318, 439), although in fact he received the first proofs only well into the summer of 1955 (12 July).[33] Only sixteen months after the event, in other words, he had been inaccurate by six to eight months.

Within *Lolita*'s fictional world, he also made at least one incontrovertible error, which immediately casts doubt on the value of the "fifty-six days." The morning Humbert comes down to check the mail is "early in September 1952" (266, 426), according to the 1955 and 1958 editions. Yet three pages later, we find "the letter was dated September 18, 1952 (this was September 22)" (269)—"this" being the day he receives the letter, hardly "early" in the month. Somebody, perhaps Nabokov himself, muted the mistake in the French translation, where the text has "vers la mi-Septembre."[34] In 1965 Nabokov altered the Russian translation by removing the "September 22" from the next chapter and bringing it forward to replace the vaguer initial reference: "for that particular morning, early in September 1952," became "ibo v to utro, 22-go sentiabria 1952-go goda" ("for that morning, September 22, 1952").[35] Several years later, Nabokov supplied to Alfred Appel, Jr., for The *Annotated Lolita,* the correction to "late in September 1952" (266).

The undoubted mistake here that persisted in Nabokov's manuscript and typescript and through readings of at least two sets of proofs (Olympia's and Putnam's, though he also read the Crest edition and presumably the Weidenfeld and Nicolson and Corgi editions) shows how little credence can be given to the unsupported testimony of "fifty-six days." A discrepancy of two weeks or so occurred within a space of three pages and was not picked up by Nabokov for more than ten years. The "fifty-six days" as evidence depends on an error of only three days over a gap of more than three hundred pages.

Not only on that, some might say. There is one other relevant change in the Russian—where, as Gennady Barabtarlo shows, dates have several times been supplied where there were none in the original.[36] In the English edition, Humbert, after finding it impossible to trace Lolita's abductor, begins a new chapter: "This book is about Lolita; and now that I have reached the part which (had I not been forestalled by another internal combustion martyr) might be called '*Dolorès Disparue,'* there would be little sense in analyzing the three empty years that followed" (255). In the Russian, the last thirteen words become "podrobnoe opisanie poslednikh trekh pustikh let, ot nachala iiulia 1949 do serediny noiabria 1952, ne imelo by smysla" (234: "a detailed description of the last three empty years, from the beginning of July 1949 to the middle of November 1952, would make no sense"). Alexander Dolinin cites this in support of his theory, as proof that there was nothing but blankness—no meeting with Lolita, no encounter with Quilty—in Humbert's life from Lolita's disappearance until this point near the end of his writing his book. Humbert is "therefore, at home, at his writing desk but not in a cell awaiting trial, as he has tried to convince his gullible readers."[37] But if this were a major piece of evidence in the reading that Nabokov wanted to imprint on his book, why did he then not transfer it back into The *Annotated Lolita* when he incorporated corrections there that he saw as necessary in the Russian?

IF  THE  PROBABILITY of a mistake in Nabokov's numerals seems high from the first, the improbability of the revisionist view seems overwhelming.

Even a reader unaware of Nabokov's capacity for error will see an immediate objection to the revisionist theory: what of John Ray, Jr.'s foreword? The 16 November date for Humbert's death, on which the whole case rests, comes from Ray, but Ray also confirms just what the case tries to deny—what Dolinin denies outright—that Humbert was in prison awaiting trial when he finished his manuscript and promptly died. Tekiner suggests that—since, presumably, Ray does not explicitly mention that Humbert's trial is for murder—the trial could be for his treatment of Lolita.[38] But Ray declares, "References to H. H.'s crime may be looked up by the inquisitive in the daily papers for September–October 1952" (6). There is nothing here or anywhere else in the foreword to imply that the inquisitive will find that the newspaper accounts utterly contradict Humbert's.[39]

In his long discussion of the implications of the fifty-six days, Dolinin of course refers to the 16 November date from which the countback starts, but curiously he never mentions the person who supplies that date and never addresses Ray's assumption that Humbert's story coincides with the known facts of the case, the details of the murder listed even in the newspapers. But to ignore evidence does not make it go away.

Connolly at least takes note of the conflicting evidence, even if only to will it into oblivion when he suggests that Humbert may have invented Ray's foreword.[40] But if that is the case, then of course Humbert does not die on 16 November 1952, there is no firm date from which to count back fifty-six days, and the discrepancy on which the whole case rests becomes nonexistent or meaningless.

Nabokov intended to indicate that Humbert died just after putting the last words to his manuscript. That is why he supplied the number of days *Lolita* took Humbert to compose, why he has Dr. Ray supply the date of Humbert's death, and why he explains in his interview with Alfred Appel that in Humbert's final paragraph he meant "to convey a constriction of the narrator's sick heart, a warning spasm causing him to abridge names and hasten to conclude his tale before it was too late" (437). If there is a discrepancy between the number of days *Lolita* took Humbert to write and the number of days until Humbert's death, that seems an error all too easy to make. Either Nabokov simply used the wrong starting point, counting from 22 September (Humbert's receipt of the letter), the one concrete date given in the novel's concluding sequence of events, rather than from 25 September (the murder), which has to be inferred from the text, or he counted correctly but he—or the typesetter—put 16 November rather than the intended 19 November for Humbert's death, making no more than the very common slip of 6 for 9. If the text read, "November 19," the argument for Humbert's having invented the last fifty pages of *Lolita* would immediately collapse. Surely it is too much to base a major reinterpretation of a novel on a single typographic character?

Nabokov always aims for exactitude. He does not allow us simply to lean on evidence, as the revisionists have to do; he makes it click into place. He has made a mistake in the dating, but what he has tried to do has his customary precision and point. Humbert admits that he has "wanted," as he says in his final paragraph, just as he feels his heart twitch, "to exist at least a couple of months longer" (311) than Quilty. In fact, since he will have only a few more hours or even minutes, he will have outlasted Quilty by fifty-six days, or eight weeks: exactly two lunar months but still just short of two strict calendar months. Playful Aubrey McFate as it were *pretends* to grant Humbert the two months he had asked for, then cuts him short, denying even that small request. That is the very exact, very Nabokovian irony of these final dates, except that somewhat—but not completely—uncharacteristically, and all too humanly, he has made a slight error.

I WOULD NOT HAVE WRITTEN this article if only one critic had proposed the revisionist hypothesis. I would have stopped here if only two or three had propelled me into print. But with six already advancing the argument, another thinking about doing so, and others inclined to entertain it, I will continue.

Dr. Ray's foreword records that Mrs. Richard Schiller dies in childbirth in Gray Star, "a settlement in the remotest Northwest" (6). How has she reached there, if Humbert does not respond to her letter that says, "I'm going nuts because we don't have enough to pay our debts and get out of here. Dick is promised a big job in Alaska" (268)? Why does Nabokov in the afterword think of Gray Star as "the capital town of the book" (318) if Lolita does not die there in childbirth? (Gray Star, presumably, is Juneau, Alaska's capital, in allusion to the old cartographic convention of stars for capital cities but also as a play on Juno, the goddess of marriage.) If Ray's foreword is accepted—and to repeat, if it is not, 16 November disappears as evidence and takes with it the whole revisionist argument—it explicitly or implicitly confirms Lolita's letter, Humbert's visit to her, Quilty's murder, and Humbert's composing the manuscript in prison while awaiting trial for the killing, all the things the revisionists try to discredit.

So too does *Lolita: A Screenplay.*

While the screenplay reinvents minor details of the novel, its main alterations seem designed precisely to convey what Nabokov regarded as crucial to the novel but likely to be lost without considerable adaptation.[41] First, and most important, Quilty's shadowy presence throughout the novel, which readers can discover only after Humbert has himself dropped the name, is signaled in the screenplay by a flash forward to the murder scene and by then making him more prominent, once the narrative returns to the beginning, from the time of Humbert's arrival in Ramsdale (at the school dance, where Quilty is presented as author of *The Nymphet*; at the Enchanted Hunters, where he is named as the drunken guest; at Beardsley School, where he is again named as author of *The Enchanted Hunters*). Second, the Edgar Allan Poe allusions, which Nabokov stresses, at the cost of some strain, are highlighted through Humbert's scholarly work and sometimes even Lolita's schooling. Third, John Ray, Jr.'s position as frame to and external commentator on Humbert's confession, places him as the sometimes comically obtrusive narrator of the whole film.

Humbert cannot narrate the film, as he does the book, for his utter ignorance of the identity of Lolita's abductor until the end is still crucial to the story. In the novel, he could introduce Quilty's presence and yet keep his identity hidden until the right moment, thereby having the satisfaction of keeping the reader in the darkness he had himself found so unlaughable. In the film, he could not be the narrator and allow Quilty to be seen on screen without repeatedly disclosing his present awareness of Quilty's role. By removing Humbert from the narration of the film and flashing forward right at the beginning to the murder, Nabokov alerts us to the identity of Humbert's foe from the start and therefore makes us vividly aware, whenever we later catch sight of Quilty, of Humbert's failure to recognize his rival until the very end.

The screenplay opens with Lolita telling Humbert where Quilty lives, showing him, in fact, a magazine photograph of Pavor Manor, which then comes to life as Humbert arrives and promptly, wordlessly, kills Quilty. Immediately afterward, the camera cuts to:

*Dr. John Ray*
a psychiatrist, perusing a manuscript on his desk. He swings around toward us in his swivel chair.

DR. RAY: I'm Dr. John Ray. Pleased to meet you. This here is a bundle of notes, a rough autobiography, poorly typed, which Mr. Humbert Humbert wrote after his arrest, in prison, where he was held without bail on a charge of murder, and in the psychopathic ward for observation. Without this document his crime would have remained unexplained. (2–3)

After Ray explains that Humbert's memoir is "mainly an account of his infatuation with a certain type of very young girl," the camera cuts to:

*Humbert's Cell in the Tombs*

He is writing at a table. Conspicuous among the reference books at his elbow are some tattered travel guides and maps. Presently his voice surfaces as he rereads the first sentences of his story.

HUMBERT'S VOICE: I was born in Paris forty dark years ago. (3–4)

Obviously, there are differences, but they seem designed primarily to make the major effects of the novel possible on the screen. Dr. Ray exists objectively before our eyes, and he describes Humbert composing the manuscript in prison after committing murder (he does not explicitly specify Quilty as murder victim: does this leave a loophole for the desperate revisionist?). By indicating Humbert's reference books, Nabokov establishes his character's effort at reliability in retelling his past. And he lets us see the murder *before* Humbert sets down his story, even lets us see Quilty asleep in Pavor Manor before Humbert first appears on screen, before Humbert reaches the manor himself. The murder, unequivocally, is not a product of Humbert's narration.

The scene of Humbert reading Lolita's letter, of which the revisionists make a great deal, is replaced by a parallel scene in the screenplay. Understandably, Nabokov has excised Rita from the screenplay as an unnecessary complication and instead shows Humbert, after he loses Lolita and all trace of her abductor's trail, teaching once again at Beardsley College. There he meets Mona Dahl, who quizzes him—years have passed—about Lolita. As Nabokov notes after this scene in an explanatory aside unimpeachably immune from revisionist skepticism: "It should now have been established that Mona has had a letter from Lolita, apparently asking her to find out if it is safe for her, Lolita, to write to Humbert" (198). Humbert picks up his mail at the university post office and heads straight to an examination he is to invigilate. He opens the letter, hears, just as in the novel, "a small, matter-of-fact, agonizingly familiar, voice" (199)—and after reading through Lolita's letter, he dashes, dazed, from the exam room.

In the novel, Humbert prepares for his unpreparedness for Lolita's letter with the great passage about endowing "our friends with the stability of type that literary characters acquire in the reader's mind. No matter how many times we reopen 'King Lear,' never shall we find the good king banging his tankard in high revelry, all woes forgotten, at a jolly reunion with all three daughters and their lapdogs. Never will Emma rally, revived by the sympathetic salts in Flaubert's father's timely tear" (267). Obviously something new is needed for the screenplay, both to prepare *us* for the surprise and to show Humbert's unpreparedness: hence the device of introducing Mona's questions, whose import we can see but Humbert cannot, and Humbert blandly opening the letter ("from a Mrs. Richard Schiller— some graduate student, I presume" [198], he had moaned in the mailroom) in the midst of the examination. Just as the novel stresses the shocked suddenness of Humbert's response—he leaves without even waking Rita from her solid morning sleep—so does the screenplay, when Humbert lurches away from his post as invigilator. For all the changes in the treatment of Lolita's letter, Nabokov has sought cinematic ways of stressing its credibility and of eliciting the same key responses in us and in Humbert.

Humbert heads for Coalmont, where the screenplay closely follows the novel. As soon as he finds out Quilty's name from Lolita, ascertains that she will never return to him, and heads off to find Pavor Manor, the screenplay's visual action ends, as Dr. Ray's voiceover explains:

> Poor Lolita died in childbed a few weeks later, giving birth to a stillborn girl, in Gray Star, a settlement in the remote Northwest. She never learned that Humbert finally tracked down Clare Quilty and killed him. Nor did Humbert know of Lolita's death when shortly before his own dissolution he wrote in prison these last words of his tragic life's story:

> HUMBERT'S VOICE *(clear and firm):* While the blood still throbs through my writing hand, you are still as much part of blest matter as I am. I can still talk to you and make you live in the minds of later generations. I'm thinking of aurochs and angels, the secret of durable pigments, prophetic sonnets, the refuge of art. And this is the only immortality you and I may share, my Lolita. (212–13)

The screenplay ends with the final two sentences of the novel intact. Once again, it strives for the very effects that the novel achieves. The reader of the novel, anxious to know what exactly did happen to Lolita and vaguely remembering the fates of some characters given in Dr. Ray's foreword, can turn back there and appreciate the poignant ironies: Lolita's death, despite Humbert's wishes for her longevity, and Humbert's sudden death, without ever learning of hers. The screenplay offers the connections that the novel invites; Nabokov planned nothing to undermine them, and a single slip in counting should not be allowed to destroy the world he created.

Revisionists could at this point try to shore up their sagging case by arguing that Nabokov would have been reluctant to undermine the status of the story in a Hollywood screenplay at the beginning of the 1960s. But he refused to undertake the screenplay at all while he could see no way to render the novel. Presumably, when he *did* undertake it, he thought he had found a means of conveying what mattered in the novel—and if the meetings with Lolita and the encounter with Quilty had never really happened in the novel, *that* would certainly matter.

Nor was Nabokov shy about undermining the status of dramatized events: the last act of *Death* (1923) may be, and almost all of *The Waltz Invention* (1938) certainly is, the delusion of the hero. He was hardly less bold in his sixties than he had been in his early twenties. The *Lolita* screenplay abounds in disruptive expressionist and self-conscious effects, like Humbert's mother flying up to heaven holding a parasol after her death by lightning, or Dr. Ray as narrator offering urgent advice to a driver in a scene he knows occurred more than a decade before ("Look out! Close shave. When you analyze these jaywalkers you find they hesitate between the womb and the tomb! [13]). Had Nabokov wanted to suggest that the final scenes of the novel were Humbert's invention, he could have done so in the screenplay. There is nothing to suggest the idea ever occurred to him.

What surprises me most about the revisionists, three of whom are Nabokov scholars I greatly respect, is that they not only have so much against their case, but so little going for it.

If their case were true, Humbert would have either invented or fantasized the visit to Lolita and the murder of Quilty. Surely invention is ruled out. Humbert, who is so unrelentingly vain, would hardly choose to invent a Lolita who makes it perfectly plain he doesn't feature in her experience of love and never has and who says that the only person she has ever really loved is the rival whom Humbert detests and whom she herself has come to think rather squalid. Nor would Humbert be likely to fabricate the murder of his rival in such a fashion that he is made to look a fool in the very act of executing the revenge for which he has so longed, as Quilty coolly mocks him ("Well, sir, this is certainly a fine poem. Your best as far as I am concerned" [302]) and even orchestrates the whole show ("the ingenious play staged for me by Quilty" [307]) that Humbert so craves to direct himself.

Above all, it seems impossible to imagine a Humbert who could construct a scene as rich in independent life as the reunion with Lolita at Coalmont. He has no gift of narrative invention, apart from his penchant for vague, self-indulgent fantasy—fondling Ginny McCoo, reliving his

Mediterranean idyll with Annabel beside Hourglass Lake with Lolita, murdering Charlotte as she swims, siring a litter of Lolitas, or savoring the bliss of sweet revenge on Lolita's abductor. Indeed it is essential to Humbert's nature that in these brief projections on the screen of his indulgence he fails to take into account the lived reality of others. Not that he is so obtuse as to be, like Hermann in *Despair*, incapable of perceiving it even after the fact—after Charlotte's discovery of the diary, after he has at last possessed Lolita, after he sees her burst into tears at the tenderness between Avis Chapman and her father. I cannot see what evidence the novel has offered that Humbert can invent a moment like this:

> "And so," I shouted, "you are going to Canada? Not Canada"—I re-shouted—"I mean Alaska, of course."
> He nursed his glass and, nodding sagely, replied: "Well, he cut it on a jagger, I guess. Lost his right arm in Italy." (276–77)

or this:

> "What things?"
> "Oh, weird, filthy, fancy things. I mean he had two girls and two boys, and three or four men, and the idea was for all of us to tangle in the nude. . . ."
> "What things exactly?"
> "Oh, things. . . . Oh, I—really I"—she uttered the "I" as a subdued cry while she listened to the source of the ache, and for lack of words spread the five fingers of her angularly up-and-down-moving hand. No, she gave it up, she refused to go into particulars with that baby inside her. (278–79)

*Imagine* that gesture, act it out. Nabokov, after decades of writing fiction and of deliberately studying gesture, can invent this, but Humbert surely cannot. Nor is there anything in these scenes that makes them smack, as Luzhin's or Hermann's or Kinbote's so plainly do, of a madman's visions.

Apart from the discrepancy in dating, the revisionists have no concrete evidence. They point to the tinge of fantasy surrounding the scenes that follow Humbert reading the letter, especially the murder scene, and argue that this proves them his invention. In the murder scene, of course, Humbert has explicitly drunk too much and is even more agitated than usual. It would be astonishing if reality were *not* skewed a little. But the revisionists simply ignore the element of fantasy that surrounds almost every scene in Lolita, from as far back as Humbert's first memory, his mother's death ("picnic, lighting" [12]), through his first glimpse of Lolita ("And, as if I were the fairy-tale nurse of some little princess (lost, kidnapped, discovered in gypsy rags through which her nakedness smiled at the king and his hounds), I recognized the tiny dark-brown mole on her side. With awe and delight (the king crying for joy, the trumphets blaring, the nurse drunk) I saw again her lovely indrawn abdomen where my southbound mouth had briefly paused" [41]), to the morning Humbert finds Lolita gone and drives drunkenly to the hospital through the "cute little town" of Elphinstone, with "its model school and temple and spacious rectangular blocks, some of which were, curiously enough, just unconventional pastures with a mule or a unicorn grazing in the young July morning mist" (248). If a jittery jostling of reality sufficed to prove that Humbert invented a scene from scratch, we would have to conclude he had invented even his own childhood and Lolita's whole existence.

It further discredits the revisionists that they cannot agree on what the discrepant dates are supposed to show Humbert has invented: all that follows the letter, but not the letter itself, nor Ray's foreword? the letter too? the foreword too? Experienced Nabokovians should know that Nabokov does not allow dual or multiple solutions: his solutions, like those of his chess problems, are exact (and, of course, not self-contradictory, like an "invented" foreword).

The revisionists seem to want to avoid the implications of their theory for Clare Quilty. None of them wants to ditch Quilty, yet without Lolita disclosing his name, there is no way for Humbert to know the identity of her accomplice. The novel stresses Humbert's long frustration in attempting to track down his identity: the cryptogrammic paper chase; the absurd stalking of Ass. Prof. Riggs; the detective who turns up a Bill Brown near Dolores, Colorado (or in the screenplay, a "Dolores Hayes, H, A, Y, E, S, . . . a fat old dame selling homemade Tokay to the Indians" [188]). Until his visit to Lolita, both novel and screenplay insist, Humbert has no inkling of the abductor's identity, despite all the clues Quilty amuses himself and torments Humbert by scattering. If the visit to Lolita is invented, then so is the identification of Quilty.[42] But if Humbert does not know the real abductor, if he is simply inventing Quilty as a rival and victim, why does someone as vain as he, as sure of his own intellectual superiority to those around him, choose to invent someone who so easily frustrates and humiliates him? If Quilty were mere invention, would Humbert not concoct something less unflattering? If on the other hand he merely follows the facts, unpleasant though they are—and takes a kind of narrative revenge on Quilty and a kind of surrogate triumph over the reader by his manipulations of Quilty's concealed appearance—what we find in the text makes perfect sense.[43]

Nor do the revisionists agree on what their theory could prove. For Leona Toker, Humbert's having invented the conclusion of his story explains why throughout the earlier part of the story we hear the voice only of the old unreformed Humbert, not the new Humbert, who loves Lolita even in her postnymphet phase, for after all the Humbert writing even the start of the story should be this "reformed" self. But this is an old problem in first-person narrative. The Gulliver of book 4 of *Gulliver's Travels* has come to hate humans and adore Houyhnhnms and horses, but none of that shows in the first three books, written after his return from that final voyage. Besides, Humbert explicitly says he has until the point of her death thought himself back into his initial relentlessly anti-Charlotte temper "for the sake of retrospective verisimilitude" (73). Why cannot he similarly mimic his unredeemedly nympholeptic state? It suits his strategy to keep his "reform" a surprise. It wins over many of Nabokov's readers, let alone Humbert's.

Dolinin and Connolly both suggest that Humbert's ability to invent a Lolita pregnant, independent, yet still loved by him reveals his new moral status, allows him to pass, in Dolinin's view, to another plane of "awareness."[44] But neither explains why Humbert should suddenly find this new moral power in an uneventful moment in his deliberately, prophylactically bland and automatic life with Rita.

Nor does either notice how incompatible is Humbert's supposedly self-propelled leap to a higher moral plane with what Humbert actually records of his own behavior in the scene he supposedly invents. He comes to Coalmont knowing that Lolita is married and pregnant. But although he assumes that her husband is Lolita's abductor, he is ready to kill him, regardless of what that would do to Lolita and the child he realizes she is bearing and would be compelled to rear on her own. Nabokov accentuates the conjunction: "The moment, the death I had kept conjuring up for three years was as simple as a bit of dry wood. She was frankly and hugely pregnant" (271). Within Humbert's narrative strategy, of course, this serves a different purpose: to mislead us into thinking for a moment that it is Lolita whom he will kill, so that when he corrects us, we will be so relieved that we will discount that he still plans to kill *someone.* He quickly disabuses us: "I could not kill *her,* of course, as some have thought. You see, I loved her" (272). Loved her enough, indeed, to plan to kill her husband. (He does not kill Dick Schiller only because he sees at once that this is not the man who spirited Lolita from Elphinstone.) How this planned murder of Lolita's unborn child's father would testify to Humbert's moral refinement, even within an invented scenario, I cannot conceive.

The revisionists indeed uniformly discount the significance of Humbert's overwhelming desire for revenge. But Humbert has always felt intense jealousy, even over the despised Valeria, let alone over Lolita, and he seethes with another kind of enraged pride at Quilty's manipulating him on the road to Elphinstone, though he himself has manipulated Lolita on roads across America for years. Humbert sees his desire for revenge as a positive, proof of his essential romanticism and dedication to Lolita, proof of his moral superiority to Quilty. He manages to convince many readers of this. Yet Nabokov has structured his whole novel to imply the parallelism between each of the quests—to possess Lolita, to erase his rival—that at the end of each part reaches its climactic and confusing satisfaction.

Despite the moral apotheosis of the scene above Elphinstone, Humbert harbors for the three years that follow a compulsion to kill Lolita's abductor, an urge as powerful as his desire for Lolita herself. Nabokov pointedly juxtaposes these two contrary impulses in Humbert in the very paragraph that introduces Humbert's dedication to murderous revenge. That paragraph ends: "To myself I whispered that I still had my gun, and was still a free man—free to trace the fugitive, free to destroy my brother" (249).[45] But it begins, in limpid prefiguration of the scene of the "moral apotheosis": "Elphinstone was, and I hope still is, a very cute little town. It was spread like a maquette, you know, with its neat greenwood trees and red-roofed houses over the valley floor and I think I have alluded earlier to its model school and temple" (248).[46] Humbert may choose for his own rhetorical purposes to make the scene of the moral apotheosis the last in his story, but Nabokov remembers that the apotheosis was conjoined for three years with an absolute determination to revenge: "I wrote many more poems. I immersed myself in the poetry of others. But not for a moment did I forget the load of revenge" (259). Even Humbert juxtaposes the contrast: "to have him trapped, after those years of repentance and rage" (297). But far too few readers stop to think what that says about the quality of his repentance.

Nabokov—and even Humbert himself—manages to make Humbert seem funny in his plans for vengeance: "on the day fixed for the execution," Humbert writes (254). As he stalks not the Rev. Rigor Mortis but his near-double, the visiting art teacher "Albert Riggs, Ass. Prof.," he discovers of course that although he seems to have ruled out everyone else, this too is not the man. Some discount the reality or the seriousness of Humbert killing Quilty because he murders someone who is in a sense his own double, a writer, a nympholept, a manipulator. But Humbert does not merely shoot his mirror image. The murder scene will indeed end up "a silent, soft, formless tussle on the part of two literati" (301), but three years before he has the least inkling of Quilty's identity, of any similarity between himself and Lolita's abductor other than their interest in the girl, Humbert vows to destroy his foe as soon as he can track him down.

In Nabokov's world, murder matters, because other people exist. A murderer acts as if another were only Other, not a self in his or her own right. A lover, per contra, can treat the Other as a self that matters at least as much as one's own. Nabokov structures *Lolita* around the contrasts and the comparisons between the girl Humbert loves and the man he hates, the one he tries to immortalize and the one he tries to obliterate, the one he at last realizes has a life of her own and the one he realizes, damn him, had such a life, was just as alive as himself, in fact far too like himself—and whom all the same he is still happy to have killed. Humbert at last loves Lolita, even though she has won free of him; he hates Quilty all the more as he finds him freer than himself. To reduce to Humbert's solipsistic fancies Lolita in her final proud but abashed independence and Quilty in his strutting irrepressibility is to gain nothing and lose almost everything— and all for the sake of one revisable digit.

### Notes

The epigraph to this chapter is from Nabokov's pseudoreview of *Conclusive Evidence* (Nabokov Archives, Library of Congress, box 5), intended at the time of writing to form a sixteenth chapter in the book version, but then omitted.

1. "'And there happening through the whole kingdom of Bohemia, to be no sea-port town whatever'

"'How the deuce could there—Trim' cried my uncle Toby; 'for Bohemia being totally inland, it could have happened no otherwise'

"—It might,' said Trim, 'if it had pleased God'" (bk. 8, chap. 19).

2. There were a couple of occasions when Bohemia had a brief toehold on the Adriatic, in the thirteenth and sixteenth centuries, and Shakespeare's source, Robert Greene's *Pandosto,* did once mention the coast of Bohemia. But Greene does not make it a turning point of the plot, as Johnson observes Shakespeare has made it.

3. Ably exposed by Richard Levin in *New Readings vs. Old Plays* (Chicago: University of Chicago Press, 1979), and many subsequent articles.

4. *The Annotated Lolita,* ed. Alfred Appel, Jr. (New York: McGraw-Hill, 1970), 257. This has the advantage over the revised *Annotated Lolita* of having the same pagination as the first American edition and the textually authoritative Vintage edition.

5. *King, Queen, Knave,* trans. Dmitri Nabokov with Vladimir Nabokov (New York: McGraw-Hill, 1968), viii.

6. Aleksandr Pushkin, *Eugene Onegin,* trans. with commentary by Vladimir Nabokov (Princeton, N.J.: Bollingen, 1964), 1:15–16.

7. *Autobiographical Acts: The Changing Situation of a Literary Genre* (Baltimore: Md.: Johns Hopkins University Press, 1976), 145–46.

8. "Time in *Lolita,*" *Modern Fiction Studies* 25 (1979): 463–69.

9. *Nabokov: The Mystery of Literary Structures* (Ithaca, N.Y.: Cornell University Press, 1989), 198–227, esp. 208–11.

10. In his essay "Dvoinoe vremia u Nabokova: ot *Dara* k *Lolite,*" revised in "Nabokov's Time Doubling: From *The Gift to Lolita,*" *Nabokov Studies* 2 (1995): 3–40 (see n. 1).

11. "'Nature's Reality' or Humbert's 'Fancy'? Scenes of Reunion and Murder in *Lolita,*" *Nabokov Studies* 2 (1995): 41–61.

12. Dieter E. Zimmer, editor's afterword to *Lolita* [in German], trans. Helen Hessel, Maria Carlsson, et al. and revised by Dieter E. Zimmer (Reinbek bei Hamburg: Rowohlt, 1996), 576–79.

13. Barbara Wyllie, "'Guilty of Killing Quilty': The Central Dilemma of Nabokov's *Lolita,*" NABOKV-L (Nabokov Internet List, discussion group, moderated by D. Barton Johnson, 21 November 1994).

14. Toker, *Mystery of Structures,* 209.

15. Brian Boyd, *Vladimir Nabokov: The American Years* (Princeton, N.J.: Princeton University Press, 1991), 613.

16. *Speak, Memory: An Autobiography Revisited* (New York: Putnam, 1967).

17. Note in *Conclusive Evidence* ms., Vladimir Nabokov Archives, Montreux, Switzerland, cited *VNAY,* 147.

18. Nabokov to Morris Bishop, 12 October 1947 (marked "46"), Vladimir Nabokov Archives, Berg Collection, New York Public Library.

19. *A Russian Beauty and Other Stories* (New York: McGraw-Hill, 1973), 220.

20. Interview of 28 June 1979.

21. *Pnin* (Garden City, N.Y.: Doubleday, 1957), 67.

22. *Ada or Ardor: A Family Chronicle* (New York: McGraw-Hill, 1969), 515.

23. Cf. Maurice Couturier, *Textual Communication: A Print-Based Theory of the Novel* (London: Routledge, 1991), 89.

24. *Ada oder Das Verlangen,* trans. Uwe Friesel and Marianne Therstappen (Rheinbek bei Hamburg: Rowohlt, 1974).

25. *Ada ou l'ardeur,* trans. Gilles Chahine with Jean-Bernard Blandenier (Paris: Fayard, 1975).

26. Cf. Brian Boyd, "Annotations to *Ada,* 2: Pt. 1 Ch. 2," *Nabokovian* 31 (1993): 39.

27. *Lolita: A Screenplay* (New York: McGraw-Hill, 1974), 21.

28. Mss., Vladimir Nabokov Archives, Berg Collection, New York Public Library.

29. *Lolita: A Screenplay* x.

30. Cf. *Lolita: A Screenplay* x–xi.

31. Cf. *VNAY* 580.

32. Tekiner, "Time in *Lolita*," 468, writes, however, "The chronology implies that Humbert is in jail for his actions toward Lolita, rather than Quilty," but does not explain how or why Humbert has been tracked down, or at what point prior to the supposed arrest for his treatment of Lolita (an arrest, of course, entirely without textual foundation) he began, as this conjecture would require, to suppress what was really happening to him, or why the conjecture does not square with the foreword. Toker, 218, suggests as one possibility (though she seems to prefer another) that "Humbert may have been arrested on the same day, almost immediately after reading Dolly's letter, and placed in a psychiatric ward 'for observation' . . . prior to being scheduled for trial," but though she rules out the murder of Quilty she does not suggest why he is being tried.

33. *VNAY* 269.

34. *Lolita,* trans. Eric Kahane (Paris: Gallimard, 1959).

35. *Lolita,* trans. Vladimir Nabokov (New York: Phaedra, 1967), 245.

36. *Aerial View: Essays on Nabokov's Art and Metaphysics* (New York: Peter Lang, 1993), 135–38. The dates become more specific for several reasons: because Nabokov's style evolved consistently towards greater chronological detail; because he felt he needed to identify for Russian readers in the late 1960s a period that was more self-evident to the Americans for whom he was writing in the early 1950s; *and* to correct inconsistencies he had noticed.

37. P. 39.

38. B. Tekiner 468.

39. Nabokov's reason for having Ray not mention murder, of course, is to avoid spoiling the sublime surprise of Humbert's first page: "You can always count on a murderer for a fancy prose style" (11).

40. P. 45.

41. Toker, *Mystery of Structures,* 210, realizes the awkwardness of the screenplay to her case but rules it out as "a totally new work. . . . The screenplay, therefore, cannot be used to settle moot points in the novel." It is indeed, as Nabokov says, "a vivacious variant" (*Lolita: A Screenplay* xiii) on the novel, not a bland transposition, but as the examples will make clear, the screenplay strives even in its changes to be true to the novel.

42. Toker is particularly confused. According to her version, Humbert does not plan ahead; his slightly reformed feelings for Lolita develop only as he suddenly begins to fantasize, from the point he writes about receiving Lolita's letter to the end

of his composing the narrative (Toker 211, 217, 218). But in that case Humbert does not discover who Quilty is until he writes the Coalmont scene, yet at the very moment she tells him who her abductor was, he comments: "Quietly the fusion took place, and everything fell into order, into the pattern of branches that I have woven throughout this memoir with the express purpose of having the ripe fruit fall at the right moment" (274). In other words, he has planned Quilty's peekaboo presence from the first.

43. Tekiner, 466 (followed by Connolly 51–52), suggests that Humbert identifies Quilty from *Who's Who in the Limelight* in the psychiatric institution where—according to her—Humbert writes up his manuscript. (Rejecting the murder, Tekiner, 468, rules out prison but does not explain why Humbert suddenly finds himself in a psychiatric institution, when his life with Rita seems perfectly stable; Dolinin is convinced that Humbert is happily sitting in his study, hoodwinking the reader.) Why Humbert should have read through the thousands of entries in *Who's Who in the Limelight* and realized the relevance of the brief Quilty entry, when he has for years come nowhere near to suspecting Quilty, seems anything but clear. True, Lolita did lie that "Quilty" was the "gal author" (223), but why would Humbert persist in reading through a fat biographical tome until he found this one clue when he had never made any connection between Lolita's disappearance and the playwright of the play in which she was to star?

44. P. 37.

45. Quilty of course has posed as Lolita's uncle in taking her from the Elphinstone hospital.

46. He has, and that description on p. 243 confirms the equation between Elphinstone and the vista of the moral apotheosis.

# Nabokov's Novel Offspring
## *Lolita and Her Kin*

ELLEN PIFER

◆   ◆   ◆

S O   F A R - R E A C H I N G   W A S   James's vision of the child's ambiguous, impure image in *The Turn of the Screw* that we must skip forward a half century to take up where he left off. We arrive at that cunning work of aesthetic enchantment created by an exiled Russian writer who, in middle age, transformed himself into a formidable American master. Vladimir Nabokov's most famous, and infamous, novel exhibits and carries to a new stage of development that same impulse or drive toward self-reflection, ambiguity, and paradox that characterizes James's innovative turn-of-the-century fictions. The slyly allusive, intensely parodic structure of *Lolita* can by now claim to have provoked as many contradictory interpretations and caught out as many readers as James's cunningly ambiguous fairy tale. In the 1950s, when *Lolita* was published first in France and then in the United States, its volatile subject matter—the sexual passion of a middle-aged European for a twelve-year-old American girl—set off a flurry of scandal.

Nabokov's novel has never fully recovered from the charges of obscenity that greeted it, despite the fact that they were quickly dismissed by the courts as well as by prominent critics. In the popular mind, the name Lolita has come to signify the cynical sophistication and sexual precocity, bordering on lewdness, of American—and Americanized—youth. Marie Winn, a social critic concerned with the fate of contemporary children, thus says:

> Once upon a time a fictional twelve-year-old from New England named Lolita Haze slept with a middle-aged European intellectual named Humbert Humbert and profoundly shocked American sensibilities. It was not so much the idea of an adult having sexual designs on a child that was appalling. It was Lolita herself, unvirginal long before Humbert came upon the scene, so knowing, so jaded, so *unchildlike*, who seemed to violate something America held sacred.

As Winn goes on to say, however, only "a single generation after: *Lolita*'s publication," Nabokov's vision appeared prophetic: "There is little doubt that schoolchildren of the 1980s are more akin to Nobokov's nymphet than to those guileless and innocent creatures with their shiny Mary Janes and pigtails, their scraped knees and trusting ways, that were called children not so long ago."[1]

Winn's statement is rife with implicit as well as explicit information about the contemporary image of childhood. As a social critic, she purports to be discussing real children, not literary types like the "fictional twelve-year-old" called "Lolita Haze." Yet in distinguishing between past and present generations, she contrasts Nabokov's young heroine with another fiction, or construction, of childhood: the innocent in Mary Janes and pigtails. We note how *her* costume, stance, and physiognomy (those scraped knees bespeaking such guileless pastimes as roller skating, hopscotch, and jumping rope) assure the adult—as little Flora's golden hair, placid face, and charming frock initially assured James's governess—of the child's sexual ignorance.

The passage says much, as well, about the way Nabokov's novel has been construed (and misconstrued) not only by the general public but by critics and reviewers. Having made her way into popular culture, Lolita has given rise to a cultural icon and a popular canard. Just as the name Frankenstein has come to signify, erroneously, the unnamed creature whom Victor Frankenstein, the protagonist of Mary Shelley's 1818 novel, conceives in the bowels of his scientific laboratory, the nymphet Lolita, conjured in the depths of Humbert's ardent imagination, gives rise to a case of mistaken identity. (Other revealing parallels between Shelley's novel and Nabokov's will be discussed later in this essay.) To the popular misconception of the nymphet as sexy teenager decked out in tight jeans and bright lipstick, both the book jackets of various paperback editions and the cinematic image of Sue Lyon—the star of Stanley Kubrick's 1962 film adaptation of *Lolita*—have undoubtedly contributed.[2] (Adrian Lyne's 1997 film version features a less vampish but even more strapping teenager, fifteen-year-old Dominique Swain, in the title role.) More surprising is the number of professional critics who, like Winn, cleave to the image of a jaded, supremely knowing twelve-year-old who has lost all claim to innocence long before Humbert comes on the scene. Apparently misled by the adolescent's stance of cool sophistication, such critics fail to note how flimsy, indeed how tragically futile, a defense it proves against Humbert's violation of both her childhood and her body.

Winn unwittingly draws attention to the perceptual haze surrounding Nabokov's child when she dubs the little girl Lolita Haze. This misnomer contradicts what the narrator already reveals in his opening lines, as he launches a hymn to the beauty of his bewitching nymphet: both her name and her image are creations of Humbert's rhapsodic imagination. Like the goddess Athena who sprang fully formed from Zeus's brow, Lolita is a mythical being. A figment of Humbert's dreaming mind, the fantasized nymphet can claim no earthly genealogy or surname.[3] Dolores Haze—the child with whom Humbert conflates the nymphet—is, on the other hand, the daughter of Charlotte Haze and her deceased husband, Harold. The identity of Dolores, or Dolly as she is known at school, is largely a matter of indifference to ardent Humbert; only sporadically does he glimpse, through the "rosy, gold-dusted" haze of his desire for the nymphet, the poignant image of the child (62).

Humbert's belated recognition of the child's identity occurs, significantly, not in the heat of passion but at a distance—recollected, so to speak, in Wordsworthian tranquillity. Only after Dolly escapes her captor, depriving him of his cherished object of desire, does Humbert begin to recognize the autonomous being—the "North American girl-child named Dolores Haze," as he ultimately identifies her—whose tender flesh was sacrificed on the altar of his obsession (285). In pursuit of his "mythopoeic nymphet," romantic Humbert can only possess, in the physical or sexual sense, the *body* of a child he has imaginatively transformed into the figment of his dreaming mind (188). That Humbert consummates his passion for the nymphet in the Enchanted Hunters hotel is apt, for he is the enchanted hunter of his own romantic tale.

## The Romantic Legacy: Enchanted Hunters and Poor Children

Like so many romantic dreamers before him, Humbert is captivated by an ideal image or vision, one infinitely more real to him than the American youngster whose childhood he destroys. Here Humbert's true precursors are not the pedophiles of psychiatric case history but those ardent disciples of romance—from Emma Bovary to Edgar Allan Poe, Don Quixote to Jay Gatsby—who in countless novels and poems suffer the fatal affliction of infinite longing, transcendent desire. Romantic love— as Poe writes in his "Annabel Lee," whose lines resonate throughout Humbert's narration—aspires to "a love that [is] more than love." The power (and poison) of romantic love springs from the paradox of ideal vision wedded to sheer impossibility. It is Humbert's longing for the unattainable, for ideal perfection—what he calls "the great rosegray never-to-be-had"—that fires his imagination and fuels his desire for nymphet beauty. As he admits, "it may well be that the very attraction immaturity has for me lies not so much in the limpidity of pure young forbidden fairy child beauty as in the security of a situation where infinite perfections"—those that can only be dreamed of or dreamed up—"fill the gap between the little given and the great promised." The vision is perfect because it remains "out of reach, with no possibility of attainment to spoil it" (266).

Only the power of imagination can "fill the gap" between the ideal and the actual. To possess his nymphet, Humbert must first eclipse the child; only when she has been, as he says, "safely solipsized"—subjugated, in other words, to the dreamer's private world of imagination—is sexual bliss assured. Only then does the nymphet worshiper enter "a plane of being where nothing mattered, save the infusion of joy brewed within [his] body." After Humbert experiences, surreptitiously and onanistically, his first sexual ecstasy with Lolita—as the child, munching an apple, lies casually sprawled on his lap—he identifies the psychic maneuvers by which he has achieved physical relief: "I had stolen the honey of a spasm," he boasts, "without impairing the morals of a minor. . . . I had delicately constructed my ignoble, ardent, sinful dream; and still Lolita was safe—and I was safe. What I had madly possessed was not she, but my own creation, another, fanciful Lolita—perhaps, more real than Lolita; . . . and having no will, no consciousness—indeed, no life of her own."[4] That Humbert's clandestine maneuvers cannot ensure the child's safety is foreshadowed by the imperial nature of his fantasies. Having successfully obliterated her autonomous identity, Humbert, like "a radiant and robust Turk," can delay "the moment of actually enjoying the youngest and frailest of his slaves," but he is clearly poised for invasion (62–64).

In thrall to his imagination, Humbert is at once captor and captive, predator and prey. Inadvertently testifying to the imagination's power to bewitch and enchant, readers of *Lolita* often fall prey to the spell cast by the narrator's mythical fantasies. Further disoriented by the abrupt shifts in narrative tone—as Humbert's voice alternates between pathos and farce, rapturous evocation and mocking self-denigration—many readers fail to heed his warning: "You can always count on a murderer for a fancy prose style" (11). In a statement at once telling and teasingly ambiguous, the narrator announces his efforts to conceal, in the very act or pretense of revealing, crucial aspects of his story. All art, like that "good cheat," Nature, is deceptive, Nabokov maintains (*Strong Opinions* 11). But Humbert's language is particularly duplicitous because he figures prominently among those he would deceive. Only gradually and with great difficulty can he bear to reveal the truth of the tale he has to tell: that at the age of thirty-seven he conceived a passion for a twelve-year-old child whom he subsequently begged and bribed, cajoled and tyrannized into sexual cohabitation—until at the age of fourteen, she managed to escape.

All the self-conscious devices for which *Lolita* is famous—most particularly, its parody of literary conventions—signal the epistemological gap between narrator and reader, between Humbert's romantic obsession and the reader's more independent perspective. But here, too, the radical nature and effects of the narrative are often misconstrued, as decades of critical commentary demonstrate.[5] In an early review of the novel, for example, Leslie Fiedler was so taken with its innovative design that he overlooked what Nabokov, in his comments on the novel, called "my little girl's heartrending fate" (*Strong Opinions* 25). Fiedler finds, by contrast, that *Lolita* "is the final blasphemy against the cult of the child." "Nowhere," he adds, "are the myths of sentimentality more amusing[ly] and convincingly parodied." In *Love and Death in the American Novel,* Fiedler takes his point further: "it is the naive child, the female, the American who corrupts the sophisticated adult, the male, the European." Nabokov's child, he concludes, is Poe's "Annabel Lee as nymphomaniac, demonic rapist of the soul."[6]

Underlying Fiedler's hyperbolic response is an assumption highly surprising in a critic long identified with cultural radicalism: the child shown to have a sexual nature or identity must be perverse. Here he serves as unwitting spokesman for that ethical conservatism or "rigorism" that Ian Watt attributed, only a few years after *Lolita* was published, to the Puritan influence on English and American culture. In *The Rise of the Novel,* Watt discusses "the tremendous narrowing of the ethical scale, a redefinition of virtue in primarily sexual terms," which took hold of the eighteen century and reached its peak during the Victorian era. As part of the Puritan legacy, "resistance to the desires of the body became the major aim of secular morality; and chastity, instead of being only one virtue among many, tended to become the supreme one."[7]

Watt's discussion sheds light on an odd but telling affinity between Fiedler's harsh language, charging Nabokov's child with nymphomania and rape, and the equally dramatic, if more sincere, expressions of outrage by James's Victorian narrator in *The Turn of the Screw*. As soon as the governess detects implications of sexual knowledge in her previously angelic wards, she assumes their absolute contamination. For all the cultural distance separating Fiedler's postwar cynicism from the governess's repressive morality, their reactions evince a mutual inflexibility, an all-or-nothing construction of the child's image: allow the child to tumble from the pedestal of blank (sexless) purity, and evil or corruption (or its modern equivalent, psychopathology) rushes in to fill the void. James Kincaid characterizes this either/or view of the child's innocence as the "dualistic" vision contemporary culture has inherited from the Victorians. Focusing on nineteenth-century literature and culture, Kincaid does not mention *Lolita* in *Child-Loving,* yet his argument sheds light on Fiedler's implicit assumption that, in Kincaid's words, the "child is either free of any whiff of sexuality or is, somehow saturated with it."[8]

To that either/or formulation even so knowledgeable a critic as Alfred Appel, Jr., appears to subscribe. "Satirized" in the novel, Appel asserts, is "the romantic myth of the child, extending from Wordsworth to Salinger. . . . *Lolita* marks its death in 1955." In his view *Lolita*'s debut was at once fatal and salutary. By the time this remarkable novel arrived on the scene, the romantic myth of the child was already moribund; in one swift blow *Lolita* relieved us of this tiresome tradition. As Appel was the first to point out, however, Nabokov's art "records a constant process of *becoming*," analogous to metamorphosis.[9] The aesthetic and linguistic process by which his fiction transforms a theme, cluster of images, or literary myth suggests— like the metamorphosis of a caterpillar into a butterfly—not so much an end as a beginning, a culmination that gives rise to new forms and images. Rather than sounding a death knell to the romantic myth of the child, I shall argue, *Lolita* renews and reinvigorates the myth, rendering the image of childhood with fresh resonance and complexity.

Before focusing on the intricacies of *Lolita*'s narrative, it may prove helpful to consider some of Nabokov's other writing, both fiction and nonfiction, that treats the image of childhood. Largely ignored by his readers thus far, the persistence of the child theme in his thought and work highlights *Lolita*'s unexpected affinities with some of Nabokov's literary predecessors, specifically Charles Dickens and Mary Shelley. While Nabokov openly expressed his admiration for Dickens's literary image of childhood, his debt to Shelley's *Frankenstein* remains implicit; yet the parallels between her bestseller and his are striking. As I will show later in this essay, the poignancy of *Lolita*, like that of *Frankenstein*, largely derives from its vision of the child's sacred innocence. To point out Shelley's debt to the English Romantic poets, whose ranks included her husband, is only to repeat what scholars and critics have long remarked. It is common knowledge that Percy Bysshe Shelley was a major influence on his wife's intellectual and artistic development and that he collaborated with her on the text of *Frankenstein*. Because *Lolita* was published a century and a half later—by a writer notorious for his parody of literary conventions and his disdain for sentimentality—the case for its romantic inheritance requires a more thoroughgoing defense. For clinching evidence, we must turn, of course, to the novel. By initially contemplating a larger frame of reference, however, readers may be better equipped to assess the evidence amply and eloquently provided by the text.

The earliest challenge to the widespread critical assumption that *Lolita* deliberately sabotages the romantic myth of the child comes from the author himself. Nearly five years before the novel appeared in print, Nabokov, with characteristic precocity, had already undermined the position his future critics would adopt. Publicly reprimanding those who "denounce" the theme of the child's innocence as "sentimental," he forthrightly accused "such people" of ignorance; they are, he declared, "unaware of what sentiment is" (*Lectures on Literature* 86). The forum for these remarks was a course on European fiction that Nabokov inaugurated at Cornell University during the academic year 1950–1951, the period during which he began to compose *Lolita* in earnest.[10] In one series of lectures Nabokov paid annual tribute for nearly a decade to the novelist who translated Romantic faith in the child's innocence into some of the finest prose fiction of the nineteenth century, Charles Dickens. Singling out *Bleak House* for detailed analysis, Nabokov drew special attention to the child theme that resonates throughout its pages.

Each year during his lecture on *Bleak House*, Nabokov took pains to criticize the casual manner in which modern readers and critics dismiss as so much "sentimentality" the theme of childhood innocence. No doubt, Nabokov told his students, the "story of a student turned shepherd for the sake of a maiden is sentimental and silly and flat and stale." In regard to Dickens's evocation of "the plight of children," however—the "strain" of "specialized compassion" and "profound pity" that "runs through *Bleak House*"—Nabokov flatly rejected "the charge of sentimentality." Instead, he praised Dickens's "striking" evocation of innocent children—"their troubles, insecurity, humble joys, and the joy they give, but mainly their misery." The "most touching pages." he avowed, "are devoted to the child theme" (*Lectures on Literature* 86–87, 65). In language that deliberately echoes Dickens's incantatory rhythms, Nabokov delivered a veritable litany of "poor children" who inhabit the novel (*Lectures on Literature* 91; see also 70, 74, 88). Significantly, he would later claim that epithet for his literary child, referring to Lolita in a 1966 interview as "my poor little girl" (*Strong Opinions* 94).[11]

## Nabokov's Offspring, Lolita's Kin

The affinities between Nabokov's and Dickens's visions of the child confirm what careful readers of *Lolita* may discover for themselves: far from sounding a death knell for the romantic myth of the child, Nabokov breathes new life into that resonant myth. For him as for his literary precursors, the child—whose innocence has not yet been ravaged by experience, whose wonder at the world is still fresh—emblematizes the human being's creative potential. In a manner that recalls Wordsworth's immortality ode, Nabokov marvels in his autobiography at "the dark-bluish tint of the iris" in his infant son's eyes. Their depth of color seems "to retain the shadows it had absorbed of ancient, fabulous forests . . . where, in some dappled depth, man's mind had been born." The birth of human consciousness, he postulates, was a sudden, glorious flowering—an intuitive leap, a "stab of wonder" by which the dreaming mind awakened to the world. Each child, in turn, repeats the miracle of that original awakening—which Nabokov calls "the initial blossoming of man's mind" (*Speak, Memory* 227–28). To borrow from F. R. Leavis's comments on Dickens, Nabokov "can feel with intensity that the world begins again with every child."[12]

As a youth and fledgling poet, Nabokov already subscribed to the luminous vision of childhood that informs his oeuvre. In 1921, while still a student at Cambridge, he wrote the following in a letter to his mother: "This little poem [I enclose] will prove to you that my mood is radiant as ever. If I live to be a hundred, my soul will still go round in short trousers."[13] For Nabokov, to gaze wide-eyed at the world as children do—and poets must—is not sentimental; grief, death, and loss are never far from view. Drawing on one of English literature's most famous children to illustrate his point, Nabokov says, "In a sense, we all are crashing to our death from the top story of our birth to the flat stones of the churchyard and wondering with an immortal Alice in Wonderland at the patterns of the passing wall. This capacity to wonder at trifles—no matter the imminent peril—these asides of the spirit . . . are the highest forms of consciousness ("The Art of Literature and Commonsense," in Vladimir Nabokov, *Lectures on Literature*, 372–74). Our childish ability to wonder at the world is, then, a form not of escape but of courage in the face of imminent peril and death.

Blessed with this capacity to wonder at trifles, Nabokov's most insightful and creative protagonists glimpse beauty and truth even in the darkest corners of their world. Though virtual prisoners of nightmarish reality, the heroes of his two most political novels, Cincinnatus C. in *Invitation to a Beheading* and Adam Krug in *Bend Sinister*—along with Fyodor in *The Gift*, Pnin, John Shade in *Pale Fire*, Sebastian Knight, even tormented Humbert, and Van Veen in *Ada*—experience those liberating asides of the spirit that constitute, for their author, the highest forms of consciousness. Nabokov's novels always describe a tension or healthy conflict between collective and individual life, between the conventional world that runs on common denominators and the singular consciousness of the individual. But at certain historical moments—as this Russian émigré and fugitive from Hitler well knew—the forces governing collective life become onerous. Seeking to suppress, manipulate, or control the creative exercise of human consciousness, the ruling powers may conspire to destroy the individual altogether. In Nabokov's fiction this unhealthy state of affairs is often signaled by the plight of children, who are inevitably the most vulnerable and easily victimized.

As *Lolita* testifies, Nabokov did not require the conditions of a police state to depict the crimes committed against society's frailest members. Still, a cursory look at his most politically explicit novels, *Invitation to a Beheading* and *Bend Sinister*, may help to clarify the significance of the child in his imaginative universe. In the grotesque police states depicted in these works, Nabokov dramatizes the intrinsic connection between a totalitarian regime's hostility to individual freedom and its lethal effect on the child. In the farcical and shoddy world of *Invitation to a Beheading*, Cincinnatus C. is the only surviving representative of creative human consciousness, the only being who harbors an "exceptionally strong, ardent and independent" inner life. Although Cincinnatus possesses the age and experience of an adult, he looks "extraordinarily youthful," even maddeningly *childlike* to his jailers (120–21, 211). Everything about him—from his "small and still young" face to his delicate limbs and "slender feet"—expresses the "impossible, dazzling freedom" of a vital imagination and memory.[14]

An active and unique inner life constitutes Cincinnatus's only crime against the state that holds him prisoner. Taunted by the radiance of an inner life they can neither possess nor control, his jailers long to "destroy utterly [his] brazen elusive flesh" (122). Betraying their hostility to consciousness at every level, the prison officials throw a party to celebrate their prisoner's impending execution. Even the food and decorations gleefully announce the doomed man's scheduled demise. A guest of honor at the banquet, Cincinnatus notices, for example, the "heap of apples" decorating the festive table. Each bloodred apple, he observes, is "as big as a child's head" (185). This seemingly casual reference abruptly announces the sentence of beheading to both Cincinnatus and the novel's readers. In the vivid image of slaughtered children, tyranny delivers its message.

In *Bend Sinister*, another novel reflecting the nightmarish world of a totalitarian regime, collective life proves so hostile to the individual and his nascent creativity that an innocent child—the philosopher Adam Krug's eight-year-old son, David—is senselessly butchered. Instead of taking him to "the best State Rest House, as had been arranged," the officials accidentally remove David to the Institute for Abnormal Children. Here he is mistakenly identified as an orphan. That mistake proves fatal to David, because the Ekwilist regime regards parentless children as a social and economic burden. From time to time, therefore, officials at the institute use a helpless orphan as a "'release-instrument' for the benefit" of the most violent criminals, who, as one medical official explains, vent "their repressed yearnings . . . upon some little human creature of no value to the community" (218). Assigned to protect Krug's son, the officials bungle the job. In a larger sense, however, David's murder is a logical outcome of this brutal regime, which denies any intrinsic value to the "human creature."

As these brief examples from Nabokov's political fictions suggest, the child's image is often implicated in the efforts of human consciousness and imagination to confront the extremes of human cruelty and suffering. Thus, in a letter Nabokov wrote to his sister at the end of World War II, he reveals how recent information about the Nazi death camps instantly evokes, in his mind and heart, an image of the children who died there. "There are things that torment too deeply," he writes, "the German vilenesses, the burning of children in ovens,—children as funny and as strongly loved as our children."[15] To Nabokov, the horrific image of those burning children brings home a terrible truth: each of those unnamed legions consumed by the camp incinerators was as unique, playful, and fiercely loved as his own young son. That Nabokov repeatedly referred to his most famous literary offspring as his "poor little girl" suggests a similar sympathy for her plight. More conclusive than any external authorial avowal, of course, is the rich evidence provided by the novel itself. *Lolita* is, without doubt, Nabokov's most extensive exploration of the child's betrayal by a world of adults.

## Nabokov's "Poor Little Girl"

Set in prosperous, postwar America, *Lolita* is remote, both politically and geographically, from the nightmarish worlds of *Invitation to a Beheading* and *Bend Sinister*. The novel testifies to the ways collective society can, even in the name of free enterprise and progressive education, conspire against the child's essential welfare and freedom.[16] In the end Dolores Haze loses not only her childhood but her life; the first of these deprivations already implies, in Nabokov's universe as in Dickens's, a betrayal of human consciousness and its creative potential.

Humbert's rhapsodic desire for his nymphet notwithstanding, Dolores Haze's experience reflects that of countless *actual* children whose plight is broadcast daily in the media: children who are sexually exploited by adults claiming to be their guardians. Like those children, who are the subjects of innumerable psychological and sociological case studies, Dolly begins by receiving little attention and less love from her mother; falls prey to notions of romance propagated by movies and magazines; succumbs to the blandishments of a handsome, adult male who adopts the role of her substitute father; and, orphaned by the death of her only surviving parent, learns to put up with her stepfather's routine sexual demands. As Humbert accurately recalls, "she had absolutely nowhere else to go" (144).

True, adolescent Lo is not a virgin when Humbert has sex with her for the first time. But Dolly Haze's experimental forays at summer camp with thirteen-year-old Charlie Holmes, the son of the camp's director, are, if not particularly savory, entirely predictable. While the adolescents' clumsy activities satirically comment on the adults who claim to be supervising them, what Charlie and Dolly get up to in the bushes is little more than child's play (138–39). Touching and vulnerable as children may be, Nabokov does not seek to portray them as genderless angels. Quite the opposite: by restoring sexual vitality to the image of childhood, he rescues it from those "debased-romantic conceptions of innocence" (to recall Peter Covency's formulation) by which late Victorianism had all but killed it. Like James's Maisie, Nabokov's children are vigorous creatures in whom the seeds of adult energy and sexuality, will and intelligence are firmly rooted.

That innocence should not be equated with sexless simplicity— a point that Fiedler and others patently ignore—is recognized even by scurrilous Humbert. When, on the road from Camp Q to the Enchanted Hunters hotel, Lolita offers her stepdad a naive imitation of a Hollywood kiss, Humbert, despite the thrill, warns himself to be careful. Wary of exceeding what he calls "the limits and rules of such girlish games," he tells the reader: "I knew, of course, it was but an innocent game on her part, a bit of backfisch foolery in imitation of some simulacrum of fake romance" (115; the German word *backfisch* means an immature, adolescent girl). Even after Humbert and young Lo have "technically," as he says, become "lovers," the adult cannot pretend ignorance of the child's vulnerability. Only in the most literal, and puritanical, sense can twelve-year-old Dolly be said to have seduced middle-aged Humbert. "While eager to impress me with the world of tough kids," Humbert says of Lolita's initial invitation to have sexual intercourse, "she was not quite prepared for certain discrepancies between a kid's life and mine. Pride alone prevented her from giving up." Naive Lo, he adds, "saw the stark act merely as part of a youngster's furtive world, unknown to adults. What adults did for purposes of procreation was no business of hers" (134–36).

Lolita's brand of naiveté—which leaves her more vulnerable, in some ways, than a child who lacks her pretense of knowing sophistication— poignantly attests to the intrusive power of the media. Forming her notions of reality from images projected on the silver screen, she has no idea that adult experiences transcend the Hollywood gestures and ritualistic movie kisses she has learned to imitate. By the time Humbert arrives on the doorstep of the Haze household, the forces of consumer culture have clearly made inroads on the child's limited experience. Spreading false cheer and empty promises, the philistine art of advertising and the mass media exert a hypnotic influence on her trustful and dreamy nature. Above all, Hollywood's images of fake romance glamorize handsome Humbert and his dark shadow, Clare Quilty, in her eyes. At once starstruck and naively trusting, Lolita, like her mother, is an easy mark for promoters and predators.

With the same naiveté that makes her prey to the media's versions of romance, twelve-year-old Dolores Haze accepts those of the adman: "She believed, with a kind of celestial trust, any advertisement or advice that appeared in *Movie Love* or *Screen Land*. . . . If some café sign proclaimed Icecold Drinks, she was automatically stirred, although all drinks everywhere were ice-cold." An avid consumer, Dolly confirms Neil Postman's observations on modern advertising, which employs "the symbols and rhetoric of religion" to deliver its message. To these "idols," which bear no "burden of logic or verification," children are particularly vulnerable.[17] Dolly Haze's unwitting faith in the adult's version of reality makes her as susceptible to the claims of the billboard as to Humbert's ploys. "She it was," Humbert explains, "to whom ads were dedicated: the ideal consumer, the subject and object of every foul poster" (150). What he fails to point out, however, is that the success of his own foul design, like the poster, depends on the child's inherent gullibility.

Just as Hollywood teaches Dolly Haze how to kiss, Clare Quilty's celebrity status thrills her adolescent heart. Years later, Quilty's promise to make her a starlet turns out to be a ruse; when she refuses to join in the orgies he stages for his amusement, Quilty loses interest in her. Yet even after she leaves him, Lolita cannot think of this "famous" man or his "sensational name" without awe (273). In the final analysis, however, it is her miserable bondage to Humbert that schools Dolores Haze in depravity and deceit. On Humbert's shoulders rests the prime responsibility, as he ultimately acknowledges, for her ruined innocence, From the moment he tells the orphan that her mother is dead and that she must comply with his sexual demands, the game is truly up: Lolita's childhood is over.

In *Lolita*, as in *Ada*, Nabokov reveals the process by which blind passion can poison the wellsprings of love—just as "the invisible worm" corrupts the rose in Blake's poem "The Sick Rose." The poet might well be speaking of Humbert or Van Veen when he writes in another poem from *Songs of Experience*:

Love seeketh only Self to please,
To bind another to its delight;
Joys in another's loss of ease,
And builds a Hell in Heaven's despite.
("The Clod and the Pebble," ll. 9–12)

Just as Blake contrasts the cruel reality of self-serving passion with the hopeful innocence of love (invoked in the poem's previous stanza), Nabokov contrasts Humbert's youthful ardor for Annabel Leigh with his destructive passion for Lolita, which "builds a Hell" for them both. Humbert's love for Annabel is mutual and trusting—innocent not of sexuality but of tyranny, rancor, and deceit. She is Humbert's willing and equal partner, not the solipsized object of his self-serving fantasy. Although Annabel, like Dolores, meets an untimely death, it is not Humbert but typhus that robs her of her childhood (15).

The fatal erosion of innocence begins the moment Humbert deprives the child of her rightful protection. Gradually, and inexorably, Lolita must assume the only role left to her, as the slave of Humbert's desire. But since Humbert is also in thrall to his passion, she shrewdly begins to counter his demands with her own. Thus he balks, but quickly pays up, when she exacts a "bonus price" of "four bucks" for a particularly "fancy [sexual] embrace." An irony writ large in the novel is the public pretense so necessary to their relationship: that Humbert is Lolita's guardian and protector. At times Humbert even allows himself to be taken in by the convenient deceit. Faced "with the distasteful task" of recounting their increasingly mercenary sexual negotiations, he even acts the pained father, bemoaning a "definite drop in Lolita's morals" (185–86).

Humbert's professed concern for Lolita's morals is painfully ironic. Canceled by his rapture for the nymphet is any real sense of responsibility for the child. Voicing his indifference to her early in the novel, Humbert says of young Dolly: "Mentally, I found her to be a disgustingly conventional little girl" who loved "gooey fudge sundaes" and equally gooey "movie magazine." Despite his disdain for American popular culture, the conventions it fosters have something in common with the "system of monetary bribes" he eventually devises to keep his Lolita in tow. In both cases the child's desire for gooey sweets and attractive toys is manipulated by adults for their private gain. With a note of condescension that suggests the disdain all con men have for their dupes, Humbert describes the twelve-year-old Dolly as "a simple child," one easily brought under "submission" by his threats (150–51).

Orphaned by her mother's death, Lolita is especially vulnerable to threats of abandonment. Humbert makes this clear in his description of their first cross-country car trip: "A simple child, Lo would scream no! and frantically clutch at my driving hand whenever I put a stop to her tornadoes of temper by turning in the middle of a highway with the implication that I was about to take her straight to [a] dark and dismal abode." As Dolly grows more obdurate, Humbert's "methods of persuasion" increase in intensity (151). Suppose she does report him to the authorities, he tells her: "Okay. I go to jail. But what happens to you, my orphan? Well, you are luckier," he pronounces with heavy irony, you "will be given a choice of . . . the correctional school, the reformatory, the juvenile detention home." As Humbert wraps up this portion of his account with a final display of rhetorical prowess, his method of persuasion speaks for itself. Syntactically tucked away in his parenthetical asides is eloquent confirmation of his victim's total surrender: "You will dwell, my Lolita will dwell (come here, my brown flower) with thirty-nine other dopes in a dirty dormitory (no, allow me, please) under the supervision of hideous matrons. This is the situation, this is the choice" (153).

Using adult knowledge and power to undermine the choice he pretends to offer her, Humbert succeeds, as he says, "in terrorizing Lo, who despite a certain brash alertness of manner and spurts of wit was not as intelligent a child as her I.Q. might suggest" (153). Here Humbert patently confuses the child's intelligence with experience. His blindness is wholly in keeping with his transgressions against her—his violation, as he ultimately admits, of the sacred rights of childhood. Inexperience, not stupidity, is what makes the child gullible; an older, more seasoned Lolita would not be so easily taken in by Humbert's false claims. It is only a matter of time, in fact, before Lolita learns to trade lies with her captor. "Eventually," he acknowledges, "she lived up to her I.Q." (184).

At the heart of Humbert's exploitation of Lolita is an irony that gradually reveals its tragic dimensions: having explored every particle of his nymphet's face and body—from the gleaming "baby folds of her stomach" to the "peppermint taste of her saliva"—he remains blind to the child's inner life and being (164, 115). Such blindness is both deliberate and self-serving. "I recall," he later says, that "it was always my habit and method to ignore Lolita's states of mind while comforting my own base self." In a brief but telling passage near the end of the novel, a remorseful Humbert recollects one of the rare times when "I knew how [Lolita] felt, and it was hell to know it" (289, 286–87). The revelation occurs when the father of Lolita's school friend Avis Chapman comes to take his daughter home. In contrast to the beautiful nymphet, Avis is "a heavy, unattractive, affectionate child" for whom Humbert feels not the slightest shudder of attraction. Invited to sit down, "Mr. Byrd" (Humbert puns on the Latin meaning of Avis's name) chats politely with Humbert while Avis "perche[s] plumply on his knee" and Lolita looks on with a smile.

Suddenly, however, "as Avis clung to her father's neck and ear [and], with a casual arm, the man enveloped his lumpy and large offspring," Humbert watches "Lolita's smile lose its light and become a frozen little shadow of itself." Holding back her tears with a grimace, the orphan rushes out of the room—to be followed, Humbert adds, "by Avis who had such a wonderful fat pink dad and a small chubby brother, and a brand-new baby sister and a home, and two grinning dogs, and Lolita had nothing" (287–88). As he recollects this scene, which sets him to "squirming and pleading" with his conscience, a remorseful Humbert concedes, in hindsight, the child's right to a dad and a dog and a chubby brother—all the "conventional" elements of an impossibly ordinary (for her) child-hood. For once, Humbert's mask of disdain slips, exposing his recognition of the child's plight.

## The Monster and the Nymphet: *Frankenstein* and *Lolita*

For most of his narrative, guilty Humbert plays on that all-or-nothing vi-sion of childhood innocence exemplified by James's Victorian governess. Claiming to have the "utmost respect" for "ordinary children," Hum-bert—who, in an effort to claim Rousseauean faith in natural innocence, even calls himself Jean-Jacques Humbert—contrasts "their purity and vul-nerability" with the nympher's sexual allure (126, 21). Turning that alleged purity to his self-serving advantage, Humbert insists that the nymphet is not really a child at all: her true nature "is not human but nymphic (that is, demoniac)." Among the "innocent throng" of "wholesome children," he explains, the ardent nympholept searches for "the little deadly demon"—and finds, with a shiver of delight, a bewitching young "Lilith" (18–22). Through this elaborate twist of rhetoric, the impossibly chaste child is supplanted by her dark alter ego—a cruel enchantress or *belle dame sans merci*—and the pedophile transported, on wings of imagination, to that "enchanted island" where the "laws of humanity" conveniently do not ob-tain (308). Taking refuge in fancy's "mossy garden" or "pubescent park," as he puts it, Humbert feels free to dally and disport at will (18, 23).[18]

The language Humbert uses to justify his conduct exposes the dark un-derside of his professed reverence for the child: "Humbert Humbert tried hard to be good. Really and truly, he did. He had the utmost respect for or-dinary children, with their purity and vulnerability, and under no circum-stances would he have interfered with the innocence of a child, if there was the least risk of a row" (21–22). Here, as though unable to bear the weight of its own false logic, Humbert's argument instantaneously collapses. In one swift aside the speaker bares his true motives, admitting that he would in-terfere with a child's innocence—that is (when the euphemism is decoded), he would tamper with her body—*only* if he could get away with it.

Betraying him at every turn, the narrator's rationalizations are as in-triguing in their self-exposure as those of his literary precursor Victor Frankenstein. Humbert's striking kinship with the protagonist of Mary Shelley's novel appears to have gone unnoticed—perhaps because the characters appear to have little in common.[19] Frankenstein, who endlessly delays marriage to his betrothed, is almost comically indifferent to the force of sexual passion that torments and consumes Humbert. Probing beneath this disparity, attentive readers may discover a telling analogy between Humbert's "deadly demon," the alluring nymphet, and Frankenstein's dreaded "daemon," the monster he laments having conceived (*Lolita* 19; *Frankenstein* 39, 40, 56, 78). Monster and nymphet—each of these "marvels" of creation, offspring of Promethean imagination, provokes torments in its creator. The true disaster, however, is one to which Frankenstein wholly and Humbert partially remain blind: the tragic betrayal of the child's original innocence. Just as Frankenstein's creature is trapped in the monstrous shape his maker fashions for him—a shape that alienates him from all humanity—the child Dolores Haze is trapped within the nymphic guise conjured by Humbert's imagination.

Conceived in the depths of Frankenstein's scientific imagination, the creature is no sooner brought to life than his maker rejects him. Recoiling in shock from the creature's grotesque appearance, Frankenstein cannot accept responsibility for the "filthy mass" of flesh and bone that he has brought to life (121). Blinded by disappointment as he formerly was by ambition, Dr. Frankenstein does not recognize what *his* author, Mary Shelley, makes clear to her readers: ugly as the creature appears, he begins life as an innocent child in a benign state of nature. With a grotesque grin wrinkling his yellow cheeks, the trusting newborn instantly stretches out a hand to his parent, as Frankenstein, overcome by repulsion, rushes out of the room (40). Much later, after suffering the misery of rejection, the creature still insists to his horrified parent that at birth he "was benevolent; my soul glowed with love and humanity" (78). Frankenstein's creature, U. C. Knoepflmacher observes, is a genuine Wordsworthian child," who delights as much as "any Romantic" in the wonders of nature.[20] As Shelley reveals, however, innocence is no proof against experience, particularly experience as cruel as that imposed on the creature not only by strangers but by the man who gave him life.

Like Frankenstein, who spurns his offspring, Humbert betrays the covenant between parent and child while exploiting his role as her self-styled guardian. When, as mentioned earlier. Humbert adopts an absurdly paternalistic note, lamenting the "definite drop" in young Dolly's "morals," readers are invited to consider the monstrous irony of his pretense. The perverse logic of Humbert's moral stance as paterfamilias is worthy of his literary precursor. Giving voice to his own brand of solipsistic fervor, Victor Frankenstein conceives of himself as "creator" not only of a single offspring but of a "new species" to follow in the wake of his initial experiment. Casting himself in the role of divine patriarch, he grandiosely declares, "No father could claim the gratitude of his child so completely as I should deserve theirs" (36). His sudden volte-face, once the supposed paragon of this superior species comes to life, is brutally comic.[21]

Cursing the "demoniacal corpse" he has brought to life, Frankenstein condemns his unfortunate offspring to isolation, misery, and, finally, rage against humanity (39). The process by which Shelley's Promethean hero projects his own "daemonic" energies—both creative and destructive— onto his creature exposes in a sharper light Humbert's hazy references to demonic enchantment. Take, for example, the scene in which Humbert, having consummated his desire for the nymphet, stands at the hotel desk waiting to check out with his "little mistress." His "every nerve," Humbert comments, is alive "with the feel of her body—the body of some immortal daemon disguised as a female child" (141). Here, as in Frankenstein's case, the narrator's rhetoric is more self-revealing than he knows. Humbert's evocation of the nymphet's mortal disguise draws attention to his own need to disguise his guilt.

Standing in the lobby of the Enchanted Hunters, Humbert strains to conceal what just took place in the hotel room upstairs, where he and the "female child" had "strenuous intercourse three times that very morning." As if that were not enough, Humbert is hiding other dreadful secrets. Not until he has safely removed Lolita from the hotel and its onlookers will he dare to tell her the truth: he has lied to her about their destination as he has lied to her about her mother. Charlotte Haze is not eagerly awaiting her daughter's arrival in some "hypothetical hospital" in a nearby town (141–42). She is dead. Lolita is a hapless and helpless orphan.

As he and the "lone child" drive away from the hotel, Humbert is suddenly gripped by a feeling of "oppressive hideous constraint as if I were sitting with the small ghost of somebody I had just killed." Temporarily awakening to the fact that the little "waif" seated next to him is no "immortal daemon," Humbert reluctantly voices his guilt. In contrast to Frankenstein, whose little brother, William, is eventually murdered by the creature, Humbert has no hideous monster to blame for the violence perpetrated against a helpless child. There is only the "heavy-limbed, foul-smelling adult" seated next to her in the car (142). No wonder he feels haunted by a small ghost: only a shade, or shadow, remains of Dolly Haze's brief childhood. The true demon is the "pentapod monster," as Humbert later describes himself, who has defiled the offspring in his charge.[22]

No sooner does this revelation occur than the processes of deflection and self-serving projection once again take over—as Humbert begins to feel "somewhere at the bottom of [his] dark turmoil . . . the writhing of desire again, so *monstrous* was [his]appetite for that *miserable* nymphet" (142; emphases added). Here the narrator's language offers a direct parody of Frankenstein's, as the scientist blames the "miserable monster" for what he himself has wrought (39). In those moments, however, when Humbert's monstrous appetite temporarily abates, he again suffers "pangs of guilt." In realizing his "lifelong dream" by having sexual intercourse with a child, he has, he admits, "plunged" them both "into nightmare" (142).

A similar descent into nightmare is traced by Shelley's narrator. Like Humbert, Frankenstein pursues his lifelong dream with solipsistic fervor— having "desired it," as he says, "with an ardour that far exceeded moderation." He, too, observes "the beauty of the dream" plunge into nightmare, a living "hell" that "even Dante could not have conceived" (39–40). (In a similar allusion to Dante's *Inferno*, Humbert describes the nympholept's strange admixture of guilt and rapture, heaven and hell as the "first circle of paradise" [285].) Seized by the Promethean ambition to create life, Frankenstein does not pause to consider the potentially disastrous consequences. Blindly he assumes that the gigantic creature he is patching together out of bits and pieces—the flesh and bones collected in charnel houses—will be "beautiful." Only after he assembles the severved limbs and body parts, stitches them together, and jolts them into life can he perceive what a dreadful "thing" he has wrought (36, 39–40). Even so, Frankenstein does not accept responsibility for the nightmare that follows. Only after his infant brother and old father, his best friend and his bride have all died does he fathom the extent of the destruction he has wrought.

The parallels between Frankenstein's "miserable monster" and Humbert's "miserable nymphet" help to clarify, as we have seen, the relationship of each protagonist to the child he victimizes. In addition, both protagonists suffer tremendous feelings of guilt, which they project onto others. Frankenstein curses the creature for the murderous actions he has set in motion; Humbert reserves his purest hatred for the "fiend" who steals Lolita from him (255, 261). At a deeper level, however, both characters recognize in their hated adversaries a mirror image of themselves. Frankenstein's hideous monster mirrors, first as a physical shape and then in his vicious actions, the scientist's monstrous disregard for moral and natural laws. By the same token, Quilty, the pervert and pedophile, serves as a nasty, even more brutish reflection of Humbert's "monstrous" lust (142). The passion enflaming both protagonists—one to usurp nature and create life, the other to usurp a child's life for his own pleasure—is mon-

strous in the most fundamental sense, a transgression, as Humbert ultimately admits, of "all laws of humanity" (308).[23]

Referring, near the end of Shelley's novel, to the "hideous narration"
he is about to complete, Frankenstein appears, at least temporarily, to take
full measure of his guilt. Repeating one of the terms he has used to deplore
the creature, "hideous," he now claims this epithet for the story he has set
in motion (42, 56, 166). With a similar sense of the hideousness he has
wrought, Humbert draws his tale to a close: "This then is my story. I have
reread it. It has bits of marrow sticking to it, and blood, and beautiful
bright-green flies" (310). Humbert's narration, like Frankenstein's, issues
from the ruins of death and decay; it resembles, metaphorically, the monster Frankenstein created, a kind of living corpse.

That the text is a body, or monstrous offspring—one that each writer,
like a modern-day Frankenstein, constructs and sends out into the
world—is a notion that Shelley asks her readers to contemplate. In her
preface to the 1831 edition of the novel, she says with a paradoxical flourish: "And now, once again, I bid my hideous progeny to go forth and
prosper. I have affection for it, for it was the offspring of happy days" (197,
192). Implicitly linking her own acts of creation—as both a writer and a
mother—with those of her Promethean narrator, she hints that, as Peter
Brooks observes, art is "a kind of controlled play with the daemonic." Significantly, however, Shelley embraces the relationship that Frankenstein
spurns—avowing her affection for the "hideous" offspring she has delivered into the world. Like a maternal expression of unconditional love,
Shelley's affection for her "hideous progeny" implicitly comments on her
protagonist's outright rejection of his: Frankenstein's failure to acknowledge, in Brooks's phrase, "the destructive potential of the creative
drive."[24] Both *Frankenstein* and *Lolita* testify to the destructive as well as the
creative power of imagination and the terrible beauty it engenders. In the
"controlled play with the daemonic" that each text invites its readers
to enter, we discover the profound extent to which imagination and will
can wreak havoc with Nature and human nature. Entering into a relationship with the demonic that is wildly out of control, each narrator produces
his "hideous" story: hideous not because his desires are grotesquely
thwarted but because human hope and innocence—embodied for both
Nabokov and Shelley in the image of childhood—have been monstrously
abused.

Describing the cross-country journey on which he and Lolita embarked,
Humbert sadly acknowledges that despite having "been everywhere," they
"had really seen nothing." He adds, "And I catch myself thinking today that

our long journey had only defiled with a sinuous trail of slime the lovely, trustful, dreamy, enormous country that by then, in retrospect, was no more to us than a collection of dog-eared maps, ruined tour books, old tires, and her sobs in the night—every night, every night" (177–78). Humbert's account concretely renders the metaphysical process by which, in Nabokov's expressed view, a world emptied of good becomes a fitting habitation for evil.[25] Indifferent to everything but his desire, Humbert has seen *nothing* of the innocent and dreamy landscape, the beneficent order of reality through which he passed like a blind man. For him, this lovely country was only a grid, a blueprint, a series of marks on a map. Such an abstract universe, emptied of love and meaning, signifies the moral vacuum that evil rushes to fill—just as the child's miserable sobs filled the silence every night. Recognizing that he has defiled both the child and the pristine beauty of the unspoiled countryside, Humbert faintly gleans the connection between the radiant source of reality and the child's innate innocence. To have robbed Dolores Haze of her childhood constitutes nothing less, in Nabokov's universe, than a crime against the cosmos.

## The Romantic Legacy Qualified

Humbert's fierce but blinkered imagination leads, paradoxically, to his transgression against the source and symbol of creative imagination: the child. For Wordsworth and Blake, Dickens and Nabokov, the child's wonder, innocence, and spontaneity constitute the image and embodiment of human freedom and creativity. In striving to attain his perfect world or paradise, Humbert deprives Lolita of her rightful childhood—and betrays the principles of romantic faith and freedom. Significantly, his capacity to transcend his solipsistic vision entails not wholesale abandonment but the searching renewal of romantic faith.

In a passage near the end of the novel, Humbert recalls a time when, overhearing Dolly talking to a school friend about death, he first realized how little he knew about the child. "And it struck me," he says, "that I simply did not know a thing about my darling's mind and that quite possibly, behind the awful juvenile clichés, there was in her a garden and a twilight, and a palace gate—dim and adorable regions which happened to be lucidly and absolutely forbidden to me" (286). Employing the fairy-tale formula of a remote and enchanting kingdom—one that faintly echoes the refrain of Poe's "Annabel Lee," with its "kingdom by the sea"—Humbert is not, for once, lamenting his lost paradise. Instead, the romantic evocation of a walled garden, or private kingdom, pays homage to the child's inner life, forever inaccessible to him.

Only in hindsight, in the process of recounting his love and loss of Lolita, does Humbert glean an image of the child as an autonomous being, an individual with the right to her own kingdom, her own universe of hopes and dreams, feelings and flights of fancy that have nothing to do with his desire. Only this gradual, painful recognition of the child's independent reality secures Humbert the moral and imaginative insight that makes his story so compelling to the reader—even a reader as wary of treating Nabokov as a "plodding moralist" as Michael Wood, who says, "If Humbert has not evoked the substantial American child as well as the solipsized . . . nymphet, there is no novel here that matters." At the end of his story Humbert's wish to protect Lolita's privacy—his instruction that his memoir "be published only when Lolita is no longer alive"—is one manifestation of his belated recognition of her autonomous being (311). That she inhabits his narrative not only as a bewitching nymphet but as a victimized child testifies, in a much more telling way, to his moral growth as well as to his guilt.[26]

Only through the medium of art can Humbert restore to the child he tyrannized—the child whose "life," as he says, he "broke"—some semblance of the freedom and autonomy he otherwise denied her (281). But as he makes clear, the consolation of art is no compensation for what she has lost: "Unless it can be proven to me . . . that in the infinite run it does not matter a jot that a North American girl-child named Dolores Haze had been deprived of her childhood by a maniac, unless this can be proven (and if it can, then life is a joke), I see nothing for the treatment of my misery but the melancholy and very local palliative of articulate art" (285). In stark language that abruptly departs from the "fancy prose style" in which most of his narrative is cast, Humbert evokes the child's right to her own life and liberty. Significantly, he now eschews the temporal terms reserved for his nymphets, grounding the child's autonomy in space, the boundless space of the North American continent, whose geographical extension and history patently invoke a universe beyond Humbert's dominion.

Humbert's admission that "Dolores Haze had been deprived of her childhood by a maniac" implicitly affirms a central tenet of romantic faith, "the conviction that," as David Grylls says, "children being innocent, the wickedest thing one can do to them is to rob them of their childhood."[27] In Dickens's *Dombey and Son*, Edith Skewton accuses her conniving mother of this very crime: "What childhood did you ever leave to me?" she demands. "I was a woman—artful, designing, mercenary, laying snares for men—before I knew myself. . . . Look at me, taught to scheme and plot when children play" (406). Victim of still fouler manipulations at the hands of her stepfather, Dolores Haze might well lay this charge at Humbert's feet. Schooled by her "mercenary" relationship with a man who pretends to be her protector, she too is forced to scheme and plot when she should be at play.

Tyrannized by a vicious adult, Dolly Haze's young life, like that of so many of Dickens's "poor children," is prematurely cut off by death. Humbert, at least, is spared the recriminating knowledge that, as John Ray, Jr., says in the novel's foreword, Mrs. Richard F. Schiller (Lolita's married name) dies at seventeen "in childbed, giving birth to a stillborn girl" (6). The reader's discovery of this grim fact adds a final note of pathos—what Nabokov calls, in his lecture on *Bleak House*, "divine" pity—to the theme of abortive childhood and thwarted innocence. As much as any work by Dickens, *Lolita* owes its poignancy and a good deal of its poetry to the vision of the child reflected in its depths. Here and throughout Nabokov's imaginative universe, the child's image shines like a beacon, a beacon that serves, among other things, to highlight this writer's unique position in the development of twentieth-century fiction. Nabokov's novels are as involuted and self-conscious as any work of postmodernist fabulation; at the same time, however, they evoke a mysterious connection, impalpable as a shaft of light, to a world that lies beyond the alleged prison house of language and the confines of the text. Readers who detect this connection can appreciate the way the novelist's art both engages and defies appearance. Like the magician whose deft fingers pluck a live bird from his hat, Nabokov beckons the real in the very act of creating illusion.

### Notes

1. Marie Winn, *Children without Childhood* (New York: Pantheon, 1983), 3.

2. For comparison of Kubrick's film with the novel and with Nabokov's published screenplay, see Ellen Pifer, "The Incomplete Metamorphosis of *Lolita*: From Novel to Screenplay and Film," in *La littérature Anglo-Américaine à l'écran*, ed. Daniel Royot and Gérard Hugues (Paris: Didier, 1993), 125–34.

3. Tapping the resources of English, French, and Russian Romanticism, Humbert's evocation of the nymphet combines the *rusalka*, the water nymph or sprite of Russian folklore, with the *neznakomka,* the incognita or alluring stranger, in the neoromantic poems of the Russian symbolist Aleksandr Blok; for a discussion of

the *rusalka* as well as of the incognita in Blok and other writers who may have influenced Nabokov, see D. Barton Johnson, " 'L'inconnue de la Seine' and Nabokov's Naiads," *Comparative Literature* 44, no. 3 (Summer 1992): 225–48.

4. Vladimir Alexandrov observes that Nabokov's later Russian translation of Lolita "makes the point even more bluntly": instead of the sentence "Lolita had been safely solipsized, the Russian version reads: "Real'nost' Lolity byla blagopoluchno otmenena" (Lolita's reality was successfully canceled; 49) (*Nabokov's Otherworld* [Princeton, N.J.: Princeton University Press, 1991], 170–71). Humbert's description of the solipsized, will-less child echoes the language of Victorian child rearing manuals, which fostered, as James R. Kincaid says in *Child-Loving: The Erotic Child and Victorian Culture* (New York: Routledge, 1992), "wax and clay" images of passive children waiting to be molded by the adult's will; as one manual bluntly put it, children "have no will of their own" (90).

5. Denis de Rougemont incorrectly argues that by "disenchanting" romantic "myth," irony ensures *Lolita*'s failure to "move" us (*Love Declared: Essays on the Myths of Love*, trans. Richard Howard [New York: Random House, 1963], 52–54). Appel more accurately employs the definition of *parody* that Nabokov provides in one of his novels—"as a kind of springboard for leaping into the highest region of serious emotion"—to characterize *Lolita*'s ultimate effects (*The Real Life of Sebastian Knight* [Norfolk, Conn.: New Directions, 1941], 91; cited in Alfred Appel, Jr., introduction to *The Annotated Lolita* [New York: McGraw-Hill, 1970], liii). Like Rougemont, Virginia L. Blum argues that Lolita's parodic structure prohibits the reader from taking the characters seriously. The plight of the abused child, in particular, is robbed of poignancy by "a text that parodies all literary conventions" and manifests a "brand of narcissism" that is "pathological" (*Hide and Seek: The Child between Psychoanalysis and Fiction* [Urbana: University of Illinois Press], 214). For a critical overview of a half century of similar charges, see chap. 1 of Ellen Pifer, *Nabokov and the Novel* (Cambridge, Mass.: Harvard University Press, 1980).

6. Fiedler, cited by Phyllis Roth in her introduction to *Critical Essays on Vladimir Nabokov* (Boston: G. K. Hall, 1984), 13; Leslie Fiedler, *Love and Death in the American Novel* (New York: Criterion, 1960), 326–27.

7. Ian Watt, *The Rise of the Novel* (Berkeley: University of California Press, 1965), 156–57.

8. Kincaid states, "The idea that children might be invested with a low-level, junior-grade sexuality—something between nothing whatever and full-fledged carnality—is seldom advanced and less often welcome" (*Child-Loving* 183).

9. Appel, *Annotated Lolita*, 1 n.2; Alfred Appel, Jr., "Nabokov's Puppet Show, Pt. II," *New Republic*, 21 January 1967, 26.

10. See Brian Boyd, *Vladimir Nabokov: The American Years* (Princeton, N.J.: Princeton University Press, 1991), 166–98.

11. For discussion of the connections Nabokov privately drew in his teaching copy of *Bleak House* between Dickens's "gentle little nymphs" and his own unfortunate "nymphet," see Ellen Pifer, "Innocence and Experience Replayed : From *Speak, Memory* to *Ada*," *Cycnos* 10, no. 1 (1993): 20–21.

12. The quote from Leavis is in his introduction to Peter Coveney, *The Image of Childhood: The Individual and Society, a Study of the Theme in English Literature,* rev. ed. (Baltimore, Md.: Penguin, 1967), 23.

13. Nabokov, cited in Brian Boyd, *Vladimir Nabokov: The Russian Years* (Princeton, N.J.: Princeton University Press, 1990), 187–88.

14. David Cowart notes that the middle-aged, eponymous hero of Nabokov's *Pnin* is sympathetically rendered as a childlike adult: "With his bald head and 'infantile absence of eyebrows'. . . , Pnin seems hairless as a baby, and in fact the author consistently characterizes him as a child: he speaks English with difficulty; he has tiny feet; and he occupies, on more than one occasion, rooms furnished for children" ("Art and Exile: Nabokov's *Pnin*," *Studies in American Fiction* 10, no. 2 [1982]: 199).

15. Nabokov, cited in Leona Toker, *Nabokov: The Mystery of Literary Structures* (Ithaca, N.Y.: Cornell University Press, 1989), 177–78.

16. For a discussion of *Lolita*'s political implications, see Ellen Pifer, "Nabokov's Discovery of America: From Russia to *Lolita*," in *The American Columbaid: "Discovering" America, Inventing the United States,* ed. Mario Materassi and Maria T. Ramalho de Sousa Santos (Amsterdam, Netherlands: VU University Press, 1996), 407–14.

17. Neil Postman, *The Disappearance of Childhood* (New York: Delacorte, 1982), 108.

18. Mark Spilka ventures on shaky ground when he equates Humbert's desire to escape to "an idyllic realm" with Nabokov's own "regressive" longing and "nostalgia" ("On the Enrichment of Poor Monkeys by Myth and Dream; or, How Dickens Rousseauisticized and Pre-Freudianized Victorian Views of Childhood," in *Sexuality and Victorian Literature,* ed. Don Richard Cox [Knoxville: University of Tennessee Press, 1984], 174–76). Blurring the distinction between *Lolita*'s author and narrator, Spilka overlooks the ways that the novel's style and structure undermine the narrator's self-serving claims.

19. Although Humbert's narrative never directly refers to *Frankenstein,* Nabokov, from childhood a voracious reader in three languages, undoubtedly read Shelley's popular classic in his youth. It is quite likely, moreover, that he would have reacquainted himself with the novel in the course of his research fot the thousand-page scholarly commentary that accompanies his translation of Aleksandr Pushkin's *Eugene Onegin.* Here Nabokov's prodigious knowledge of the English Romantics—Byron, Wordsworth, and Percy Bysshe Shelley—as well as their European precursors, contemporaries, and epigones is both obvious and well documented. Nabokov, in his commentary on the translation of *Eugene Onegin,* refers to Shelley's "widow" when glossing a line (chap. 3, stanza 9, l.8) of Pushkin's novel in verse:

"According to his widow," Nabokov comments, "one summer evening [the poet] heard the skylark and saw the 'glow-worm golden in a dell of dew' mentioned in his famous ode" (2:344).

20. U. C. Knoepflmacher, "Thoughts on the Aggression of Daughters," in *The Endurance of Frankenstein: Essays on Mary Shelley's Novel*, ed. George Levine and U. C. Knoepflmacher (Berkeley: University of California Press, 1979), 100–101.

21. Philip Stevick discusses the "problematic comedy" of Shelley's novel, which belongs to "a class of works" that "generate simultaneously mythic seriousness and uncomfortable laughter" ("Frankenstein and Comedy," in *The Endurance of Frankenstein*, ed. Levine and Knoepflmacher, 222).

22. Joyce Carol Oates detects in Humbert's reference to the nymphet as "some immortal daemon disguised as a female child" a "cultural relationship" between *Lolita*, the manuscript of which Nabokov evidently finished in the spring of 1954, and William March's *The Bad Seed* published in that same "watershed" year. She implies that "although Nabokov the aesthete would have distanced himself from March," he shares something of the latter's demonic vision of childhood ("Killer Kids" (*New York Review of Books*, 6 November 1997, 20). To the contrary: not only Nabokov's aesthetics but his ethical and epistemological understanding of reality— in which the child embodies human creativity and freedom—place him in diametric opposition to March's deterministic vision of the "bad seed," the child's genetic predisposition to evil.

23. For an extended comparison of Quilty and the creature in their function as doubles, see Ellen Pifer, "Her Monster, His Nymphet: Nabokov and Mary Shelley," in *Nabokov and His Fiction: New Perspectives*, ed. Julian W. Connolly (Cambridge: Cambridge University Press, 1999), 158–76.

24. " 'Godlike Science/Unhallowed Arts': Language, Nature, and Monstrosity," in *The Endurance of Frankenstein*, ed. Levine and Knoepflmacher, 220, 217.

25. Alexandrov observes that Nabokov regarded human evil not as the manifestation of some vital force or *presence* but as the outcome or effect of *absence*—the absence of good (*Nabokov's Otherworld* 53–55). His discussion draws on the essay in which Nabokov declares his "irrational belief in the goodness of man," adding; "Now 'badness' is a stranger to our inner world; it eludes our grasp; 'badness' is in fact the lack of something rather than a noxious presence; and thus being abstract and bodiless it occupies no real space in our inner world" (Vladmir Nabokov, "The Art of Literature and Commonsense," in Nabokov's *Lectures on Literature*, ed. Fredson Bowers [New York: Harcourt Brace, 1980], 373, 375–76).

26. Michael Wood, *The Magician's Doubts: Nabokov and the Risks of Fiction* (London: Chatto and Windus, 1994), 7, 115. On this point Nabokov says, "I do think that Humbert Humbert in his last stage is a moral man because he realizes that he loves *Lolita* [*sic*]," but "it is too late, he has destroyed her childhood" (cited in David

Rampton, *Vladimir Nabokov: A Critical Study of the Novels* [Cambridge: Cambridge University Press, 1984], 202 n.34). For a discussion of the liberating power of love in Nabokov's universe, see Ellen Pifer, "Shades of Love: Nabokov's Intimations of Immortality," *Kenyon Review,* no. 2 (Spring 1989), 75–86.

27. David Grylls, *Guardians and Angels: Parents and Children in Nineteenth-Century Literature* (London: Faber and Faber, 1978), 140.

# "So Nakedly Dressed"

## The Text of the Female Body in Nabokov's Novels

### JENEFER SHUTE

◆ ◆ ◆

W AS SHE REALLY PRETTY, at twelve? Did he want—would he ever want to caress her, to really caress her? Her black hair cascaded over one clavicle and the gesture she made of shaking it back and the dimple on her pale cheek were revelations with an element of immediate recognition about them. Her pallor shone, her blackness blazed. The pleated skirts she liked were becomingly short. Even her bare limbs were so free from suntan that one's gaze, stroking her white shins and forearms, could follow upon them the regular slants of fine dark hairs, the silks of her girlhood. The iridal dark-brown of her serious eyes had the enigmatic opacity of an Oriental hypnotist's look (in a magazine's back-page advertisement) and seemed to be placed higher than usual so that between its lower rim and the moist lower lid a cradle crescent of white remained when she stared straight at you. Her long eyelashes seemed blackened, and in fact were. Her features were saved from elfin prettiness by the thickish shape of her parched lips. Her plain Irish nose was Van's in miniature. Her teeth were fairly white, but not very even.[1]

This description, from Vladimir Nabokov's novel *Ada*, is of a twelve-year-old girl as perceived by her close coeval and "cousin," Van, whose inchoate and reluctant desire is now beginning to articulate itself. In order to name itself, his desire has first to articulate an image of the desired object—limb by limb, sentence by sentence. The portrait thus produced—an inventory of desire, a catalog of the constituted body—is a familiar rhetorical place in fiction as in poetry and painting; in Nabokov's work, however, it has attained unusually high levels of self-conscious elaboration and investment. Two novels in particular—*Ada* and *Lolita*—are punctuated by this recurrent *topos,* this inventory of the female form, this cartography of desire. But how, precisely, is it constituted? How, in Nabokov, does desire articulate itself—utter itself—and articulate the desired Other, hinge together, limb by limb, the locus of the female body?

In both *Ada* and *Lolita*, the female body upon which the most intense rhetorical elaboration is lavished is an immature one—or, more accurately, the body of a child irradiated by a sexuality powerless yet to name itself. Since this sexuality is still mute, still only potential, the body has not yet constituted itself as an object of desire. Here, then, is one major distinction between Nabokov's evocation of the female body and the venerable tradition to which it belongs: the body, because not quite adult, has not yet constituted itself as an object to be looked at. As John Berger points out, in Western culture, to be a woman is to be viewed:

> Men look at women. Women watch themselves being looked at. This determines not only most relations between men and women but also the relation of women to themselves. . . . A woman must continually watch herself. She is almost continually accompanied by her own image of herself. . . . Thus she turns herself into an object—and most particularly an object of vision: a sight.[2]

In the case of Nabokov's nymphets, however, the girl-woman has not yet constituted herself as an object of visual consumption, and it is the male viewer who, like an artist or magician, must create from this recalcitrant material a landscape of desire. Humbert Humbert states this quite explicitly. In order to recognize that magical creature, the nymphet, he says:

> You have to be an artist and a madman, a creature of infinite melancholy, with a bubble of hot poison in your loins and a super-voluptuous flame permanently aglow in your subtle spine . . . in order to discern at once, by ineffable signs . . . the little deadly demon among the wholesome children; *she* stands unrecognized by them, and unconscious herself of her fantastic power.[3]

Nabokov's evocations of the immature female body in *Lolita* and *Ada* thus deliberately trace the social process whereby this body, out of its own initial unconsciousness, is constituted as an object of desire; in David Packman's words, "The body as text is unaware of its meaning, which is produced in the reading."[4]

"Was she really pretty, at twelve?" Van wonders about Ada, implicitly calibrating his own desire against more general definitions of the desirable. The extended description that follows is presented as if in answer to this question—and yet the question is never resolved, for parallel to the catalog of conventional, even clichéd, tokens of feminine beauty (cascading black hair, dimple, white skin, silkiness, hypnotic eyes, long eyelashes) is a series of terms marked by neutral-to-negative affect: "thickish," "plain," "parched," "fairly white, but not very even." Yet such terms do not undermine the articulation of desire here; quite the contrary, since this evocation of a body in its particularity and imperfection attests all the more strongly to the power of the desire that celebrates it—and to the power of the desirer, the Pygmalion of this mute and intractable material.

Paradoxically, however, the articulation of this body in all its uniqueness and particularity is itself highly conventionalized. As Roland Barthes suggests, "Meanings abound in the portrait, proliferating through a form which nonetheless disciplines them: this form is both a rhetorical order (declaration and detail) and an anatomical cataloguing (body and face): these two protocols are also codes."[5] In Nabokov's evocation of Ada, these two codes coincide in the rhetorical strategy of enumeration, an inventory whose organization is emphasized by anaphora: "her black hair," "her pallor," "her long eyelashes," "her features," "her plain Irish nose," "her teeth," and (even) "her bare limbs." Such an inventory of the female body, each fragmented part promoted to a temporary fetish, has become familiar from a number of genres, primarily pornography. In pornography, however, the inventory has a strict sexual logic—the logic of the striptease, proceeding from outside to inside, from the peripheries of the body to the sexual center, from metonymic foreglimpses to final, climactic exposure.

Nabokov's inventory has no such logic, wandering seemingly at random from hair to clavicle to dimple to cheek to limbs to shins to forearms to hairs to irises to eyes to eyelashes to lips to nose to teeth. Besides metonymic relations between several of these terms (dimple/cheek, hairs/forearms, irises/eyes, eyelashes/eyes), this inventory's only formal logic seems that of exclusion: excluded are precisely those parts of the body most frankly sexual. But while Nabokov here seems to avoid the obvious pornographic trope of the striptease, he subtly reinvests his language with its defining features: sexual looking and the unveiling of the body.

Ada's body is described in such a way that looking at it becomes a kind of caress, a sustained substitute for the doubtful gesture of the second sentence. This equivalence between looking and touching is asserted quite overtly ("one's gaze, stroking her white shins and forearms"), but is also more subtly enforced by tactile evocations such as "moist," "parched," and "silks." What is not so clear, however, is precisely who is looking: within the passage's omniscient third-person narration, a number of potential viewers are suggested: "Did *he* want . . . to caress her?" "*one's* gaze, stroking her"; "when she stared straight at *you*"; "an element of immediate recognition"—but for whom? What defines this projected community of voyeurs—in which the reader is implicated—is the capacity to respond predictably to the sustained visual caress of Nabokov's prose. The implied reader here—like the implied viewer in the Western tradition of the nude—is obviously male.

From this perspective of male desire—distributed among author, character, and reader—description becomes a kind of undressing. Clothing is sketched in but effectively erased in the same sentence: "The pleated skirts she liked were becomingly short." Beneath this clothing, which is both there and not there, the body strips itself of its own potential disguises: Ada's hair "cascades" over her clavicle, covering it, yet she makes a gesture of "shaking it back"; her "bare" limbs are "free from suntan," which somehow makes them barer. For all this, however, the body is never naked: stripped and exposed but still dressed in its own tactile nudity, the "silks of her girlhood." As John Berger suggests:

> To be on display is to have the surface of one's own skin, the hairs of one's own body, turned into a disguise which, in that situation, can never be discarded. The nude is condemned to never being naked. Nudity is a form of dress.[6]

As both Berger and Barthes imply, description—especially of the female body—can never be neutral, never innocent. It partakes always, with varying degrees of self-consciousness, of prior codes: the nude, the portrait, the inventory, the striptease, and so on. Not only is the woman's body made into an object—as Nabokov's syntax makes perfectly clear here—but it is an object defined by certain codes, an object of art.

The particular art being invoked in this description of Ada may not be immediately apparent, but as the prose develops, so does an image, an image in black and white: "black hair," "pale cheeks," "blackness," "pallor," "dark hairs," "white shins," "dark-brown," "crescent of white," "blackened," "fairly white." Any possible suggestion of color is systematically drained: flesh tints pale to "white" on limbs "free from suntan," and an entire rainbow is cancelled in "iridal dark-brown." Black-and-white Ada "stare[s] straight at you," this being the only moment when the looked-at-object becomes subject and looks back—but with the "enigmatic opacity" of a hypnotist's gaze or the gaze, perhaps, of a face in a photograph.

Such an appeal to a prior code of the image is made even more explicit in a parallel passage from *Lolita*, where Humbert describes his first glimpse of the nymphet:

> It was the same child—the same frail, honey-hued shoulders, the same silky supple bare back, the same chestnut head of hair. A polka-dotted black kerchief tied around her chest hid from my aging ape eyes, but not from the gaze of young memory, the juvenile breasts I had fondled one immortal day. And, as if I were the fairy-tale nurse of some little princess (lost, kidnapped, discovered in gypsy rags through which her nakedness smiled at the king and his hounds), I recognized the tiny dark-brown mole on her side. With awe and delight (the king crying for joy, the trumpets blaring, the nurse drunk) I saw again her lovely indrawn abdomen where my southbound mouth had briefly paused; and those puerile hips on which I had kissed the crenulated imprint left by the band of her shorts—that last mad immortal day behind the "Roches Roses." The twenty-five years I had lived since then, tapered to a palpitating point, and vanished. (41)

Here, desire is quite explicitly imagined as rediscovery, the desired body a replication of a previous one: as Barthes suggests, beauty "cannot assert itself save in the form of a citation."[7] Citation and replication are the major rhetorical modes here, as Lolita's body becomes a replication of another, its discovery a rediscovery, and that very rediscovery a replaying of the persistent tradition: the recognition scene in myth and fairy tale.

Humbert's invocation of this code of recognition accounts for two major differences between this passage and the one from *Ada*: its tense structure and its sense of gender. By invoking the trope of rediscovery, Nabokov plays here with time and tense, oscillating between perfect and pluperfect in a way quite different from the linear inventory of the *Ada* passage. Moreover, in this oscillation between past and present, between fantasy and actuality, distinctions become obscured and gender boundaries more permeable: Humbert, for instance, turns into a "fairy-tale nurse," while the girl-child's body is described as "puerile." These linguistic transformations, which include a kind of neutering generalization ("it" was the same "child"), tell a good deal about the ambiguous sexuality of obsessive nymphet love. Despite these important differences, however, the basic rhetorical structure of the passages from both *Ada* and *Lolita* remain essentially the same, with the major strategies of anatomical inventory, visual caress, and verbal unveiling more overt, if anything, in Humbert's prose.

Unlike the more equivocal description of Ada, Humbert's evocation of Lolita leaves no doubt about who is looking—"my aging ape eyes," "I recognized," "I saw again"—and the reader, uninvited, becomes a voyeur of Humbert's own voyeurism. *Voyeurism* is the appropriate term here, for the inventory of the fragmented fetish-body in this passage has the pornographic logic—absent or only implied in *Ada*—of the striptease. Beginning at the shoulders and working downward from hair to back to breasts to abdomen to hips, the sequence imitates the "southbound" logic of sexual desire, increasing the verbal excitation ("the king crying for joy, the trumpets blaring") until both language and desire reach their climactic "vanishing point."

Also according to the logic of the striptease, clothing reveals more than it conceals: the "kerchief" hides from present view, but not from fantasy ("the gaze of young memory"), Lolita's "juvenile breasts"; the fairy-tale princess's "gypsy rags" do not cover so much as permit discovery; other clothes disappear completely, leaving only a ghostly afterimage: "the crenulated imprint left by the band of her shorts." Once bared in this way, the body becomes an object of tactile assimilation ("fondled," "silky," "crenulated") which—as the language of touch modulates into that of taste ("honey," "chestnut," "drunk," "mouth")—lends itself at last to complete consumption.

The major rhetorical strategy, then, is one whereby, through the inventory of the fragmented fetish-body and the appeal to prior codes of the image (photography, striptease, fairy tale), the immature female body is transmuted into an appropriate image for male consumption. This strategy characterizes Nabokov's descriptions throughout *Lolita* and *Ada*, including those passages where the girl/woman is ostensibly described as agent rather than object. In *Ada*, for example, there is an extended description, again through Van's eyes, of Ada engaged in an absorbing activity:

On those relentlessly hot July afternoons, Ada liked to sit on a cool piano stool of ivoried wood at a white-oilcloth'd table in the sunny music room, her favorite botanical atlas open before her, and copy out in color on creamy paper some singular flower. She might choose, for instance, an insect-mimicking orchid which she would proceed to enlarge with remarkable skill. Or else she combined one species with another (unrecorded but possible), introducing odd little changes and twists that seemed almost morbid in so young a girl so nakedly dressed. The long beam slanting in

from the french window glowed in the faceted tumbler, in the tinted water,
and on the tin of the paint-box—and while she delicately painted an eyespot or the lobes of a lip, rapturous concentration caused the tip of her
tongue to curl at the corner of her mouth, and as the sun looked on, the
fantastic, black-blue-brown-haired child seemed in her turn to mimic the
mirror-of-Venus blossom. Her flimsy, loose frock happened to be so deeply
cut out behind that whenever she concaved her back while moving her
prominent scapulae to and fro and tilting her head—as with air-poised
brush she surveyed her damp achievement, or with the outside of her left
wrist wiped a strand of hair off her temple—Van, who had drawn up to her
seat as close as he dared, could see down her sleek *ensellure* as far as her
coccyx and inhale the warmth of her entire body. (99)

Here, unlike the previous two passages, Ada is agent—syntactically at
least, since she is the subject of most of the sentences' active verbs. Con-
spiring against the syntax, however, are a number of rhetorical strategies
that contrive again to reduce her to an object—more specifically, an object of art. The art (the image code) appealed to in this case is not difficult
to identify, since the same code is invoked both in the constitution of the
image and in the image itself. As Ada paints, with "rapturous concentration," the image that conjures her is itself painterly.

In this painterly image, the emphasis is on light and color. With impres-
sionist precision, Nabokov specifies several different qualities of light—
"sunny," "glowed," "beam," "slanting"—and, unlike the previous black-
and-white picture of Ada, this image is delicately tinted: "ivoried," "white,"
"in color," "creamy," "tinted," "paint-box," "black-blue-brown." As Ada
paints "some singular flower" in color on "creamy paper," so she in turn is
painted in color on the white background of her "ivoried" seat and "white
oil-cloth'd table." Although color is suggested throughout the image, only
in the description of Ada herself are individual colors named and then in
a generous profusion, an iridal explosion: "fantastic, black-blue-brown-
haired child." In her extravagant beauty, Ada seems to resemble the
"mirror-of-Venus blossom" that she is painting—girl mimicking blossom
mimicking butterfly in a mimetic chain similar to that of art itself. In a
final magical transformation, what she is painting ceases to be solely blossom or butterfly, but—with its delicately painted "eyespot" and the "lobes
of a lip"—a face: an image, perhaps, of her own, which is being painted
even as she paints.

But who is painting Ada here? The function of looking and seeing seems
even more diffuse here than in the previous passage from this novel, where

it was distributed among author, character, and reader. Van is certainly looking—he "could see down her sleek *ensellure*"—but then so is Ada, as she "surveys" her painting, which seems to look back at her from its painted "eyespot," while the sun "looks on" at everything. This circuit of looking is completed by the typically Nabokovian notion of the mirror ("the mirror-of-Venus blossom") and of mimicry, another kind of eyed exchange.

Within this context of ubiquitous and reciprocal eyeing, the by-now-familiar visual caress of the female body is carried out. Tactile evocations such as "hot," "cool," "sleek," and "damp" remind us that Ada is, after all, "so nakedly dressed": an oxymoron that succinctly expresses the complex relation between clothing and nudity upon which Nabokov's verbal striptease depends. As in the previous descriptions, the girl's clothing here is characterized more by its flimsiness and incompleteness—a "loose" frock "deeply cut out behind"—than by its stubborn presence. An aid, rather than an obstacle, to the imagination, it obligingly allows not only visual access—"could see down her sleek *ensellure* as far as her coccyx"—but also a metonymic foreglimpse of the body's complete consumption.

This foreglimpse, in which Van is able to "inhale the warmth of her entire body," underlines the basic paradox implicit in all of this inventorying of the fragmented female body. In this particular description, Ada's body is even more fragmented than in previous ones: "a strand of hair," "the corner of her mouth," "the outside of her left wrist," "the tip of her tongue." The fragments are smaller, more specific, more scattered—and even less imbued with a recognizably sexual logic. Part anatomist, part artist, the male gaze roams seemingly at random from mouth to hair to scapulae to head to wrist to temple to coccyx. What is missing (again) is the body's sex—in this case, however, not absent but merely displaced. By a kind of metaphoric migration, the sex absent from the fragmented body recurs elsewhere in the image: in the orchid, the delicately tinted "lobes of a lip," the "mirror-of-Venus" upon which such "rapturous concentration" is lavished. By an etymological accident, the orchid (which Ada proceeds to "enlarge with remarkable skill") evokes also the male sex; its fantasied femaleness is confirmed later, however, in Van and Ada's first sexual encounter, when "impatient young passion . . . did not survive the first few blind thrusts; it burst at the lip of the orchid" (121).

Yet, despite this displacement and fragmentation, despite the stripping and scattering of the female body, what is desired ultimately—and paradoxically—is articulation: articulation of a whole body from all its parts, articulation of the body in the articulation of desire. For at the end of the inventory of the fragmented body, the displaced and scattered body, is placed always the promise of a whole: in Ada's case, "the warmth of her entire body." As Barthes points out, the female body in art comes to be known only as

> a division and dissemination of partial objects. . . . Divided, anatomized, she is merely a kind of dictionary of fetish objects. This sundered, dissected body . . . is reassembled by the artist (and this is the meaning of his vocation) into a whole body, the body of love descended from the heaven of art.[8]

But, as Barthes point out, this "redeeming body remains a fictive one," because of the stubborn linearity of language. In order to evoke a whole body, language has to keep listing its parts, as if a complete inventory could somehow articulate itself into an unbroken totality. This is, for Barthes, the "spitefulness of language":

> Language undoes the body, returns it to the fetish, . . . the sentence can never constitute a *total*; meanings can be listed, not admixed; the total, the sum, are for language the promised lands, glimpsed *at the end* of enumeration, but once this enumeration has been completed, no feature can reassemble it.[9]

In order to articulate a whole body, the body of desire, language, locked into its linearity, has to keep multiplying fragments; the promised prospect of the whole becomes yet another item in an inventory.

In Nabokov's art, the female body is a peculiarly privileged *topos*, a rhetorical landscape visited again and again. Yet the more it is invoked, the more it eludes him, receding always into a perspective of prior codes (the nude, the photograph, the striptease, the fairy tale, the painting) and fragmenting beneath the pressure of the very language that aims to articulate it. The (male) artist is able always to articulate his desire but never the desired body; this is, as Humbert Humbert recognized, both his prison and his power.

### Notes

1. Vladimir Nabokov, *Ada* (New York: McGraw-Hill, 1969), 58. Subsequent references to this edition will be given in the text.

2. John Berger, *Ways of Seeing* (Harmondsworth, England: Penguin, 1972), 47, 46.

3. Vladimir Nabokov, *The Annotated Lolita,* ed. Alfred Appel, Jr. (New York: McGraw-Hill, 1970), 19. Subsequent references to this edition will be given in the text.

4. David Packman, *Vladimir Nabokov: The Structures of Literary Desire* (Columbia: University of Missouri Press, 1982), 26.

5. Roland Barthes, *S/Z* (London: Jonathan Cape, 1975), 60.

6. Berger, *Ways of Seeing,* 54.

7. Barthes, *S/Z*, 33.

8. Barthes, *S/Z*, 112.

9. Barthes, *S/Z*, 113–14.

# "Ballet Attitudes"

## Nabokov's Lolita and Petipa's The Sleeping Beauty

### SUSAN ELIZABETH SWEENEY

◆  ◆  ◆

VLADIMIR NABOKOV'S AESTHETIC is usually associated with literature or painting, not dance; he did not care for music and once remarked that he "was never much interested in the ballet" (*SO* 171). He came from a musical family, however, complete with a brother, Sergey, who was a balletomane, and a cousin, Nicolas Nabokov, who was "a musician with a deep knowledge of ballet" (Balanchine and Mason 120). More important, Nabokov himself was quite familiar with this form of theatrical storytelling. He cites the history of Russian dance in his commentary on Pushkin's *Eugene Onegin* (2:84–92), often includes dancers and acrobats as figures in his own fiction, beginning with *Mary* (1926; trans. 1970), frequently refers to Serge Diaghilev's Ballets Russes and premier danseur Vaslav Nijinsky, and alludes to dance, dancers, and dance steps throughout his most famous novel, *Lolita* (1955). In this essay I argue that the most celebrated classical Russian ballet—Marius Petipa's *The Sleeping Beauty* (1890)—influenced Nabokov's art in general and provided an important subtext for Lolita in particular.

## Choreographing *Lolita*

Nabokov's novel alludes to various modes of theatrical production, from pantomime, puppetry, *commedia dell'arte*, opera, and cinema to the embedded text of Clare Quilty's play *The Enchanted Hunters. Lolita* refers to dance, in particular, as a form of dramatic expression. Humbert records Dolly's "various girlish movements" in considerable detail and often compares them to "a ballet sequence" or "a ballet attitude" (42, 55, 233). He asks himself, for example, "Why does the way she walks—a child, mind you, a mere child!—excite me so abominably? Analyze it. A faint suggestion of turned-in toes. A kind of wiggly looseness below the knee prolonged to the end of each footfall. The ghost of a drag" (41). He also notices the way that she has learned to "fold her arms, and step on one toe with the other, or drop her hands loosely upon her still unflared hips," when skipping rope (163–64), as well as her manner of riding a bicycle: "rising on the pedals to work on them lustily, then sinking back in a languid posture while the speed wore itself off" (188). He studies the "exquisite clarity of all her movements" on the tennis court (231). He explains that whenever she was engaged in conversation, "her feet gestured all the time: she would stand on her left instep with her right toe, remove it backward, cross her feet, rock slightly, sketch a few steps, and then start the series all over again" (187). Humbert also describes Lolita's actual dance steps. She takes drama, music, and dance lessons while they are living in Beardsley, and he likes to watch her "mimetic actions" as she responds to various imaginary stimuli in an acting exercise or her "leg-parted leaps" as she dances for him in order to earn a promised reward (230). He is so aware of the "naked rhythms" of Lolita's body that from the mere sound of her "bare feet practicing dance techniques" downstairs, while he plays with Gaston Godin upstairs, he is able to reconstruct every single movement that she makes: "and-one, and-two, and-one, and-two, weight transferred on a straight right leg, leg up and out to the side, and-one, and-two, and  . . .  she started jumping, opening her legs at the height of the jump, and flexing one leg, and extending the other, and flying, and landing on her toes" (182).

Nabokov's novel not only lovingly choreographs Lolita's various gestures, postures, and steps, it also alludes to ballet as a specific way to express meaning through stylized patterns of rhythmic movement. The studio of Humbert's friend Gaston Godin, for example, features photographs of composer Peter Ilyich Tchaikovsky, who wrote the music for *The Sleeping Beauty*, and dancer Vaslav Nijinsky, who performed with Diaghilev's Ballets Russes (181). The novel also depicts murder in oddly terpsichorean terms. Humbert imagines his proposed drowning of Lolita's mother, Charlotte Haze, as being "like some dreadful silent ballet," with "the male dancer holding the ballerina by her foot and streaking down through watery twilight  . . .  and only when the curtain came down on her for good, would

I permit myself to yell for help" (86–87). When Humbert eventually kills his double, Quilty, he presents that murder, too, as a kind of dance—with himself making "a kind of double, triple, kangaroo jump, remaining quite straight on straight legs" and then executing "a ballet-like stiff bounce" (303), while his victim, Quilty, rises in the air "higher and higher, like old, gray, mad Nijinski" (302).[1]

## Nabokov and *The Sleeping Beauty*

Because of Humbert's emphasis on Lolita's "essential grace" and "the pattern of her motions" (233, 237), because of her own "interest in dance" (202), and the narrative's extensive use of ballet imagery, it is not surprising that when she falls ill Humbert buys her, among other gifts, two books, *The History of Dancing* and *The Russian Ballet* (242).[2] *The Russian Ballet*, in particular, would probably devote considerable space to *The Sleeping Beauty*. Marius Petipa's famous ballet is one of the most popular versions, in any art form, of Charles Perrault's French fairy tale "La Belle au bois dormant" (1697). *The Sleeping Beauty* represents the "grandest, fullest, and finest achievement" of the classical ballet tradition (Porter 140), the spectacular apotheosis of late nineteenth-century Russian aristocracy (which appears, within the ballet, as a fairytale version of the French court of Louis XVI), and, indeed, the inspiration for a generation of Silver Age Russian artists in various fields (Krasovskaya 20; Scholl 27, 36–39). Petipa's ballet helped to shape modern Russian dance and modernist aesthetics, and, I will argue here, also influenced Vladimir Nabokov.

In his childhood, Nabokov may have seen *The Sleeping Beauty* at St. Petersburg's Maryinsky Theatre; by the early years of the twentieth century, it was a regular offering there. The Nabokovs regularly attended such musical and theatrical performances (Boyd, *Russian Years*, 40) and "had many acquaintances who painted and danced and made music" (Nabokov, *SO*, 171). More significantly, the family knew several of the painters in the *Mir Iskusstva* circle—Mstislav Dobuzhinsky, Leon Bakst, Alexandre Benois, and Konstantin Somov—whose admiration for *The Sleeping Beauty* eventually led them to form the Ballets Russes (Boyd, *Russian Years*, 39; Scholl 43–45; Souhami 12). Dobuzhinsky, who became a lifelong friend, taught drawing and painting to the young Nabokov (SM 92, 94). Bakst, who identified seeing *The Sleeping Beauty* with "the start of his artistic life" (Souhami 11), did the "rose-and-haze pastel portrait" of Nabokov's mother that hung in his father's study and that is reproduced in *Speak, Memory;* Nabokov's parents collected Bakst's other works, too, including "a number of watercolor sketches made for the Scheherazade ballet" (*SM* 190). They also collected the paintings of Somov and Benois, who was an art critic for *Rech'*, the daily newspaper that Nabokov's father edited, and who was the member of this circle most fascinated by *The Sleeping Beauty* (Boyd, *Russian Years,* 39; Scholl 45). Many years later, when Nabokov was asked to name his favorite Russian artists, he cited Dobuzhinsky, Benois, and Somov, who had flourished, he said, in "the experimental decade that coincided with my boyhood" (*SO* 170; cf. *SM* 236). Given the Nabokov family's ties to these painters, who so admired Petipa's classic ballet; the ballet's fairyland setting and assorted characters from the rest of Perrault's *Contes du Temps Passés*, which would have made it an appropriate treat for a little boy who had been raised on European fairy tales and was devoted to them (V. Nabokov and D. Nabokov 78; *SM* 26); and the ballet's widespread popularity and influence, which continued throughout his childhood, it is quite likely that young Nabokov would have been taken to see *The Sleeping Beauty.* He may not have enjoyed it completely, however; he later remarked of Tchaikovsky, the ballet's composer, that his "cloying banalities have pursued me ever since I was a curly-haired boy in a velvet box" (*SO* 266).

Even more suggestive is the fact that Nabokov may have also seen the Ballets Russes' modernist revision of Petipa's classic ballet. During his years at Cambridge, Nabokov would have had the opportunity to attend, in London, either their 1919 performance of a pas de deux from *The Sleeping Beauty* or their 1921 production of the entire ballet, entitled *The Sleeping Princess*, staged by Nicholas Sergeyev with scenery and costumes by the Nabokovs' acquaintance Leon Bakst, additional choreography by Nijinsky's sister, Bronislava Nijinska, and additional music by Igor Stravinsky (Balanchine and Mason 393; Lifar 254, 257, 258–259). Such an occurrence may seem unlikely at first, especially considering Nabokov's later assertions of indifference toward dance. And yet his brother Sergey—who was also at Cambridge during this period and with whom Nabokov spent more time there than ever before—was very fond of ballet and especially of Diaghilev's Ballets Russes, and he made a point of attending every one of the company's premières, dressed for the occasion in a black cape and carrying a cane (Boyd, *Russian Years*, 174). Nabokov himself was then romantically involved with Marianna Shreiber, a ballerina from St. Petersburg who was living in London (Boyd, *Russian Years*, 174, 181), and on one occasion during this period he even danced a foxtrot in London with Anna Pavlova, the première danseuse for the Maryinsky Theatre and later for the Ballets Russes (*SO* 171; Boyd, *Russian Years*, 165). He had spent the fall of 1921, moreover, "reading seventeenth-century French tomes" (Boyd, *Russian Years*, 186); it may have amused him to attend the full-length production of a ballet based upon a seventeenth-century French fairy tale, which opened at the Alhambra Theatre that November and ran for at least three months (Beaumont 476). Nabokov was also extremely homesick for Russia during his years at Cambridge. Surely he would have been likely to attend, with either his balletomane brother or his ballerina girlfriend, one of the Ballets Russes' London performances of the most famous classical Russian ballet.

## Envisioning the Sleeping Princess

Whether Nabokov saw *The Sleeping Beauty* as a child, as an adult, or both, it is apparent that the ballet's story, staging, and choreography influenced his conception of *Lolita*. That novel, like its precursors "A Nursery Tale" ("Skazka," 1926) and *The Enchanter* ("Volshebnik," 1939), employs fairy tales in general and Perrault's seventeenth-century tale of "La Belle au bois dormant" in particular, as pretexts—in both senses of the word—for its protagonist's pedophiliac fantasies.[3] But *Lolita* is much more fully developed and more artfully self-reflective than those earlier stories, and, as we have already seen, it often uses ballet imagery to describe both Lolita's movements and Humbert's desire for her.[4] It is appropriate, then, that this novel alludes not only to Perrault's tale but also to the famous Russian ballet based upon it. Indeed, *Lolita* echoes specific aspects of the plotting, characters, scenery, and choreography of *The Sleeping Beauty*.[5]

From the very beginning of his narration, Humbert Humbert describes his desire for little girls with imagery that specifically suggests Petipa's *The Sleeping Beauty*. He sees himself, in the opening pages, as a "certain bewitched traveler" who has come upon "an enchanted island" (16) and as a "lone voyager" who has fallen utterly "under a nymphet's spell" (17)—just as the prince in *The Sleeping Beauty*, spellbound by a vision of the sleeping princess, embarks upon a voyage in order to obtain her for himself. Humbert may have directly borrowed his imaginary temporal geography from the scenery of Petipa's ballet: "I substitute time terms for spatial ones. In fact, I would have the reader see 'nine' and 'fourteen' as the boundaries—the mirrory beaches and rosy rocks—of an enchanted island haunted by those nymphets of mine and surrounded by a vast, misty sea" (16). Indeed, the appeal of this "intangible island of entranced time" (17), for Humbert, is his belief that it somehow resists time's passage, just as the castle in the ballet does. The punningly named Hourglass Lake—which appears later in the novel as an actual setting and as the site of Humbert's erotic fantasies about Lolita—alludes even more precisely to the magic lake that the ballet's prince must cross in order to reach that enchanted realm where time has stopped.

Humbert's pedophilia originated, he explains, in his childhood romance with Annabel Leigh, whom he loved in "a princedom by the sea" until their parting and her death four months later (9). He presents their romance as a fairytale enchantment and even describes himself as remaining in thrall to Annabel, the progression of his erotic attachments essentially stopped, "until at last, twenty-four years later, [he] broke her spell by incarnating her in another" (15). When Humbert first glimpses Lolita in her mother's backyard, moreover, he recognizes her—in a parody of the recognition scene that commonly occurs in fairy tales and folklore—as the very same "little princess" untouched by time (39), just like the young heroine of *The Sleeping Beauty.*

After Humbert first sees Lolita and decides to rent her mother's vacant room, he continues to associate her with fairy tales in general and *The Sleeping Beauty* in particular. Studying a list of students in her class, for example, he rhapsodizes over his discovery of "'Haze, Dolores' . . . in its special bower of names, with its bodyguard of roses, a fairy princess between her two maids of honor" (52). The names that surround hers—"Rose Carmine," "Mary Rose Hamilton," and "Rosaline Honeck," among others—suggest to him her "bevy of page girls," "handmaids and rosegirls" (51–52, 194, 257). More specifically, they recall the maids of honor in *The Sleeping Beauty,* who surround the princess as she dances the famous "Rose Adagio" in the first act. The ballet's choreography, scenery, and costuming consistently associate the princess with roses; in the "Rose Adagio," in particular, she appears in rose-colored silk and is gently turned, while standing on point, by four princes who each present her with a rose (Balanchine and Mason 401–2; Krasovskaya 33). Humbert's imagery of roses, bowers, fairy princesses, and maids of honor echoes this scene; at the same time, his comment as he contemplates the list of Lolita's classmates—that he alone is "elected" to recognize her among their names (53)—suggests that he identifies himself with the enchanted prince who will one day wake the princess from her slumber.

Throughout the first part of the novel, Humbert conceives of Lolita's innocence as just such a magic sleep. He "conjure[s] up a dreaming and exaggerating Dolly in the 'latency' period of girlhood," imagining himself as a "wily wizard," "incubus," or "fairytale vampire" who can enjoy her without her knowledge (124, 49, 71, 139). More precisely, "Humbert the

[in]Cubus"—like his predecessor, the protagonist of *The Enchanter*—fantasizes about ogling, caressing, and kissing a child in her sleep (71). He
dreams about either "gorg[ing] the limp nymphet with sleeping pills" during her mother's absence or "administering a powerful sleeping potion to
both mother and daughter so as to fondle the latter through the night
with perfect impunity," sedating them "so thoroughly that neither sound
nor touch should rouse them" (80, 71, 94). He even imagines Lolita becoming pregnant from such encounters, an outcome that does occur in the
earliest variants of the Sleeping Beauty folktale (Opie and Opie 81–83). Indeed, Humbert often couches these disturbingly necrophiliac fantasies in
fairytale terms; he pictures Lolita, for example, "hardly breath[ing] in her
sleep, as still as a painted girl-child" (71). He imagines her clothes, too, in a
metonymic state of entranced slumber: they wander "to various parts of
the house to freeze there like so many hypnotized bunnies" (81), like the
transfixed fauna of the castle in *The Sleeping Beauty*. Still later, after Humbert
marries Lolita's mother and she conveniently dies, he dreams of at last
being able to spend "forty nights with a frail little sleeper at my throbbing
side" (109).

Humbert tries to fulfill this fantasy only once before their night at the
Enchanted Hunters hotel. One "bewitched Sunday" (288), while her
mother is at church, he secretly masturbates as Lolita sprawls across his
lap. He presents this encounter, too, in fairytale terms—alluding to "Cinderella," for example, when he observes that Lolita has lost her slipper, and
to "Beauty and the Beast" when he contrasts his "gagged, bursting beast
and the beauty of her dimpled body in its innocent cotton frock" (59). He
also evokes tales of enchanted slumber. He describes Lolita reclining at full
length and even biting into a red apple, like Snow White. He compares
himself to a magician who has "divert[ed] the little maiden's attention"
with his patter, sleight of hand, and hypnotic power, and to a sorcerer who
has cast her under a "special spell" by reciting song lyrics and garbling
them as if talking "in his sleep" (58, 59, 60). Later he calls himself a successful "conjuror," because he thinks he achieved orgasm in her presence after
rendering her unaware of it (62). And yet Lolita remains wide awake in this
scene—and more aware, perhaps, than he realizes, given her squirming,
her flaming cheeks, and the "sudden shrill note in her voice" (61).

Indeed, it is the would-be enchanter himself—as in Nabokov's eponymous novella—who seems spellbound by the "mysterious change [that]
came over [his] senses . . . a new plane of being where nothing [else]
mattered" (60). Humbert is bewitched, moreover, by the very image that
he himself has conjured up: that of an idealized, incorruptible, insensible

child who can be "safely solipsized" (60). He muses, "What I had madly possessed was not she, but my own creation, another, fanciful Lolita—perhaps, more real than Lolita; overlapping, encasing her; floating between me and her, and having no will, no consciousness—indeed, no life of her own" (62). Humbert's lonely enjoyment of his construction of Lolita—which occurs long before they are "technically lovers" (132)—specifically recalls the prince's pas de deux with the princess's image in the second act of *The Sleeping Beauty.*

According to the libretto, this dance occurs between the prince and an image of the princess that the Lilac Fairy has conjured up for him before he voyages to the entranced castle (Vsevolozhsky 370–71).[6] The pas de deux is thus a "ballet blanc," or vision scene, which occurs solely within his mind (Scholl 25). Humbert similarly fantasizes about the image of his "princess" throughout the first part of the novel, "pressing to [his] face Lolita's fragrant ghost," mooning over her name in the list of schoolchildren, embracing her specter in a dream set of Hourglass Lake, picturing her clothes as "phantom little Lolitas," and even masturbating in her presence, "a performance that affected her as little as if she were a photographic image rippling upon a screen" (39, 47, 108, 62).

## Some Enchanted Evening

Humbert thus possesses his "fairy princess" in imagination before he does in reality—just as the prince in *The Sleeping Beauty* does. And Humbert's opportunity to fully realize his fantasies, which occurs at the Enchanted Hunters hotel after Lolita's mother has died, parallels the prince's eventual arrival at the princess's castle. From its first appearance, the hotel suggests the palace of the ballet. Finding the hotel is an "exasperating ordeal" because Humbert keeps losing his way "in the maze" of directions that he receives from passersby (116), recalling the prince's efforts to reach the enchanted castle. Soon, however, "after falling under the smooth spell of a nicely graded curve, the travelers bec[o]me aware of a diamond glow through the mist, then a gleam of lakewater appear[s]—and there it [is], marvelously and inexorably, under spectral trees, at the top of a graveled drive—the pale palace of The Enchanted Hunters. A row of parked cars . . . seem[s] at first sight to forbid access; but then, by magic," one car backs out of its parking space (117). The "spell," the "palace," and the apparently impenetrable barrier that yields "by magic"—all suggest *The Sleeping Beauty.* Moreover, the dark mist and gleaming water recall the ballet's famous entr'acte, which dance historians describe as set in a "pall of opaque vapor" streaked by "silvery light" (Beaumont 471): "a slowly paced interlude during which the fairy's magic barge passed slowly across the lake, surrounded by a panorama of dense forest and splendid vistas of the enchanted palace . . . rising high on the summit in the distance" (Balanchine and Mason 406–7).

Once they have arrived at the hotel, another balletic scene—Lolita's "slow-motion walk" in their hotel room (120), which Nabokov identified as one of the "subliminal co-ordinates" by which he plotted the novel ("On a Book Entitled *Lolita*" 316)—also seems to refer specifically to *The Sleeping Beauty*. In this passage, which is yet another lovingly detailed account of Lolita's motions and gestures, Humbert watches as she approaches a suitcase full of new clothes, "lifting her rather high-heeled feet rather high, . . . bending her beautiful boy-knees while she walked through dilating space with the lentor of one walking under water," and "very slowly stretching [a garment] between her silent hands as if she were a bemused bird-hunter" examining his catch. The wordless, "slow-motion" effect, the imagery of hunter and prey, and the references to an "enchanted mist" (120) may allude to the tempo, choreography, and setting of the prince's dance with the vision of the princess. In that pas de deux—which is characterized by motions of flight and capture and set in a misty forest glade—"he pursues her softly, patiently, yet never catches up to her" (Balanchine and Mason 406; cf. Beaumont 470; Krasovskaya 40; Scholl 25–26). Humbert's description, however, casts Lolita herself as the hunter. This discrepancy may reflect the reversal of roles that he attempts to suggest throughout his narration. But Nabokov may also have had in mind a dance that appears at the end of *The Sleeping Beauty*: the pas de deux between another fairytale character, the Enchanted Princess, and the Bluebird. In this dance, the Enchanted Princess tiptoes up to her prey, who continually leaps away, "the fingers of his outstretched arms flutter[ing] in semblance of the wings of a bird," before he briefly allows her to capture him (Beaumont 473).

Humbert's rapturous descriptions of the hotel's interior and inhabitants also echo the scenery and the minor characters of *The Sleeping Beauty*. The dining-room murals depict enchanted hunters in an enchanted wood, like the one surrounding the princess's castle; other aspects of the decor recall the ballet's flowery and roseate imagery, from the hotel lobby's "floral carpet" to the bedroom's "Tuscan rose chenille spread and . . . frilled, pink-shaded nightlamps" (117, 119). The hotel is staffed by storybook servants and inhabited primarily by "old ladies" in "floral dresses,"

who are in town for a flower show (117, 126). Humbert and Lolita dine surrounded by such "scattered old ladies" and later share an elevator with
"two withered women, experts in roses" (121, 122). These elderly women
recall the Cherry Blossom Fairy, the Carnation Fairy, and the Lilac Fairy,
among others, who attend the princess's christening at the beginning of
the ballet and are "experts in roses," in a sense, because of the prophecies
they make about her future and the fact that she herself is identified as a
rose. Indeed, Humbert describes Lolita herself, in these hotel scenes, as a
"blossom-like vision." The ballet's benevolent Lilac Fairy, in particular, appears as an "ancient lady swathed in lilac veils" who tells Lolita something
that Humbert cannot hear (118). Carabosse—the evil, ugly, hunchbacked
fairy godmother who crashes the party at the christening and later appears
in disguise to tempt the princess with a forbidden spindle—is represented
by Clare Quilty, Humbert's rival, nemesis, and doppelgänger. Quilty, after
all, is an unbidden guest at the hotel and appears there in several disguises
(*AnL* 349). The role of Carabosse, moreover, is traditionally performed by a
male dancer. (This cross-gendered casting may explain Quilty's androgy-
nous name and his collaboration with the ambiguously gendered Vivian
Darkbloom.) And Quilty, too, is an expert in roses, judging by a remark he
makes to Humbert: "That child of yours needs a lot of sleep. Sleep is a rose,
as the Persians say" (127). This observation neatly combines Quilty's own
sexual interest in Lolita with the imagery of rose bowers and endless slum-
bers from *The Sleeping Beauty.* More important, it echoes the curse with
which Carabosse, the ballet's evil fairy, brings about the princess's one hundred years of somnolence.

Lolita's sleepiness, once she arrives at the hotel, is also described in
terms of the ballet. After they are served dessert among the enchanted
murals. Humbert produces a magic "philter"—a bottle of purple sleeping
pills—in "a strange and monstrous moment," which parallels that moment in *The Sleeping Beauty* when Carabosse offers the princess a forbidden
spindle. Humbert tells Lolita that the pills are made of "summer skies
. . . and plums and figs, and the grapeblood of emperors"; their "violet
blue" hue may also allude to the Lilac Fairy, who alters Carabosse's curse so
that the princess does not die but instead falls into a long, long sleep.[7]
Humbert also observes that these capsules are "loaded with Beauty's
Sleep" (122), a phrase that neatly puns on the title of *The Sleeping Beauty* and
the notion of a "beauty sleep."

Once Lolita has swallowed the supposed sedatives, Humbert leads her
upstairs to their hotel room at the Enchanted Hunters. He describes her increasing lethargy, moreover, by choreographing the slowness of her move-

ments—her slow-motion, "watertread[ing]" walk, her "swaying" body (122), her "lolling" head, the "slow fingers" with which she removes a hair ribbon, and the drowsiness with which she raises one foot to fumble at her shoelaces (123)—in ways that recall the princess's "faltering steps" after she pricks her finger in the ballet (Beaumont 467). Indeed, Humbert's description of Lolita as his "tottering, dazed rosedarling" seems to allude directly to the princess's movements in this scene (122). Their hotel room, meanwhile, has become a "strange pale-striped fastness where Lolita's old and new clothes reclined in various attitudes of enchantment on pieces of furniture that seemed vaguely afloat" (130–31), just as in the ballet the entire palace becomes entranced once the princess falls asleep. More precisely, the "pale-striped fastness" suggests both a state of deep slumber—that is, "a fastness of sleep that a whole regiment would not have disturbed" (128)—and "the vertical lines and turreted spires of a castle," like that depicted in the ballet's painted scenery (Beaumont 471). The apparel that Humbert sees there in "various attitudes of enchantment" echoes earlier descriptions of Lolita's belongings frozen like "hypnotized bunnies" in her mother's house (81) and of the new clothes, like "phantom little Lolita's dancing, falling, daisying, all over the counter," that he bought her at an "enchanted" store earlier that day (108). The entire hotel has become a fairytale fastness of sleep, in which everything, it seems, is under the same spell: the reclining clothes, the floating furniture, the cocker spaniel "swooning" in the lobby, and the "hunters in various postures and states of enchantment" in the dining-room murals (117, 121). Those balletic "attitudes" and "postures" of "enchantment" (131, 121), in particular, suggest the staging at the end of *The Sleeping Beauty*'s first act, in which the Lilac Fairy "gestures with her wand in the direction of the castle, and the groups of people on the threshold and on the staircase suddenly fall asleep, as if struck with slumber. Everything falls asleep" (Vsevolozhsky 369).

## The Ridiculous Lover

Lolita's slumber that night, however, is not as deep as Humbert had expected. At one point he remarks wistfully, "She was again fast asleep, my nymphet, but still I did not dare to launch upon my enchanted voyage. *La Petite Dormeuse ou l'Amant Ridicule*" (129). Alfred Appel says that this French title mocks eighteenth-century engravings, but that no such picture exists (*AnL* 381 n. 2). By now, however, it should be clear that Nabokov is alluding once again to Perrault's seventeenth-century French fairy tale and, more specifically, to Petipa's ballet *The Sleeping Beauty*, in which the prince embarks on just such an "enchanted voyage" in order to arrive at the castle and wake the sleeping princess. The "ridiculous lover," moreover, refers to all of those would-be suitors who try—like Humbert himself—to wake the princess from her innocent slumber before the time is ripe.

As Lolita's lover, of course, Humbert is indeed both ridiculous and tragically premature. From the beginning, he has found it difficult to imagine himself as her fairytale consort: "What a comic, clumsy, wavering Prince Charming I was!" he remarks en route to the Enchanted Hunters (109). These three particular adjectives seem to link Humbert's inadequacy with a lack of expressiveness, grace, and agility, as if he had indeed been miscast in the role of *The Sleeping Beauty*'s prince, who, in the Ballets Russes' 1921 production of the ballet, was actually named "Prince Charming" for the sake of the English audience (Beaumont 455). The morning after Humbert's night with Lolita at the Enchanted Hunters, moreover, completely inverts the climactic arousal from enchantment in *The Sleeping Beauty*. Lolita, again, is already wide awake; it is actually Humbert who "feign[s] handsome profiled sleep" and gives "a mediocre imitation of waking up," when she nuzzles him and they "gently kiss" (132, 133). More important, it is Lolita, recently introduced to sex at summer camp, who seduces him—although she is unaware of that act's implications or the ways in which he will exploit it in the second part of the novel.

The rest of *Lolita* reveals the sad and grotesque aftereffects of Humbert's attempt to play the part of the prince in *The Sleeping Beauty*. The tone shifts abruptly, as the fairytale fantasies of part 1 give way to the "singular and bestial cohabitation" of part 2 (287). Indeed, subsequent scenes of Lolita in bed range from Humbert bringing her coffee each morning and withholding it "until she ha[s] done her morning duty," to "her sobs in the night— every night, every night—the moment [he] feign[s] sleep" (165, 176). At the same time, however, the second part of *Lolita* parodies both its protagonist's fantasies and its own plot in the embedded play of *The Enchanted Hunters*, which is yet another variation on Petipa's *The Sleeping Beauty.*

## Enchanted Hunters

According to Humbert's sketchy synopsis, Quilty's play concerns "a farmer's daughter who imagines herself to be a woodland witch, or Diana, or something, and who, having got hold of a book on hypnotism, plunges a number of lost hunters into various entertaining trances before falling in her turn under the spell of a vagabond poet." Humbert, noticing the title, assumes that play, hotel, and murals all refer to "some banal legend," some bit of "New England lore" unknown to him. He does not realize that the hotel's name derives from a muralist's "chance fantasy" or that the play's title indicates that Quilty was at the hotel when Humbert tried to stage his own fairytale fantasy there (200). He dismisses the play itself as "a dismal kind of fancy work, with echoes from Lenormand and Maeterlinck and various quiet British dreamers." Its "dancing nymphs, and elves, and monsters" (201), in particular, recall the nineteenth-century ballet-féerie tradition that led to *The Sleeping Beauty*, a ballet that concludes with a panoply of fairytale characters (Puss in Boots, Bluebeard, Cinderella, Beauty and the Beast, and others from Perrault's *Contes du Temps Passés*), who have come to pay their respects to the prince and princess.

Even more strikingly, the enchanted hunters of the play's title—which resonate throughout the imagery and wordplay of Nabokov's novel—also echo Petipa's ballet. *The Sleeping Beauty* specifically portrays the prince, for example, as an enchanted hunter. The entire second act is devoted to his hunting expedition, complete with "the merry tarah-ti-rarah-ri-rarah of lustily blown hunting horns" (Beaumont 468) and a series of hunting minuets danced by huntsmen and huntresses, and it concludes with the pas de deux, characterized by movements of flight and pursuit, in which the Lilac Fairy entrances him with the princess's image (Krasovskaya 40). Nabokov apparently borrowed the notion of an enchanted hunter from *The Sleeping Beauty*, and he acknowledged that borrowing—along with all of his other debts to Petipa's ballet—with his embedded parody of just this kind of theatrical or literary appropriation of fairy tales, in the form of Quilty's play *The Enchanted Hunters.*

Nabokov's use of such pretexts and his parody of such literary conventions, according to Edmund White, can be compared to the works of two of his Russian contemporaries in other fields, music and dance: Igor Stravinsky, who created a "crisp collage built up out of radical juxtapositions," and George Balanchine, who "eliminated mime, a fussy port de bras, story and decor to make plotless ballets that distill the essence of the Petipa tradition" (White 25–26). Alfred Appel also once suggested, while interviewing Nabokov, that his work was comparable to that of Stravinsky and Balanchine (*SO* 171–72). With his usual combination of artfulness and accuracy, Nabokov only replied that he knew "Mr. Stravinski very slightly" (*SO* 172)—this silently correcting Appel's transliteration—and that he could not "understand why the names of most of the people with whom I am paired begin with a B," but that this name, at any rate, should be spelled "Balanshin, not Balanchine" (171).[8]

White's and Appel's implicit linking of Nabokov with these other great Russian modernists is especially interesting because Stravinsky and Balanchine also, in their own ways, rewrote or responded to Petipa's *The Sleeping Beauty*. (Stravinsky devised additional music for the Ballets Russes' 1921 London performance, and Balanchine composed his *Ballet Imperial* as a tribute to Petipa's and Tchaikovsky's collaboration.) Nabokov, for his part, apparently associated just such artistic revision with the original source for Petipa's ballet: in *Lolita*, he specifically cites "Sleeping Beauty" as a fairy tale "arranged and rearranged many times" for theatrical production (201). He himself revised Perrault's tale—and Petipa's terpsichorean version of it, in particular—one more time in the plot, characters, imagery, and setting of *Lolita*.

### Notes

1. Nabokov was obviously familiar with Nijinsky's special talents, principal roles, and eventual insanity. He may have had in mind Nijinsky's performance as the Faun in *L'Apres-Midi d'un Faun*, since in Gaston Godin's photograph of him the dancer appears as "all thighs and fig leaves" (*AnL* 181–82); that ballet complements the mythological imagery of nymphs and fauns underlying Humbert's notion of the "nymphet."

2. Appel says that both books actually exist (*AnL* 421 n. 1); I have been unable to verify this claim, although I have located volumes with similar names. The title of another book that Humbert brings Lolita, *Clowns and Columbines*, alludes to two stock characters in classical ballet (242); indeed, Harlequin, Columbine, Pierrot, and Pierrette are the first storybook characters to greet the newly married prince and princess in the Ballets Russes' 1921 production of *The Sleeping Beauty* (Beaumont 472).

3. This essay is part of an ongoing project in which I develop this argument more fully. See Sweeney, "Fantasy, Folklore, and Finite Numbers in Nabokov's 'A Nursery Tale,'" *Slavic and East European Journal* 43, no. 3 (Fall 1999): 511–29; "Looking at Harlequins: Nabokov, the World of Art, and the Ballets Russes," in *Nabokov's World*, ed. Jane Grayson, Arnold McMillin, and Priscilla Meyer, vol. 2 of *Reading Nabokov* (Basingstoke, U.K., and New York: Palgrave, 2002), 73–95; and *"The Enchanter* and the Beauties of Sleeping," *Nabokov at Cornell*, ed. Gavriel Shapiro (Ithaca, N.Y.: Cornell University Press, in press).

4. One of their earliest encounters, for example, occurs as Humbert, sitting

with Lolita and her mother on a dark porch, fondles her as well as "a ballerina of wool and gauze which she played with and kept sticking into my lap" (45).

5. For detailed descriptions of the ballet's story, staging, and choreography, see Vsevolozhsky's original libretto; Krasovskaya's description of the 1890 première; Beaumont's account of the Ballets Russes' 1921 version; discussions of Bakst's role in that production as costume and scenery designer by Souhami (11–27) and Spencer (189–214); and Balanchine and Mason's synopsis of the ballet's basic story and its various productions (393–410).

6. The original libretto, more precisely, explains that the Lilac Fairy produces this vision by waving her wand toward some rocky cliffs, "which open to reveal Aurora and her girlfriends, asleep," as the sun's rays "illuminate her with a rosy light"; later the princess's image disappears into a cleft in the rocks (Vsevolozhsky 370). *Lolita* may allude to this staging, perhaps, in "the violet shadow of some red rocks forming a kind of cave" (13), the setting for Humbert's last tryst with Annabel Leigh and a leitmotif in the novel (16, 39).

7. This may be why Nabokov's Russian translation of Lolita consistently replaces the colors purple and umber with lilac and violet blue (Cummins 362).

8. Nabokov may also have known Balanchine slightly; his cousin Nicolas Nabokov was close to Balanchine and collaborated with him on the ballet *Don Quixote* (Balanchine and Mason 119–20). At any rate, Nabokov probably did not know either man well; after he emigrated to America he was not interested in meeting other Russians, and that apparently included Ballanchine and Stravinsky (Boyd, *American Years,* 22).

## Works Cited

Balanchine, George, and Francis Mason. "The Sleeping Beauty." In *101 Stories of the Great Ballets,* 393–420. Rev. ed. New York: Doubleday, 1989.

Beaumont, Cyril W. "The Sleeping Princess." In *Complete Book of Ballets: A Guide to the Principal Ballets of the Nineteenth and Twentieth Centuries,* 454–82. New York: Grosset, 1936.

Boyd, Brian. *Vladimir Nabokov: The American Years.* Princeton, N.J.: Princeton University Press, 1991.

———. *Vladimir Nabokov: The Russian Years.* Princeton, N.J.: Princeton University Press, 1990.

Cummins, George. "Nabokov's Russian *Lolita.*" *Slavic and East European Journal* 21, no. 3 (Fall 1977): 354–65.

Krasovskaya, Vera. *Marius Petipa and "The Sleeping Beauty."* Trans. Cynthia Read. *Dance Perspectives,* vol. 49. New York: Dance Perspectives Foundation, 1972.

Lifar, Serge. *A History of Russian Ballet: From Its Origins to the Present Day.* London: Hutchinson, 1954.

Nabokov, Véra, and Dmitri Nabokov. Interview with D. Barton Johnson and Ellendea Proffer. *Russian Literature Triquarterly* 24 (Winter 1991): 73–85.

Nabokov, Vladimir. *The Annotated Lolita.* Ed. with introduction and notes by Alfred Appel, Jr. Rev. ed. New York: Vintage, 1991. Cited in text as *AnL.*

———. *The Enchanter.* Trans. Dmitri Nabokov. New York: Putnam, 1986.

———. *Lolita.* 1955. Rpt. New York: Vintage, 1989.

———. *Mary.* 1926. Trans. Michael Glenny with Vladimir Nabokov. New York: McGraw-Hill, 1970.

———. "A Nursery Tale." In *The Stories of Vladimir Nabokov,* 161–72. Trans. Dmitri Nabokov. New York: Knopf, 1995.

———. "On a Book Entitled *Lolita.*" In *Lolita,* 311–17.

———. *Speak, Memory: An Autobiography Revisited.* New York: Putnam's, 1966. Cited in text as *SM.*

———. *Strong Opinions.* New York: McGraw-Hill, 1973. Cited in text as *SO.*

Opie, Iona, and Peter Opie. *The Classic Fairy Tales.* London: Oxford University Press, 1976.

Porter, Andrew. "Musical Events: The Nureyev Session." *New Yorker,* 5 May 1973, 140–46.

Pushkin, Aleksandr. *Eugene Onegin: A Novel in Verse.* Trans. with commentary by Vladimir Nabokov. Rev. ed. 2 vols. Princeton, N.J.: Princeton University Press, 1975.

Scholl, Tim. *From Petipa to Balanchine: Classical Revival and the Modernization of Ballet.* New York: Routledge, 1994.

Souhami, Diana. "The Sleeping Beauty and the Ballets Russes." In *Bakst: The Rothschild Panels of the Sleeping Beauty,* 11–27. London: Philip Wilson, 1992.

Spencer, Charles. "The Sleeping Prince." In *Leon Bakst,* 189–216. London: Academy, 1978.

Vsevolozhsky, Ivan Alexandrovich. "Libretto of the Sleeping Beauty." Trans. Roland John Wiley. In *A Century of Russian Ballet: Documents and Accounts, 1810–1910,* 360–72. Oxford: Clarendon, 1990.

White, Edmund. "Nabokov: Beyond Parody." In *The Achievements of Vladimir Nabokov,* 5–27. Ed. George Gibian and Stephen Jan Parker. Ithaca, N.Y.: Cornell University Press, 1984.

# Artist in Exile

## The Americanization of Humbert Humbert

JOHN HAEGERT

◆　　◆　　◆

> That is the true myth of America. She starts old,
> old, wrinkled and writhing in an old skin. And
> there is a gradual sloughing off of the old skin, to-
> wards a new youth. It is the myth of America.
> —D. H. Lawrence, *Studies in*
> *Classic American Literature*

I AM AN AMERICAN WRITER, born in Russia and educated in
England where I studied French literature, before spending fifteen years
in Germany."[1] Thus Vladimir Nabokov described the circuitous process,
begun twenty-four years earlier, of evolving a new American identity and
adapting it to his European past. Readers of *Lolita* (1955) have long noted a
comparable effort of assimilation in the creation of his only "American"
novel and of its émigré protagonist, Humbert Humbert. Despite his persistent disclaimer that "there is nothing autobiographic in *Lolita*,"[2] Nabokov's
critics have repeatedly stressed the many striking affinities between
Humbert's uneasy life in Ramsdale and Beardsley and his creator's early
émigré years in the northeastern United States.[3] It has often been observed
that Humbert's fervid desire for the eternal nymphet is similar to, if not actually derived from, the many quests for some imperishable ideal embodied in Poe, Hawthorne, and, indeed, in much subsequent American fiction.[4] Humbert's energetic pursuit of his "ultraviolet darling" across the
American dreamscape has also received pointed attention, and, of course,
Nabokov's own Homeric attempts to master the *poshlost* and dreary philistinism of middle-class American life have become all but legendary in our
time.[5]

Questions spring to mind when so overt an appeal is made to American themes and sources. In what ways may *Lolita* be expressive not only of Nabokov's perennial concerns (namely, art and the aesthetic imagination) but of a new and pressing interest in securing an American identity? What does that vague term *American novel* mean, after all, and of what use is it when applied to the work of a writer so conspicuously international in outlook? In light of Nabokov's concerted attempt to reclaim America for his own creative purposes, it may prove fruitful to reexamine *Lolita*, both as an American novel and as a work of émigré fiction, in an effort to see how its celebrated theme of the wayward artist is imbued with a characteristically American resonance.

It is a commonplace, and rightly so, that *Lolita* underscores the enduring conflict between the claims of the imagination—especially when it is drawn to some aesthetic ideal—and the obligations and infringements of everyday reality.[6] Exploring this tension in depth, the novel deals centrally with Humbert's fantastic attempt to revive the past and incarnate an impossible vision of imperishable bliss. That the vision thus embodied is actually a human child, and an all-American one at that, is for Humbert only a minor obstacle in an otherwise all-consuming passion: the gradual absorption of Lolita into a changeless realm "where nothing mattered, save the infusion of joy brewed within my body."[7] So conceived in the novel, Humbert's crazed obsession with Lolita is less a matter of physical desire than of aesthetic compulsion and less a matter of either than of metaphysical envy. As Alfred Appel has argued, Humbert's insatiable need to "fix once for all the perilous magic of nymphets" (136) is not merely cause for amusement, it is an occasion for Nabokov's "devastating criticism of the reflexive attempt to move out of time."[8] The novel traces his farcical attempt to thwart time, then, but also his developing sense of doom before time's irresistible encroachments. The countermovement to its theme of nympholeptic bliss is Humbert's growing awareness, throughout part two, that his idealizing efforts have been both aesthetically futile and morally transgressive, insofar as they have led him to inflict his desires on Lolita and thus deprive her of her childhood and her status as an independent being.[9]

Whether Humbert really achieves such awareness has been widely contested, of course. Some would have it that for once John Ray, Jr.—the fictitious pedant who "preambulates" the narrative—is reliable when he describes the book as "a tragic tale tending unswervingly to nothing less than a moral apotheosis" (7), while others see Humbert's "confession" as nothing more than a virtuoso performance, an artfully contrived *apologia* designed to stimulate his readers' sympathies and recast his misdeeds as the aberrations of genius. My aim here is not to resolve this issue but to point out that the perplexing ambiguities inherent in Humbert's motives are not confined to his "aesthetic" interests, properly so-called, nor even, strictly speaking, to his relationship with Lolita; insofar as they define his character, they arise as well from his ambivalent role as an émigré hero, a wandering, ill-fated exile uneasily suspended between two conflicting sets of cultural values. In the final analysis, as has been said, *Lolita* is not only or even primarily "'about' literary originality, creative language, art in general, or *any* similar abstraction."[10] As a novel of character (rather than a self-reflective fiction like *Pale Fire*), it is chiefly concerned to demonstrate the complexities of human behavior and experience in a particular time and space, including, it should be noted, the very American space to which Humbert Humbert feels himself condemned.

Behind all the familiar oppositions of the book—the conflict between Lolita as demonic temptress and Lolita as prepubescent brat, the conflicts between art and Nature and between imagination and reality—looms the greatest and most potent of American polarities: the legendary conflict between New World possibilities and Old World sensibilities. And Humbert himself is the pivotal figure in Nabokov's interpretation of this most fundamental of American myths. Humbert does not of course "represent" Europe any more than Lolita "embodies" America: as Nabokov insists in his afterword to the first American edition, nothing is more alien to the spirit of the novel than the "idiotic" imposition of such allegorical equivalences. As an émigré protagonist, on the other hand, Humbert serves to qualify the equally allegorical view that *Lolita* is essentially a timeless fable of the artistic life. Recent criticism, for example, stressing the psychoautobiographic sources of Humbert's story, has often contended that in the portrayal of his feckless hero, Nabokov was in part attempting to exorcise an unwanted "double": the solipsistic artist who is indifferent to human needs and human suffering.[11] In this view, Humbert's molestation of Lolita is symptomatic of the artist's own voyeuristic velleities and desires, his "unnatural" tendency to preempt and transform reality, to arrest it—as we have seen—at a moment of imaginative perfection. My own consideration of the text as an exemplary work of émigré fiction is meant to offer a complementary argument, namely, that Humbert's evolving attitude toward Lolita reflects (to use no stronger a word) his creator's changing and generally much-improved estimate of American life. Viewed from this perspective, as we shall see, Humbert's ambivalent search for "his" lost Lolita in the last third of the book enacts an émigré's quest for a truer vision of his host environment—an America no longer seen as a nubile nymphet in need of European refinement but as an estimable independent spirit requiring (and deserving) a national identity of its own.

To specify the émigré character of Humbert's life does not, of course, give a complete account of *Lolita*, but it can help to illuminate the novel's unique and in many ways anomalous position in American literature. There is a Humbert Humbert in all of us, a capacity for pride and its consequence, damnation. And this pride is of the most inviting and seductive kind—not pride of place or position or wealth but pride of the intellect, the beguilingly insidious idea that we know more than others and are somehow wiser and better than they are. Other people should automatically admire us, and our inner life should likewise be a kind of pleasing dream, without the prehistoric monsters or the modern gargoyles always looming in the shadows behind us or around us. Pride and its deceptiveness are, of course, the subject of much serious literature, from *Oedipus Rex* through *Faust* to *Remembrance of Things Past.* But in *Lolita*, this legendary theme acquires a unique cultural importance through its association with the other great legend, Humbert and Lolita's, which is in part the legend of America as a whole and of its historical relationship to Europe.

Again it would be a mistake to oversimplify the Old World–New World antithesis in *Lolita*, as if the novel were an extended vindication of American vulgarity (Lolita) over European gentility (Humbert), or vice versa. As Nabokov pointedly remarked in refuting the charge of anti-Americanism leveled against the book: "In regard to philistine vulgarity there is no intrinsic difference between Palearctic manners and Nearctic manners. Any proletarian from Chicago can be as bourgeois (in the Flaubertian sense) as a duke" (317).[12] I would add, however, that the complex issue of Humbert's intellectual pride and moral depravity is often simplified by regarding it as a purely "aesthetic" problem, to be pondered apart from the peculiar historical and cultural circumstances underlying it. To understand the cause of his obsessive behavior toward Lolita, we must consider his character not only as a self-conscious "poet"—the usual view—but as a cultural exile: an American ethnic hero, albeit a very sorry one, whose ignoble fate it is to wander aimlessly with Lolita along the margins and byways of American society, sans roots, sans family, sans anything save his glorious memories of an older European world.

In that shimmering Riviera world, the splendid Hotel Mirana owned by Humbert's father "revolved as a kind of private universe, a whitewashed cosmos within the blue greater one that blazed outside" (12). To be sure, the privileged world of the Mirana—with its wealthy American ladies leaning toward him "like Towers of Pisa"—does not represent Europe, pure and simple, for, obviously, all the other characters and places associated with his youth are European as well. Yet it represents one of its most distinctive features, and since it constitutes Humbert's earliest and fondest memory, it is also the most plainly evocative one. There is also a recurring perspective in the novel as a whole through which the circumstances and events of Humbert's early life become generalized and at which level Europe is not merely a "salad of racial genes" (like his Franco-Austrian father) but an integration, any one of whose parts is representative and typical. For example, when Humbert recounts the sad story of his Annabel "phase," he reflects, somewhat pompously even for him: "Our brains were tuned the way those of intelligent European preadolescents were in our day and set, and I doubt if much individual genius should be assigned to our interest in the plurality of inhabited worlds, competitive tennis, infinity, solipsism and so on" (14). Presumably "individual genius" is not required of such preadolescents because an archetypal genius, European and upper class, animates their various nationalities, knitting them together in their knowledge of things like infinity and solipsism, to which their brains are precociously "tuned."

The importance of Europe in *Lolita*, however, is not merely that it provides a unified perspective on Humbert's early life. It also underlies and informs all of his subsequent impressions of America. In explaining the origin of his incurable nympholepsy, for example, Humbert argues that his infatuation with Lolita was prompted by an earlier "prototype"—the half-English, half-Dutch Annabel—whose tragic and untimely death had introduced him to the idyllic raptures of unrequited love and impelled him to "incarnate" her being in another: "All I want to stress is that my discovery of [Lolita] was a fatal consequence of that 'princedom by the sea' in my tortured past. Everything between the two events was but a series of gropings and blunders, and false rudiments of joy" (42). The argument may well be specious, not to say self-serving, as some have suggested, but it underscores a tendency toward narrative repetition and reconstruction that is entirely characteristic of Humbert and that, in its own way, is premonitory of that wider pattern of Nabokovian parody and coincidence for which the novel itself has been alternately celebrated and condemned.[13] Culturally speaking, the argument suggests what is obvious enough in other ways throughout the book: that Humbert regards his new American life as a mere succession of "gropings and blunders" and America itself as a pale imitation or parody of "prototypical" Europe.

Thus America is generalized and an "American character" is adduced in the "horrible hybridization" of the Haze household. Humbert is prospecting for suitable lodgings in Ramsdale and wondering how, in heaven's name, he can elude the predatory Charlotte. He then recapitulates the hopeless decor of her home:

> I could not be happy in that type of household with bedraggled magazines on every chair and a kind of horrible hybridization between the comedy of so-called "functional modern furniture" and the tragedy of decrepit rockers and rickety lamp tables with dead lamps. I was led upstairs, and to the left— into "my" room. I inspected it through the mist of my utter rejection of it; but I did discern above "my" bed René Prinet's "Kreutzer Sonata." And she called that servant maid's room a "semi-studio"! (39–40)

For Humbert, the "hybridization" here is an ordeal, which his "old world politeness" obliges him to endure. In its way it is expressive of that wider hybridization—of past and present, Old World and New, Europe and America—that for Nabokov typifies American middle-class life (especially in the East) and that so accurately defines the deracinated condition of his hero.

Thus when Humbert, the émigré scholar, first arrives in New York, he is compelled to pursue two incommensurable jobs—one devising and editing perfume ads for his uncle's company, the other composing a comparative history of French literature for English-speaking students. "As I look back on those days," he reflects, "I see them divided tidily into ample light and narrow shade: the light pertaining to the solace of research in palatial libraries, the shade to my excruciating desires and insomnias of which enough has been said" (34). It is as if the incongruities of his émigré life serve to objectify the inner divisions of his psychic life. Still later, in the wake of a nervous breakdown, he sets out with an expedition into the Canadian wilderness, attaching himself as a "recorder of psychic reactions." (The decisively American caste of the expedition is enhanced by the site of their weather station, based on "Pierre Point in Melville Sound"!) Even under the "translucent" Arctic sky there would seem to be no reprieve from the horrible hybridization of his new life. Notwithstanding the sexual favors of the camp nutritionist, Humbert is alternately bemused and appalled by the motley conditions of the camp itself, where, among other staples of American life, supplies are said to include "the *Reader's Digest*, an ice cream mixer, chemical toilets, and paper hats for Christmas" (35).

By the time he reaches Ramsdale and his "fate," therefore, Humbert's initiation into the hybrid texture of American life is well under way, if by no means complete. What it has taught him can be readily surmised not only from his reaction to Charlotte's home, already cited, but from his early descriptions of Lolita herself. More than anything else, we are told, she is a maddening "mixture" of discordant qualities. On the one hand, she is all "tender dreamy childishness" and innocence; on the other, she is said to embody an "eerie vulgarity," which combines "the blurry pinkness of adolescent maid servants in the Old Country" with the harsh corruption of their counterparts, the "very young harlots disguised as children in provincial brothels." These qualities in turn, of course, get all "mixed up" in Humbert's mind with the immemorial memory of Annabel, his "Riviera love," "so that above and over everything there is—Lolita" (46–47).

It would appear that Humbert's so-called portrait of Lolita—her alleged individualization of "the writer's ancient lust"—is itself a highly hybridized affair, one that mixes an equal and abundant measure of cant, hypocrisy, egotism, and willful self-delusion. Moreover, it is as much a cultural statement as an aesthetic one and constitutes an extended variation on Humbert's view of America as a whole. Encoded in his attempt to portray her fatal attractiveness and demonic charm, therefore, is an émigré perspective that laments the insubstantiality of American society and, by implication, apostrophizes Europe. Thus in emphasizing "what is most singular" about Lolita, he does just the opposite, that is, he treats her "twofold nature" as a transcendental type or category—the enigmatic "nymphet"—to the exclusion of anything materially concrete about her, including her own national identity. In such a perspective even her quintessentially American vulgarity, so amusing to most readers, is only an analogue of an earlier European decadence. Hence Humbert's exclusive reliance upon continental prototypes and precursors ("adolescent maid servants in the Old Country") as a means of mitigating her corruption and of reattaching it to that saturnalia of "nymphic" symptoms by which Lolita and her like are separated from their ordinary, earthbound sisters. In the middle-class world of Ramsdale, evidently, American vulgarity is an excusable offense only when accompanied by a European pedigree.

From Humbert's point of view, it might be said, all regions of America are necessarily middle class, in the sense that they seek to mimic in a makeshift and thoroughly middling way the ostentatious splendors of Europe. (Consider his description of Pavor Manor, for example, Quilty's home in Parkington: a combination brothel, pleasure palace, and medieval castle.) Seldom in his account, therefore, is American life shown to be a distinct if variable experience, worthy of sustained exploration and discovery. More often than not, it is portrayed as a ghostly and degenerate version of his European past as when, for instance, he strives to create "a morning illusion of Venice when actually it was Pennsylvania and rain" (147) or when, attempting to replicate "the crisp charm, the sapphire occasion and rosy contingency of my Riviera romance" (169), he is confounded by the foul weather and "matter-of-fact mist" of the New England coast. Indeed, every time that Humbert tries to recapture some memorable moment of his European "phase," he invariably encounters obstacles and disappointments, which come as a series of abrasive shocks to his émigré sensibility and make him feel like the displaced person that he is. Thus in his relationship with Lolita—Nabokov's strictures notwithstanding—we see European culture and experience trying to suppress and "solipsize" American Otherness, the Old World expressing its incestuous disdain for the New. So fervent is Humbert's desire to recast Lolita in the role of her European predecessor, complete with stage props and dramatic settings, that there is something faintly onanistic in his efforts. After wresting her away from Ramsdale, for example, he deliberately intensifies his lust by resorting to imaginary reconstructions and reminders of his original "Riviera romance." In his words: my "search for a Kingdom by the Sea, a sublimated Riviera, or whatnot, far from being the impulse of the subconscious, has become the rational pursuit of a purely theoretical thrill" (169).

Rational or not, Humbert's energetic embrace of Old World stereotypes in preference to native American realities inspires fierce and prolonged resistance, not only from his nubile quarry but from the hybrid culture of which she is a part. For in a very real sense, it is not Lolita or even Quilty who is his chief antagonist and "nemesis" (as Humbert would have us believe). Rather, the agent of his undoing is his own inability—cultural as well as aesthetic—to participate in the plenitude of American life on its own terms, without some mediating vision of Europe to direct and control it. In the light of such visions, not only American culture is anomalous and disordered. Seemingly, the enormous continent itself—with its immense profusion of forests, deserts, and mountains ("altitudinal failures as Alps go")—is but a grotesque distortion of a more serene and civilized European ideal. Recalling his "hopeless hauntings of public parks in Europe," for example, Humbert expresses his dismay at the difficulty of ravishing nymphets in the "never Arcadian" American wilderness:

> But in the wilds of America the open-air lover will not find it easy to indulge in the most ancient of all crimes and pastimes. Poisonous plants burn his sweetheart's buttocks, nameless insects sting his; sharp items of the forest floor prick his knees, insects hers; and all around there abides a sustained

> rustle of potential snakes—*que dis-je,* of semi-extinct dragons!—while crab-
> like seeds of ferocious flowers cling, in a hideous green crust, to gartered
> black sock and sloppy white sock alike. (170)

In the spectral glow of memory, even his immediate impressions of the land prove disconcertingly surreal.

Inevitably, then, the New World that emerges in *Lolita* is a world already mired in *poshlost* and suffused with satire. For Humbert, obviously, it is the middle-class world of Ramsdale and Charlotte Haze, with her passion for "culture" and exotic books. Less obviously but more generally, it is the rootless American world at large, represented by the myriad motor courts, movie theaters, public parks, and roadside restaurants that litter the landscape throughout part two and whose purely commercial culture embraces both the pornography of a Clare Quilty and the "progressivism" of a Miss Pratt, headmistress of the Beardsley School for Girls, where America's future mothers are forever instilled with the utilitarian value of "the Four D's: Dramatics, Dance, Debating and Dating" (179). Although Nabokov often expressed delight in its creation, it should be emphasized that the New World so hilariously and savagely evoked in the novel is a world directly presided over by Humbert, not his creator.[14] (Sensitive to this point, Nabokov often underscores the discrepancy between his own and Humberts views by having the latter repeatedly avow either the vagueness or the artfulness of his recollections.) Insofar as we have a vision of America in the book, it is a vision not once but twice removed from reality—a Nabokovian rendering of a character's reminiscence. And, like so many other elements in Humbert's self-serving account, it is largely a fictionalized projection, the effect of which is to enhance his émigré memories and legitimize his émigré desires.

Whatever the precise degree of Humbert's unreliability, there can be no doubt that his denigration of America is designed, at least in part, to rationalize his relationship with Lolita and endow his criminal conduct with a sense of high heroic purpose. So committed is he to the monumental task of self-exoneration that he comes to see himself—and so to portray himself—as a kind of émigré quester in an alien wasteland, seeking the coveted grail of his European past amid the resplendent ruins of America. Traveling with Lolita during their first cross-country odyssey, he recalls how "treasured recollections of my father's palatial hotel sometimes led me to seek [in vain] for its like in the strange country we traveled through" (149). Later "that mad year" (August 1947 to August 1948), as Lolita's mutinies grow more frequent and ferocious, he tries to improve her temper by teaching her tennis; in the process he is able to forget his troubles and, for a few halcyon moments, "relive the days when in a hot gale, a daze of dust, and queer lassitude, I fed ball after ball to gay, innocent, elegant Annabel" (164). Such moments of self-forgetfulness are admittedly few and far between, but they point to a persistent pattern of his émigré life. As its more or less circular movement attests, Humbert's vertiginous flight with Lolita across America (beginning with "a series of wiggles and whorls in New England" and "petering out in the college town of Beardsley" [156]) brings him not renewal but regression, not a new beginning but only another return—the eastward arc of their travels describes a journey back to America's New England origins when Europe still exerted an irresistible hold on American life. Consequently, Humbert's extensive and often-quoted account of their itinerary (156–68) is not, properly speaking, a description at all. For all its vaunted accuracy and amplitude, it amounts to little more than an exotic clutter of American names spanning the continent in featureless profusion, like the faded entries in a collection of "ruined tour books." Only in retrospect—after his nymphet has departed—does America slowly begin to impress itself on his consciousness as a distinct cultural presence with a coherent sense of place independent of his émigré dreams of an earlier world. Until then, its only apparent function in his wandering life is to provoke his fantasies and increase his homelessness. "We had been everywhere. We had really seen nothing," Humbert sadly recalls. "And I catch myself thinking today that our long journey had only defiled with a sinuous trail of slime the lovely, trustful, dreamy, enormous country that by then . . . was no more to us than a collection of dog-eared maps, ruined tour books, old tires, and her sobs in the night" (177–78).

Thus in comparing himself throughout the book to Poe as well as to much greater artists such as Virgil, Dante, and Petrarch ("nympholepts" all), Humbert is not merely establishing ample erotic precedent for his own misconduct. He is also identifying himself as one of a noble company of spiritual explorers whose illustrious peregrinations throughout human history he can liken to his own. Humbert as pilgrim embodies a crucial dimension both of the New World experience and of his own illicit relationship with Lolita. Imprisoned in the present indicative of his new American life, he is nonetheless driven, as we have seen, to repeat the past, to search for some supreme, unutterable consummation whose final object lies far beyond and above the nubile, mortal clay of Lolita, who is its ostensible object. Lolita, it has often been said, is valuable to Humbert not only as sexual object but as aesthetic possibility: her "nymphetage" and inexperience allow her to be "safely solipsized" by Humbert's haunted imagination. This is certainly true, yet even here, in the "umber and black Humberland" of their private and secluded world, Nabokov has rung in his own character- istic cultural complexities. For at the center of their relationship lies not only the relationship between Europe and America, but also the ambigu- ous interaction between the contradictory impulses of Europe that led to the original settling of America: commercialism and transcendentalism. The contradictory nature of the two impulses has been described by Van Wyck Brooks (who could well have been Humbert's philosopher in these matters) in *The Wine of the Puritans*:

> You put the old wine [Europeans] into new bottles [American continent] . . . and when the explosion results, one may say, the aroma passes into the air and the wine spills on the floor. The aroma or the ideal, turns into transcendentalism and the wine or the real, becomes commercialism.[15]

Throughout American history, Van Wyck Brooks suggests, the two im- pulses have a way of being both radically exclusive and mutually confus- ing, the one melting into the other: the human faculty of wonder, on the one hand, and the power and beauty of things, on the other. Perhaps no one better understood these competing drives of the American psyche than William Carlos Williams, who in his imaginative reconstruction of America's colonial past, *In the American Grain*, accords them definitive ex- pression in two antithetical figures of American life and legend: Benjamin Franklin and Daniel Boone. For Williams, Franklin's deification of "indus- triousness" and "frugality" expresses a purely commercial desire to domi- nate and improve the environment, to render it amenable to practical use, whereas Boone's near-mystical attachment to the Kentucky wilderness suggests a purely "aesthetic" perception of the land in all its wondrous plenitude and Otherness: "The beauty of a lavish, primitive embrace in savage, wild beast and forest rising above the cramped life about him pos- sessed him wholly. Passionate and thoroughly given he avoided the half logic of stealing from the immense profusion."[16] While Williams's sympa- thies as a poet are obviously with Boone, the historical perspective gener- ated by his book compels a conclusion quite similar to Brooks's: as the country grew older and as Americans themselves became more conscious of their national identity, these once archetypal attitudes toward the New World become blurred and indistinct, often manifesting themselves at the same time, indeed in the same person.

*Lolita* dramatizes this continuing ambiguity directly in the life of Hum- bert and retrospectively by a glance at rural America at the end of the novel. It does so especially in the once-notorious chapter 13 (part one), which describes Humbert's first—and conceivably last—ecstatic moment with Lolita, a moment when his imagination seems on the verge of entering an earthly paradise. As Lolita sits squirming on his berobed lap in the Haze living room, Humbert triumphantly reflects:

> I entered a plane of being where nothing mattered, save the infusion of joy brewed within my body. What had begun as a delicious distension of my innermost roots became a glowing tingle which *now* had reached that state of absolute security, confidence and reliance not found elsewhere in conscious life. With the deep hot sweetness thus established and well on its way to the ultimate convulsion, I felt I could slow down in order to prolong the glow. Lolita had been safely solipsized. (62)

The emphasis in the passage on Humbert's "joy" and "security" hardly needs commenting, nor does the sexuality, immature in Lolita's case and illicit in Humbert's, nor the solipsizing process whereby Humbert seeks to enter an ideal realm "where nothing mattered." For these are the central symbols of his émigré life: the cultured European imagination trying to transfigure the as-yet-unfinished, though potentially beautiful American object. But, of course, Lolita can be neither solipsized nor transfigured completely, any more than the north Atlantic coast can be transformed into a "sublimated Riviera" or the American wilderness into an "Arcadian" paradise. Behind the rhetorical rapture of his prose, Humbert's moment of ecstasy remains a purely onanistic act, a solitary indulgence in which Lolita herself is both idealized and ignored, elevated and exploited.

The conflicting impulses at work in Humbert's "moment" accurately identify his character and condition in the New World. Confronted with the raw material and "immense profusion" of the land, he is impelled to reconstruct them in his own image, to impose his outworn idealizations upon them; in the process, as the novel makes clear, he robs them of their native beauty and individual identity. (He may scoff at the protective mimicry and hybridization of American life, but have not his own idealizations of Lolita been at bottom a form of mimicry, a way of replicating his European past—as exemplified by Annabel—and grafting it to his American present?) The ambiguities inherent in Humbert's motives derive then not merely from his contradictory attitudes toward art, sex, and fate or even from the moral implications of his "confession"—important as these are to any overall estimate of his character. As much as anything, the ambivalence of his behavior reflects a self-conscious attempt to reconcile the equal but divergent interests of his émigré heart: the commercial impulse to dominate and exploit things and the transcendental impulse to idealize and transform them.

This ambidextrous attempt is inscribed on nearly every page of Humbert's narrative, completely mixed with intermittent recognitions of failure. Early in his "confession," we hear of the exalted artistry and sublime madness required to appreciate the nonhuman nature of nymphets; two pages later he alludes to that "incomparably more poignant bliss" (20) unceasingly bestowed by the ardors of nympholepsy; and on the next page he solemnly salutes Virgil, Dante, and Petrarch as his illustrious predecessors in the privileged art of pedophilia. Yet only two pages after that we find him sternly rebuking himself for his "degrading and dangerous desires" (23). Indeed, in the very passage devoted to the poignant bliss of nympholepsy, he also refers to "the dimmest of my pollutive dreams" (20). Midway through the book, he is describing his sexual appetites as "monstrous," yet within thirty pages he reiterates his contention that "there is no other bliss on earth comparable to that of fondling a nymphet" (168). These are not isolated examples, either, for almost every page reveals Humbert's maddening ambivalence toward his own behavior, as well as his conflicting attitudes toward Lolita. As the incarnation of his émigré dreams, Lolita is nothing less—and ultimately nothing more—than his adored enchantress, an "ultraviolet darling" made miraculously manifest to his unworthy and unsuspecting eye; this Lolita must be carefully preserved and protected. But, as a flesh-and-blood child, she is little more than the wayward daughter of Charlotte Haze, an all-American brat of dubious taste and even more dubious virtue; this Lolita must be carefully suppressed and controlled. "To the wonderland I had to offer," Humbert complains of this other Lolita, "my fool preferred the corniest movies, the most cloying fudge. To think that between a hamburger and a humburger, she would— invariably, with icy precision—plump for the former. There is nothing more atrociously cruel than an adored child" (168). The conflict that Humbert is vainly attempting to resolve, in other words, consists in his contradictory impulses toward the idealization of Lolita (which he achieves only in fantasy or in the quiet "refuge of art") and the subjugation of her to the practical imperatives of adult experience and consciousness. These impulses are, in an important respect, the same impulse. They both imply the repudiation of Lolita as an autonomous being, and they are both symptomatic as well of his perennial inability to adopt a consistent posture toward his new American life.

To the extent that Humbert's passion for Lolita embodies an unstable union of spirit and substance, of dream and reality, his relationship to her represents a dramatization of the basic thesis proposed by Brooks and Williams: that America had produced an idealism so impalpable that it lost touch with reality and a materialism so intractable that it became corrupt. (Hence Humbert's endless ambivalence toward his own obsessions, and hence too his curious identification with Clare Quilty, whom he regards first with aversion as his "nemesis" and then with affinity as his "brother.") The novel as a whole offers another elaboration on this American legend, with the impossible idealism trying to actualize itself, to its utter destruction, in the gross materiality. As Humbert acknowledges, in one of his most impressive moments of self-analysis in the book: "It had become gradually clear to my conventional Lolita during our singular and bestial cohabitation that even the most miserable of family lives was better than the parody of incest, which, in the long run, was the best I could offer the waif" (289). Yet he imagines still—so resilient is his passion, so enduring are his delusions—that even in death, if only in death, they will find eventual union in the consoling eternity of art: "I am thinking of aurochs and angels, the secret of durable pigments, prophetic sonnets, the refuge of art. And this is the only immortality you and I may share, my Lolita" (311).

Thus Nabokov multiplies the ambiguities and ironies of Humbert's life, but does so in a way that deeply implicates his aesthetic obsessions with his temporal fate as an émigré in an unsettled, expanding, traditionless culture. No one knows better than Humbert, of course, that nothing could finally match the splendors of his own imagination—least of all a churlish and wily nymphet determined to resist him—and the novel suggests finally that not only had his aesthetic vision of Lolita been corrupted but that it was, in part anyway, necessarily corrupted, for it asked too much. Nothing of this earth, even the most beautiful of earthly objects, could be anything but a perversion of it. *Lolita,* it is often said, is a powerful demonstration of this view and constitutes a severe and fundamental challenge to the aesthetic ideal. Yet even here, in portraying his hero's downfall, Nabokov may properly be said to generate an essentially émigré perspective on events. After Lolita runs off, therefore, Humbert slowly begins to reconstruct her true and quintessentially American worth. He recalls her moments of unguarded inwardness and grace, her untutored sensitivity and depth—as well as his own tyrannical authority and possessiveness. Too late, he reflects that there was in her "a garden and a twilight, and a palace gate—dim and adorable regions which happened to be lucidly and absolutely forbidden to me, in my polluted rags and miserable convulsions" (286). But perhaps most significant of all, it is in the context of his newly awakened affection for the "lovely, trustful, dreamy, enormous" American continent that Humbert's dramatic reappraisal of Lolita begins—a point symbolically strengthened by the fact that she makes good her escape from him on the Fourth of July. The terms of that emerging affection may be best suggested by a final quotation, one of Nabokov's recorded favorites, taken from the conclusion of the novel. Having just murdered Quilty—his "nemesis" and his "brother"—Humbert recalls the time, soon after Lolita's disappearance from his life, when he had stopped along a mountain road in Colorado. Looking into "its friendly abyss," he heard a "melodious unity" of children's voices emanating from the valley town below:

> What I heard was but the melody of children at play, nothing but that, and so limpid was the air that within the vapor of blended voices, majestic and minute, remote and magically near, frank and divinely enigmatic—one could hear now and then, as if released, an almost articulate spurt of vivid laughter, or the crack of a bat, or the clatter of a toy wagon, but it was all really too far for the eye to distinguish any movement in the lightly etched streets. I stood listening to that musical vibration from my lofty slope, to those flashes of separate cries with a kind of demure murmur for background, and then I knew that the hopelessly poignant thing was not Lolita's absence from my side, but the absence of her voice from that concord. (310)

Worthy of comparison with Huck Finn's "lonesome" eloquence on the river or even with Nick's imaginative reconstruction of the legendary Dutchmen at the end of *Gatsby*, the passage comprises one of those rare aboriginal moments—usually pastoral and invariably elegiac—of which modern American literature is so fond and whose recurrent expression runs from Hawthorne and Melville through Twain and Faulkner, Hemingway and Bellow. In *Lolita*, as in the works of these classic American writers, the primary purpose of this narrative moment is to provide a countermovement to the main events, a journey back to man's Edenlike beginnings in the American landscape.[17] While its lyric poignancy and power have often been noted, its true significance seems to me preeminently cultural, deriving from Humbert's unfettered awareness, at last, of a native American reality "unsolipsized" by his émigré imagination. Indeed, it is as though, having divested himself of his Old World pretensions and preconceptions, he can finally see Lolita—and America—for the slightly tawdry, hybrid beauties they have always been.

## Notes

1. Vladimir Nabokov, *Strong Opinions* (New York: McGraw-Hill, 1973), 26.

2. *Strong Opinions,* 77.

3. See, for example, Alfred Appel, Jr., "Backgrounds of *Lolita,*" *Triquarterly* 17 (1970): 17–40. Appel's essay appears in somewhat different form as part of his introduction to *The Annotated Lolita* (New York: McGraw-Hill, 1970), xxxiii–lviii.

4. Several critics have remarked on the affinities between Humbert 's legendary nympholepsy and the visionary element in classic American literature, but see especially Martha Banta, "Benjamin, Edgar, Humbert, and Jay," *Yale Review* 60 (Summer 1971): 532–49; also Lucy Maddox, *Nabokov's Novels in English* (Athens: University of Georgia Press, 1983), 66–85.

5. Nabokov's fascination with *poshlost* ("corny trash, vulgar clichés, philistinism in all its phases") is ventilated at length both in his study of Gogol (*Nikolai Gogol* [New York: New Directions, 1944], 63–74), and in a *Paris Review* interview of October 1967, reprinted in *Strong Opinions,* 100–101. On Nabokov's imaginative mastery of American *poshlost,* see Alfred Appel, Jr., "The Road to *Lolita*; or, The Americanization of an Émigré," *Journal of Modern Literature* 4 (1974): 3–31.

6. See, for example, Andrew Field, *Nabokov: His Life in Art* (Boston: Little, Brown, 1967), 323–51; Alfred Appel, Jr., "*Lolita*: The Springboard of Parody," in *Nabokov: The Man and His Work,* ed. L. S. Dembo (Madison: University of Wisconsin Press, 1967), 106–43; and Harold Brent, "*Lolita*: Nabokov's Critique of Aloofness," *Papers on Language and Literature* 11 (1975): 71–82.

7. *Lolita* (New York: Putnam, 1955), 62. Subsequent references to this edition will be incorporated in the text.

8. Alfred Appel, Jr., *Nabokov's Dark Cinema* (New York: Oxford University Press, 1974), 251.

9. The moral vision of *Lolita* is persuasively discussed by Martin Green, "The Morality of *Lolita,*" *Kenyon Review* 28 (June 1966): 352–77; and by Robert J. Levine, "'My Ultraviolet Darling': The Loss of Lolita's Childhood," *Modern Fiction Studies* 25 (1979): 471–79.

10. Robert Merrill, "Nabokov and Fictional Artifice," *Modern Fiction Studies* 25 (1979): 454.

11. See in this connection Douglas Fowler's discussion of *Lolita* in his *Reading Nabokov* (Ithaca, N.Y.: Cornell University Press, 1974), 147–75; and Ellen Pifer's chapter "Singularity and the Double's Pale Ghost: From *Despair* to *Pale Fire,*" in her *Nabokov and the Novel* (Cambridge, Mass.: Harvard University Press, 1980), 97–118.

12. As is well known, Nabokov always regarded with disdain and suspicion the idea that art—least of all *his* art—could ever survive as a creature of cultural affiliation or national identity. "The writer's art is his real passport," he suavely asserted.

"I have always maintained . . . that the nationality of a worthwhile writer is of secondary importance" (*Strong Opinions* 63). In describing the essence of his own achievement, therefore, Nabokov always carefully refrained from using ethnic labels or cultural stereotypes, as if to portray himself as a defiantly global artist endowed with gifts of imagination and language far exceeding the nourishing traditions of any particular soil or society.

13. Favorable and unfavorable reactions to Nabokov's extensive use of parody and artifice in *Lolita* are represented, respectively, by Appel's several articles on the work incorporated in his introduction to *The Annotated Lolita* and by Max F. Schulz, "Characters (contra Characterization) in the Contemporary Novel," in *The Theory of the Novel: New Essays,* ed. John Halperin (New York: Oxford University Press, 1974), esp. 144–47.

14. As Nabokov humorously quips in his afterword: "Humbert is a foreigner and an anarchist, and there are many things, besides nymphets, in which I disagree with him" (317). Too often an unintended consequence of the few cultural analyses of Humbert's American experience is the collapse of this elementary distinction—as in Appel's otherwise illuminating essay, "The Road to *Lolita*; or, The Americanization of an Émigré."

15. Van Wyck Brooks, *The Wine of the Puritans* (London: Sisley, n.d.), 17–18.

16. William Carlos Williams, *In the American Grain* (New York: New Directions, 1925), 136.

17. On the ideological development of this theme in American literature and culture, see R. W. B. Lewis's valuable study, *The American Adam: Innocence, Tragedy, and Tradition in the Nineteenth Century* (Chicago: University of Chicago Press, 1955).

# Lolita and the Poetry of Advertising

RACHEL BOWLBY

◆ ◆ ◆

L I K E *Lady Chatterley's Lover, Lolita* was the subject of a major literary-social controversy at the turn of the 1960s involving the relation of unconventional sexuality to an indeterminate borderline between literature and pornography. The public scandal then found its way right into the book. My British Corgi paperback, for instance, is padded with soundbite testimonials at the back from leading literary experts divided by country and ranging from Lionel Trilling's early defense in *Encounter* ("not about sex, but about love") to Bernard Levin ("certain of a permanent place on the very highest shelf of the world's didactic literature").[1] There is also the afterword, "On a Book Entitled *Lolita*," written by Nabokov at the end of 1956, in the wake of initial reactions to the first publication in Paris.[2]

But the scandalous accompaniments are not confined to later additions and editions. *Lolita* also has its spoof foreword purportedly written by one John Ray, Jr., Ph.D., both defending the book's artistic qualities and placing them in the context of worthy moral deterrence: we can be "entranced with the book while abhorring its author" (7). Ray's concluding paragraph decisively categorizes the work as a "case history" capable of wide and socially beneficial influence : " 'Lolita' should make all of us—parents, social workers, educators—apply ourselves with still greater vigilance and vision to the task of bringing up a better generation in a safer world" (7).

Nabokov begins his own declaration by referring to the foreword as "my impersonation of suave John Ray" and by preempting its own reading as "an impersonation of Vladimir Nabokov talking about his own book."

All of this accompanying material, some of it there in the original version of the novel, would make it practically impossible not to read *Lolita* in the light of a moral question and a potential scandal. The framing texts act as warning signs or obligations to establish a context for *Lolita* even as they ostensibly exhort the reader to take it on its own aesthetic terms. (Ray's conscientious foreword is recognizably a parody, and Nabokov defends himself against the barrage of moralizing readings, which he rejects in the name of literary autonomy.) There is thus not even the illusion of an innocent reading of this novel.

The trouble with *Lolita* can be provisionally stated simply in terms of the plot. Where *Lady Chatterley's Lover* involves a question about the defensibility of the heroine's behavior, here it is the male fictional narrator who is implicitly on trial, not for his murder of Clare Quilty (the crime that has finished him off within the novel), but for his feelings for and treatment of someone who is not just female but too young, and not just young but legally his daughter. According to Lévi-Strauss, incest—the word that Lolita herself baldly utters within the text (126)—is the last, or the first, taboo of human culture.[3] In this sense alone it is a million psychic miles from the stock-in-trade transgressions of a novel of adultery, even with the added barrier of class. Denis de Rougemont, for whom the literature of passionate love always depends for its power on an opposition between social custom and the erotic, saw in incest the one remaining taboo available to the late twentieth-century imagination; Trilling's defense mentions de Rougemont's hypothesis as though in legitimization of this particular theme, and later de Rougemont himself wrote about *Lolita* in these terms.[4]

Throughout its history, *Lolita* has been the subject of arguments veering between the two poles of literary value and pornographic reprehensibility. Ray's defense of the defense—artistic *and* didactic—follows an ancient and honorable tradition, going back to Horace's definition of the functions of literature as a combination of pleasing and teaching, not one rather than the other.[5] But contemporary criticism tends to separate these, taking moral values as not just distinct from but incompatible with those associated with art. More than that, it is in breaking with the moral standards of society that literature's distance from a banal conformity can be measured. Literature's autonomy depends on such a separation, exempting it from moral criteria applicable elsewhere and removing it from any suggestion of having itself an educative function.

In this context, early praise of *Lolita* characteristically made the case by pointing to the difference between art and life. Gabriel Josipovici, for instance, wrote:

> If, from one point of view, Humbert is forced into writing the Memoir by the fear of impending madness and the impossibility of ever possessing Lolita in the flesh, if, that is, the Memoir is simply a poor substitute for the living girl, from another point of view the shift from life to art is the logical outcome of his discovery that he had somehow gone wrong in his previous attempts at capturing the elusive beauty of nymphets. It is not a poor substitute but the true and only way of capturing Lolita and fulfilling his poetic longings.[6]

There is no hint yet here of a defense against the charge that Humbert might have been violating Lolita in "capturing" her in life or on the page; the case being made, interestingly, is in relation to an implied suggestion that literary fulfillments in relation to women—or nymphets—might be thought to be only substitutes for the real thing "in the flesh." We shall come back to this distinction between the real and the fake, which is crucial within the novel as well as in its readings.

A later phase of criticism made use of Russian formalism and its development within French structuralism to affirm the separation between life and art as one between worldly morals and textual autonomy. As David Packman put it:

> According to Donald E. Morton, Humbert "has used Lolita in his private and subjective way for his own pleasure—and presumably without her knowledge or cooperation." One could argue that as he composes his memoir, Humbert might share Morton's implicitly dim view of his manipulation of the nymphet. However, quite another, more formal view of the matter is certainly possible. The Russian Formalist notion of motivation permits this other view, from which moral implications are absent. One might say that Lolita has indeed been "safely solipsized" in that she has become a functional element in the construction of a sequence, a bit of narrative.[7]

The rhetoric of this betrays something bordering on anxiety in the need to find an approach that will let the reader off any moral hooks, literally licensing him ("permits") to forget the problem, which nonetheless remains in the breezy energy of its refusal and in the need to seek permission for a different approach at all.

More recently, in the wake of feminist criticism, the question of the relations between literature and pornography and their inseparability from a more general cultural misogyny has become less easy to ignore or to relegate to a quick dismissive paragraph. This has been intensified by a sense that structuralist, formalist, and then deconstructive approaches have the effect of bracketing off ethical issues by their concentration on a text assumed to be operating in its own world apart from a real one situated somewhere else. But curiously, this then tends to produce a kind of double approach: textual reading plus moral reading, with the separation remaining in place.

Thus Rodney Giblett, having developed an analysis of *Lolita* in terms of its parody of the genre of fictional confession, moves off in a quite different direction by pointing to the way that "the pleasure it produces for the implied reader is . . . compromised by its production of the sexuality of the pubescent girl and the pleasure that that produces for the middle-aged nympholept."[8] He then stages a kind of replay of the Quilty-versus-Humbert wrestling match between male doubles by pitting Terry Eagleton and Fredric Jameson against each other as two Marxist critics with opposite notions of the political value of textual sexuality. By the end, Giblett's arena has shifted markedly from his formalist beginnings:

> The construction of this pleasure has both an historical lineage and a politics of gender and generation. By tracing that lineage and enouncing those politics, the material grounds of possibility of pleasure can be critically transformed and the domain of pleasure reinstituted as a site for left-political intervention.[9]

The ethical and political imperative has now taken over completely from the early analysis of the pleasures of parody "compromised" by its unacceptable content. However worthy the conclusion, the very separation of the two kinds of approach—either an unself-conscious text-for-text's-sake literary *jouissance* at the expense of the girl or the treatment of texts and, in particular, this text, as primarily a place for a politics constituted elsewhere and in advance, not a place for pleasure—has the effect of leaving the problem as it was: either pleasure or political correctness, but not both at once.

In a similar vein, Elizabeth Dipple begins by celebrating the postmodern playfulness of *Lolita* and then turns to worrying about its theme:

> In the late 1980s when the misuse of children is so much before us, the plot of *Lolita* causes uneasiness and many readers stubbornly deny its higher forum of aesthetic excellence. In other words, Nabokov *should* perhaps, at least on one level, have a more exacting moral in tow.[10]

The firmness in the attribution of stubbornness here puts Dipple herself more in the moralist's place than in that of the advocate of "aesthetic excellence." In the next sentence, further, the emphatic *should* shows the ways in which the separation of ethics from aesthetics always seems to imply that what is moral is prescriptive in some easily recognizable way, with the word "moral" suggesting a general injunction to be followed in the reader's real, as opposed to reading, life.

Dipple goes on to argue that the book is indeed a moral work, for all of its literary pleasures and ironies, because the narrator does acknowledge that he has wronged the girl: "This final admission that HH had been guilty of a larger crime than the literary murder of his Quilty-Guilty alter ego necessarily moves the novel into a higher ethical category."[11] "Higher" ethics are represented by the replacement of "his narrow sexual obsession . . . by a genuine love and moral apprehension of the person in front of him." More than this, even: "in a very real way, the killing of his guilty Quilty opens Humbert Humbert to a relinquishment of solipsism, and to a selfless poetic act—the immortalizing of a girl who, like him, like Nabokov, like all readers caught in the mesh of time, is subject to death."[12] What is striking here is the way that every trace of irony, postmodern or not, seems to have disappeared in the thoroughly prepostmodern appeal to the authenticity of such categories as the whole person, real love (as opposed to base sex), and the pathos of poetic immortality in the face of inevitable human death. This is related to the prevailing use of a language of high and low: the "higher ethical category" and the "higher forum of aesthetic excellence" of the first quotation.

Once again, it seems as though it is difficult to talk about ethics in relation to *Lolita* without setting up a division that renders literature—in its supposed divorce from real people and mature attitudes—irresponsible, childish, or at best salutary (a consolation for mortality). This same impasse—the difficulty of bringing the moral and the aesthetic together—forms the starting point for Linda Kauffman's challenging reinterpretation, which, like Dipple's, explicitly sets itself in the context of the 1980s' focus on issues of child sexual abuse.[13] Kauffman seeks to avoid the stark alternatives that suggest that a text be seen either as simply copying a world awaiting transcription (the representational fallacy) or as sublimely independent of the social and ethical questions its story may suggest or require. The first, habitually, would be the moralizing version of the kind exemplified by the John Ray foreword, where the acknowledged enchantments of literature are merely added as ornament or distraction to texts that, in other ways, may perfectly well tell it like it is or was—in this instance, the "lesson-for-our time" case history. The second version would be the supposed moral insouciance of the often-cited "aesthetic bliss" invoked by Nabokov's afterword (332). Unlike Dipple, Kauffman does not see a moral awaiting retrieval from Nabokov's text, but she suggests that it might be "possible . . . in a double movement to analyze the horror of incest by reinscribing the material body of the child Lolita in the text and simultaneously to undermine the representational fallacy by situating the text dialogically in relation to other texts."[14]

Reading much more against the novelistic grain than Dipple, Kauffman then finds not the compensatory immortalization of Lolita's body but its violation: "By thus inscribing the female body in the text . . . one discovers that Lolita is not a photographed image, or a still life, or a freeze frame preserved on film, but a damaged child."[15] Kauffman reaches this conclusion by way of recent medical literature on father-child incest, which serves more as corroboration than as intertextual counterpoint. It is as though the moral point can only be made, despite every recognition of the difficulties, by returning to a form of referential appeal—"this is the way it is"—which once again implies that there are some things (some bodies, some acts) that, although inscribed or reinscribed "in" a text, nonetheless carry a meaning independent of it.

It is in one sense ironic that this should be true of incest, of all crimes, since—as Lévi-Strauss demonstrated—though the prohibition is apparently a cultural universal, its specific exclusions are infinitely variable. It is worth noticing, too, that Humbert is not Lolita's father in any of the ordinary ways, either biologically or adoptively—he did not bring her up—which emphasizes the arbitrary aspect in all human relationships, including those that do connect blood relations. Paternity is here quite literally a legal form in relation to which bodily desires and acts will come to take their meaning. Far from being a natural or obviously "material" question of bodily affects, the incest taboo, for Lévi-Strauss, both inaugurates and epitomizes the symbolic order of human culture, "placing" persons in relation to one another, in terms of permissions and prohibitions that are unconnected with nature.

This is not to say that Lolita is not a damaged child but to suggest that that phrase gives too much away, from Kauffman's own point of view, to a particular normative cultural fiction, one parodied within the novel and through the Ray preface, which would have it that there is a state of perfect health and wholeness—proper individuality and proper human relations—from which it is possible to make clear-cut demarcations as to just where the damages begin. The extremity of the Lolita case becomes more, not less, forceful as a critique of sexual values if it is acknowledged that it is not without relation to the sanitizing fictions of faultless human growth and relationship.

Apart from the divisions of guilt and innocence, seducer and victim, real love and perverse sexuality, there is another area in which *Lolita* seems to have suggested to its readers the existence of sharp antinomies, and in this case they are usually taken to be more or less those intended by the author. For the novel apparently stages a manifest clash between the literary values of Humbert and the vulgar, consumerly values of Lolita, which is reinforced through the familiar opposition of the European visitor and the all-American girl. In this antithesis, Lolita does not so much represent innocence and virginity as the crude embodiment of a different kind of victim, one subject to and made over in the image of a mass culture with which she has completely identified; and the narrator, far from representing the force of exploitation, can be associated with an aesthetic authenticity whose plausibility gives the novel its power because it distracts the reader from what would otherwise appear as a simple assault.

Linda Kauffman implicitly connects these two versions of the antithesis:

> Materialist critiques of the novel could focus on the rampant consumerism of American society in 1955, since Lolita is the ideal consumer, naive, spoiled, totally hooked on the gadgets of modern life, a true believer in the promises of Madison Avenue. Yet a materialist *feminist* perspective enables one to see something that has not been noted before: Lolita is as much the object consumed by Humbert as she is the product of her culture. And if she is hooked, he is the one who turns her into a hooker.[16]

As the juxtaposition shows, consumer culture and violent seduction are seen to be discursively interchangeable, the first as "rampant" as a rapist in commonplace critiques, and the victim in the second equivalent to a commodity and then to a prostitute. But as we shall see, the equivalences are not so straightforward: Humbert does not enjoy Lolita in the way in which she might enjoy a soda pop or a new dress; and if she is "hooked" on consumer culture, that does not imply vulnerability so much as pleasure.

In a more extended discussion of this aspect, Dana Brand sees the novel as a fairly unequivocal and justifiable critique of consumerism through aestheticism.[17] The normative discourses epitomized by advertising are at once overpowering and alienating for subjects who, by implication, would otherwise be whole: "only Humbert the foreigner is able to resist the influence of these new and powerful forms of coercion."[18] What distinguishes advertising from art is that the former promises, deceptively, to deliver its goods, while the latter is knowingly independent of the real world.

Brand quotes the passage in which Humbert describes the emptiness of night-time Main Street in Appalachia, covered with store signs and brand names, and finds him transforming it into something other than its native commercial character:

> A world of shop windows, signs, laxative and lubrication advertisements becomes a beautiful realm of anthropomorphic colored light in Humbert's consciousness. The advertising message in the light is of no importance to him. The name of the liquor store is of less importance to him than the fact that the letters on its sign are "sherry-red." The name of the lubrication is important only for what it suggests to him. By aestheticizing the objects he sees, Humbert neutralizes the coercive power they have as signs in commercial American culture.[19]

Yet the power of the brand name of the lubrication oil to suggest something else is not incompatible with its function as an advertisement but is just what is supposed to happen: in advertising terms, the name has made an impression, has led to an association with other words and ideas.[20] "Sherry-red," moreover, is just the sort of neologistic compound that might be invented by an advertising copywriter—or the founder of the European literary tradition, for that matter. Homer's "wine-dark" sea would seem to be a perfect adjective for the nocturnal liquor store, were it not that Brand has intriguingly metamorphosed what Nabokov gives as a "camera shop" (297).

L E T   U S   T R Y to disentangle these devious and diverse analogies and distinctions among aesthetic, consumer, and moral values as they appear within the novel. We may begin on the relatively secure ground of a literary erotic tradition, by looking at the way that *Lolita* leads us in one direction to read it in relation to the motif of the *passante*, or passing woman, the one and only woman, no sooner identified by the male narrator than she is placed definitively out of reach, to return only in the aesthetic form that restores her to a kind of immortality: "You see I loved her. It was love at first sight, at last sight, at ever and ever sight" (284).[21]

In the hectic passage across practically every state of America in the late 1940s and early 1950s, in the company or in quest of the irreplaceable object of the narrator's adoration, we are met at every turn by the names of those who represent the European literary and artistic tradition, which he has left behind geographically but which continues to shape the landscape of his desire for the Lolita he never fully possesses as his own: Poe, Baudelaire, Coleridge, Dante, Petrarch, Botticelli, Proust, Rimbaud, Virgil. In one aspect, at least, *Lolita* looks as though it is presenting itself as the continuation, if not the culmination, of a search for the image of feminine perfection in a woman who will necessarily pass on or away, whose very unattainability will be the cause of her continuing power to move the narrator's desire. In this novel, the postulate of the woman's inaccessibility seems to be taken to the furthest possible limit, if not off-limits, in the embodiment of the ideal in the form of a barely pubescent girl. Here, the loved one is fated to disappear not because she may die or because she may leave or never meet him, but because her life span as a "nymphet" is limited to just a year or two. Unlike Dorian Gray, Lolita cannot become the unchanging incarnation of her moment of youthful perfection. As a girl, moreover, she cannot be had, either legally or in the fantasy of a love that would be shared, and the tragedy of the novel derives partly from the way in which the distance between the two is so clearly maintained even after and in spite of its physical crossing.

At the same time, *Lolita* also departs from some of the standard components of the *passante* romantic scenario. The declaration of unconditional love "at first sight, at last sight" occurs not at the start but after Humbert has controlled (and then lost control of) her life for some years and when she no longer looks like the girl for whom he originally fell. Possession is followed, not preceded, by a quest (after Lolita goes off with Quilty). And far from being an encounter between strangers walking on a city street, the meeting of Lolita and Humbert takes place in an utterly familial setting: on the lawn of the suburban house where they will soon be living together. This is a novel in which there is almost no walking at all; the car has taken over as the vehicle of undirected cruising. Only the occasional standardized Main Street figures as a distant replica of the city.

Only the young prostitute in Paris to whom Humbert is fleetingly attached before he marries Valeria shows the qualities of the *passante as flâneuse*: "a slim girl passed me at a rapid, high-heeled, tripping step, we glanced back at the same moment, she stopped and I accosted her" (24). It is as though the older setting of the scene has been relegated or confined to the meeting with the actual streetwalker, which does not function in the same way because the dramatic condition of inaccessibility is replaced by its opposite, the assumption of availability. But Monique's appeal is real nonetheless, and it is in her walk. The same is partly true of the American girl Lolita:

> Why does the way she walks—a child, mind you, a mere child!—excite me
> so abominably? Analyze it. A faint suggestion of turned-in toes. A kind of
> wiggly looseness below the knee prolonged to the end of each footfall. The
> ghost of a drag. Very infantile, infinitely meretricious. (45)

In the reverse process to Norbert Hanold's in Jensen's *Gradiva*,[22] the passion
for a step here turns into the wish to analyze what produces it, and the
"meretricious" hint at the end operates as a dim echo of the whorish associations of the city to which the suburban girl has no connection.

The encounter with Lolita lacks both mystery and anonymity: there is
no wonder in Dolores Haze's presence in her own backyard. And where
the scene is without the uncertainties that mark the urban version, it does
more than merely domesticate by the provision of identities on both sides:
it also introduces new kinds of dissymmetry by the wide separations of age
and culture. So we have the seemingly unbreachable gaps that will show
up throughout the novel: between the older man and the naive girl; between the European and the American; between high culture and consumerism; and, as the version of this last that is most to the fore, between
true literature and trash. All of these polarities, as they appear in the novel,
have in common a distinction—at least at first sight—between the original and the derivative or the fake. They bring together a wide range of
themes, which might seem to take us too long a way from the vicissitudes
of love and literature, just as these two appear to be distant from the questions of contemporary consumerism and national cultures.

Such are the distinctions that the narrator seems to want to maintain,
in his constant demarcation of his own preoccupation with romantic love
and aesthetic culture, as opposed to Lolita's indifference to these and her
obsession with all of the accoutrements of American consumerism. In this
context, it becomes significant that Lolita is not the first love, but very deliberately—in the order of narration, as well as in the order of the narrator's life—situated as second. She is the follow-up—at once replacement
and perfect version—for the European Annabel Leigh, introduced on the
first page as Lolita's "precursor." Rather than Lolita being the one who
passes away, it is Annabel who actually dies, her ghost returning in the
form of Lolita so that "I broke her spell by incarnating her in another" (17).
The Annabel/Lolita relation, in which it is not clear which is the "true"
love, sets up, from the beginning, the question about orders of priority between pairs of terms that runs throughout the book.

The America from which Lolita emerges is presented as a place of
pseudovalues promoted through how-to-books, movies, magazines, and

consumerism of all kinds, and it is consistently set against the authentic culture of the European outsider. References to techniques for inculcating norms or establishing norms to be inculcated abound. There is the bizarre experiment of the "American ethnologist" (33) in California in which Humbert's former wife and her new man participate; there is the research unit to which the narrator is attached as a "recorder of psychic reactions" (36) soon after he first arrives in the country; and there are the numerous asides against psychoanalysis or psychiatry as methods of diagnosis and cure that operate according to inflexible, mechanically applied standards. Lolita's mother uses a "Know-Your-Child" book (113), and the educational program at the school that Lolita attends in Beardsley is directed toward the acquisition of the skills of "adjustment" with a curriculum summarized like an advertising jingle as "the four D's: Dramatics, Dance, Debating, and Dating" (186) and deliberately cast as a rejection of European cultural priorities: "with due respect to Shakespeare, we want our girls to *communicate* freely with the live world around them rather than plunge into musty old books" (187). Humbert's self-appointed mission to raise the level of Lolita's culture is met with a rejection that implies that the process of institutional conditioning against high culture is in any case unnecessary: "my attempt to refine her pictorial taste was a failure" (210), and "I could never make her read any other books than the so-called comic book or stories in magazines for American females. Any literature a peg higher smacked to her of school" (183).

Humbert always situates himself as having the overview of high and low, of culture and its debased forms, as opposed to the American females, who are identified so completely with the second. So when Lolita's mother, Charlotte, demands details of his former life and lovers, he is able to use this as a strategy:

> Never in my life had I confessed so much or received so many confessions. The sincerity and artlessness with which she discussed what she called her "love-life," from first necking to connubial catch-as-catch-can, were, ethically, in striking contrast with my glib compositions, but technically the two sets were congeneric since both were affected by the same stuff (soap operas, psycho-analysis and cheap novelettes) upon which I drew for my characters and she for her mode of expression. (85)

Charlotte lives entirely in the world imagined by the sensational genres of her culture; the narrator's art, against her "sincerity and artlessness," consists both in superior aesthetics and in the duping he mentions "ethically" as a difference.

This normative culture is manifest at every turn in the travelling across America that occupies much of the space of the novel. In the succession of motels, diners, museums, and movies, the narrator suggests that there is nothing to be seen but a perfectly predictable standardization amid the semblance of variety produced by equally homogeneous publicity:

> We came to know—*nous connûmes*, to use a Flaubertian intonation—the stone cottages under enormous Chateaubriandesque trees, the brick unit, the adobe unit, the stucco court, on what the Tour Book of the Automobile Association describes as "shaded" or "spacious" or "landscaped" grounds. . . .
>
> *Nous connûmes* (this is royal fun) the would-be enticements of their repetitious names—all those Sunset Motels, U-beam Cottages, Hillcrest Courts, Pine View Courts, Mountain View Courts, Skyline Courts, Park Plaza Courts, Green Acres, Mac's Courts. There was sometimes a special line in the write-up, such as "Children welcome, pets allowed" (*You* are welcome, *you* are allowed). (153–54)

The self-consciously Flaubertian and even more self-consciously "Chateaubriandesque" references that frame the description reinforce the assumed difference from the literature of the tourguide, the equivalent American aesthetic being the offer of the landscape as a "landscaped" place to stay. Seriality—"their repetitious names"—goes with verbal appeals whose worthlessly "would-be" status appears to be self-evident.

The account of the trip then comes to resemble a shopping list of things that can be dutifully checked off once each purchase is completed: "The various items of a scenic drive. Hundreds of scenic drives, thousands of Bear Creeks, Soda Springs, Painted Canyons. Texas, a drought-struck plain. Crystal Chamber in the longest cave in the world" (165). The different stages of the prescribed itinerary are thus all on the same plane, distinguished only insofar as they are amenable to being arbitrarily designated as different from anything else:

> The object in view might be anything—a lighthouse in Virginia, a natural cave in Arkansas converted to a café, a collection of guns and violins somewhere in Oklahoma, a replica of the Grotto of Lourdes in Louisiana, shabby photographs of the bonanza mining period in the local museum of a Rocky Mountains resort, anything whatsoever. (160)

Set alongside each other in this way, all of the items can be represented as unique and therefore of value, "worth the visit." Roland Barthes describes the operation of this logic in photography, which to begin with "photographs the noteworthy . . . but soon, by a familiar reversal, it decrees as noteworthy what it photographs."[23] In the passage above, the Lourdes "replica" and "shabby photographs" take this a stage further by suggesting that the copy becomes the object of interest in its own right.[24]

It appears at first sight as though this secondariness of simulation might apply only and characteristically to the American scene, which is contrasted, for instance, to the real Lourdes of France, to a Europe that is viewed other than by the standards—the norms and the serial repetitions—of America. But the Europe that seems to figure as a backcloth of authenticity to this artificially "scenic drive" through the theme park of the New World is also shown as complicit in this construction of America:

> By a paradox of pictorial thought, the average lowland North-American countryside had at first seemed to me something I accepted with a shock of amused recognition because of those painted oilcloths which were imported from America in the old days to be hung above washstands in Central European nurseries. (160)

The correction to this initial view, American in origin but European in its mediated context of reception, is not a true, unbiased view but a sense of "Claude Lorrain clouds" or "a stern El Greco horizon . . . somewhere in Kansas" (161), both perspectives equally filtered through European aesthetic stereotypes.

This conversion from American kitsch to European art as a frame in which to see the American landscape acknowledges that the mode of viewing is relative to a culturally informed predisposition, but it still maintains unchallenged the opposition of value between high and low art and between the New and the Old Worlds. Yet the account of Humbert's early years completely blows apart this distinction by depicting a slice of Europe that is as much a place of images and consumerism as the America he will later discover. His father owns "a luxurious hotel on the Riviera," and he has a mother described, in a word that both exemplifies and gives priority to the significance of images in relation to their subjects, as "very photogenic" (11). Her death "in a freak accident (picnic, lightning)" is placed in the generic context of a sensational news story, a formulaic "tragedy" rather than a tragedy, along the lines of those Humbert will condescendingly summarize as the stuff of Lolita's trash reading.

What the crossings of American and European images suggest is that the European side cannot maintain its status as a place of origin, or rather, that this value accrues to it only insofar as the perceived secondariness of the New World and its culture of seriality and simulation is necessary to the postulation of Europe's priority and authenticity. These qualities then themselves become effects produced only in relation to this initial assumption of America-the-reproducible. If this structure is particularly evident in the fantasies of tourism, it can also be seen in the book's fascination throughout, as a theme and in its own use of language and narrative forms, with questions of literature and genre.

Ostensibly, the division is clear-cut between high and low literature, with the narrator setting himself up as the representative of the European literary tradition—both by the constant erudite references and in his professional work as a writer of scholarly papers and histories of poetry. Clare Quilty, the playwright who is Humbert's rival for Lolita, is opposed to this in every respect: he is American, popular, famous, and contemporary in his productions. At the same time, the distance that separates Humbert from Lolita is measured not just in terms of age but in his conception of her according to the whole European tradition of poetic idealization of the beloved woman, from Virgil and Catullus onward, against which is set her absorption in the sentiment and melodrama of magazine stories and her indifference to his attempts to "raise" her level.

The plot draws loudly on Proust. Just as Albertine comes after Gilberte, the childhood sweetheart, so Lolita is second to Annabel. After Lolita's departure, there are direct allusions to the comparable situation in Proust: where one book of *A la recherche du temps perdu* is called *Albertine disparue,* Humbert muses about calling one part of his *Dolorés Disparue* (267); where another is named *La Fugitive,* so is Lolita (217). Alongside this, and as though to mark the distance all the more intransigently, the novel also includes numerous references to the plots of American movies and magazine stories. Unlike the European works mentioned, these are never represented as having a particular author. Instead, they are defined in terms of a formulaic resemblance, which makes them wholly predictable and, by implication, undistinguished. At one point, on the basis of the "one hundred and fifty or two hundred programs" seen in the first year of traveling around, Humbert proceeds to give summaries of the standard plots of Lolita's three favorite genres:

> musicals, underworlders, westerners. In the first, real singers and dancers had unreal stage careers in an essentially grief-proof sphere of existence wherefrom death and truth were banned and where, at the end, white-haired, dewy-eyed, technically deathless, the initially reluctant father of a show-crazy girl always finished by applauding her apotheosis on fabulous Broadway. (179)

Similar treatment is then given to "underworlders" and "westerners"; in the case of the musicals, it seems obvious that the narrator is tetchily asserting the superior artistic value of "death and truth" as that which is categorically unacceptable for the "unreal" wish-fulfilling plot of the film.

Throughout the journeying across the continent, the narrator shows his distance from American culture partly by scattering in-jokes and impossible coincidences, which turn out to be a foretaste of the game he will play in the chase with Lolita's abductor, Quilty, who leaves verbal clues all over the place. Key words like "haze," "quilt," and "enchanted" (from the name of the inn where he spends his first night with Lolita) keep appearing. The world seems to shrink to a place where everyone has some direct connection to everyone else, and so they encounter "an elderly, but still repulsively handsome White Russian, a baron they said . . . who had known in California good old Maximovich and Valeria" (164), Humbert's first wife and her new husband, last encountered back in Paris.

But this puzzle feature indicates too that we should perhaps be wary of adhering too readily to the distinctions between the literary and the vulgar or the cultured and the consumerly, which the novel seems to be encouraging us to make on Humbert's authority. Literature as no more than quiz-style wordplay has none of the poignant or pretentious associations of literature as a great continental tradition of poetic passion.

There are many other ways in which *Lolita* does not sustain its apparent literary distinctions. At the level of specific incidents, there are many moments when the forms and fantasies of film are invoked without the polemical distance that sets them apart from the narrator in other places. For instance, on the night in the Enchanted Hunters: "I seemed to have shed my clothes and slipped into pyjamas with the kind of fantastic instantaneousness which is implied when in a cinematographic scene the process of changing is cut" (135). A mode of narration peculiar to film is used not as an example of the lack of realism or truth, but rather the reverse, as the frame in which to understand an experience whose reality is itself shaped by film. Again, "the davenport scene" (66) earlier is given a deliberately filmic turn: "nothing prevented me from repeating a performance that affected her as little as if she were a photographic image rippling upon a scene and I a humble hunchback abusing myself in the dark" (66). On the one hand, the cinematic parallel accentuates both the inaccessibility and the continuing intactness of Lolita; on the other hand, it produces the cinema as the modern medium for picturing the image of the feminine ideal. In a parody of the mechanical element, Humbert then makes the whole episode into a technological recording, repeatable any number of times and suspended indeterminately amid a past, present, and future indistinguishable from one another.

The cinematic frame gives Humbert a representation of himself as both spectator and performer, and this is a structure that recurs numerous times in the novel. In this passage, Humbert, the resident of the small town of Beardsley, projects himself as a series of viewers curious about himself:

> I used to review the concluded day by checking my own image as it prowled rather than passed before the mind's red eye. I watched dark-and-handsome, not un-Celtic, probably very high-church, Dr. Humbert see his daughter off to school. I watched him greet with his slow smile and pleasantly arched thick black ad-eyebrows good Mrs. Holigan, who smelled of the plague (and would head, I knew, for master's gin at the first opportunity). With Mr. West, retired executioner or writer of religious tracts—who cared?—I saw neighbor what's his name, I think they are French or Swiss, meditate in his frank-windowed study over a typewriter, rather gaunt-profiled, an almost Hitlerian cowlick on his pale brow. (198)

And so on for another page, culminating with "letting in a queerly observant schoolmate of Dolly's: 'First time I've seen a man wearing a smoking jacket, sir—except in movies, of course'" (199).

For Humbert, as much as for Lolita's friend, cultural types are the model for placing someone, identifying them according to familiar parameters. Whether fascistically "gaunt-profiled" or seductively reproducing the ideal of the "dark-and-handsome" or the "ad-eyebrows" blessed with three further adjectives, Humbert's self-surveillance involves looking at himself as the image of the screen character with which he can be safely identified.

Everyone in the novel is seen and evaluated, and sees and evaluates themselves, at two removes or more, according to their acting of parts copied from parts acted in movies or bestselling stories. Charlotte engages in "a make-believe conversation about a fake book about some popular fraud" (46). A similar accumulation of artifice characterizes Lolita's behavior; hers looks nothing but a weak derivative of an already weak model as she rushes into his arms with her "innocent game . . . in imitation of some simulacrum of fake romance" (119). The four levels of this—from romance to fake to simulacrum to imitation—leave the hypothesis of nonfaked romance looking like a very dead letter beneath the successive layers of masquerade. But Humbert himself is always part of the same show, knowingly acting up, appealing to Lolita with his movie-star good looks and to her mother with consciously simulated "old-world politeness" (41), put on in identification with her American fantasy of Europe.

In a similar fashion, the overall plot of *Lolita* is copied as much from the world of the movies as from the more venerable European literary tradition from which it seems at first to take its direction. The farcical side of the double chase in which first Humbert is pursued by Quilty and then Quilty by Humbert is in part, of course, a parody of the "low" genres of the thriller or detective novel, and the narrator seems to be keeping himself well above them:

> I now warn the reader not to mock me and my mental daze. It is easy for him and me to decipher *now* a past destiny; but a destiny in the making is, believe me, not one of those honest mystery stories where all you have to do is keep an eye on the clues. (222)

But the various doublings also have the effect of making a mockery of the supposedly original romantic story and troubling the security of the narrator's ironic distance. The Quilty subplot, with its exaggerated male rivalry and reversals, functions as the comedy to the tragedy of the main story. As the popular, successful writer, living his flamboyantly debauched his life in his *Playboy*-style mansion, Quilty is at once Humbert's double—they are both addicts of sex and literature, and they each pursue the other—and the one who serves to undercut the ideals of the pedantic high-culture critic by manifesting them in a satirically low form. The symmetry in the positions of Quilty and Humbert, both in turns the pursuer and the pursued, puts them on a level; by bringing to the fore the rivalry between the two men, it also relegates Lolita to the status of an object of exchange, the contingent occasion for their competition. This trivialization matches the way that the time with Lolita is repeated almost stage for stage with the homophonic but otherwise completely unresembling Rita (Humbert lives with her for two years and drives all around America with her).

That there is more than a hint of self-parody in these aspects of the plot is suggested from the other side by the details Humbert gives of his own literary activities:

> I switched to English literature, where so many frustrated poets end as pipe-smoking teachers in tweeds. . . . I published tortuous essays in obscure journals. I composed pastiches. . . .
>
> A paper of mine entitled "The Proustian theme in a letter from Keats to Benjamin Bailey" was chuckled over by the six or seven scholars who read it. (18)

Knowledge of literature is not sacrosanct: it can be played around with for fun and deployed as a professional skill like any other (writing textbooks and college teaching).

For, in spite of all of the narrator's protestations to the contrary, the driving force of the novel's language, what pushes it from one motel to the next and through all the vicissitudes of the impossible search for Lolita, is not so much its recognizable continuation of a literary tradition as its incorporation into the mass-cultural modes that make up Lolita's American world. After her disappearance, there is a moment where Humbert gets rid of "an accumulation of teen-magazines" (267) from the car:

> You know the sort. Stone age at heart; up to date, or at least Mycenaean, as to hygiene. A handsome, very ripe actress with huge lashes and a pulpy red underlip, endorsing a shampoo. Ads and fads. . . . Invite Romance by wearing the exciting New Tummy Flattener. Trims tums, nips hips. Tristram in Movielove. Yessir! The Joe-Roe marital enigma is making yaps flap. Glamorize yourself quickly and inexpensively. Comics. Bad girl dark hair fat father cigar; good girl red hair handsome daddums clipped moustache. Or that repulsive strip with the big gaggoon and his wife, a kiddoid gnomide. *Et moi qui t'offrait mon génie.* . . . I recalled the rather charming nonsense verse I used to write her when she was a child: "nonsense," she used to say mockingly, "is correct." (267–68; emphasis and second ellipses in original)

The sentence preciously marked off in French sits pathetically with the poem in celebration of advertising language that surrounds it; neither the supposed proffering of a nebulous *génie* nor the distance-taking "you know the sort" at the start can make any appeal against the vitality of the catch phrases and "nonsense," which works through a racy pleasure in verbal play of all kinds.

Over and over again, the language of consumption, which on the surface is spurned as obviously inferior to the traditions of great literature, seems to take over the poetic force of the novel as though against the grain of the narrator's own intentions. In one sense this is presented as an identification with Lolita's own desires, so that in the afternoon prior to picking her up from summer camp, the fascination with the girl is shifted by an easy transfer onto "buying beautiful things for Lo":

> Goodness, what crazy purchases were prompted by the poignant predilection Humbert had in those days for check weaves, bright cottons, frills, puffed-out short sleeves, soft pleats, snug-fitting bodices and generously full skirts! Oh, Lolita, you are my girl, as Vee was Poe's and Bea Dante's, and what little girl would not like to whirl in a circular skirt and scanties? (113)

The alliteration of *p*, followed by the fashion-item list of fetishistic details in the style of magazine copy and then the concluding apostrophe, is perfect in its rhythmic precision, which naughtily makes "Dante's" the cue for "scanties" so that the esteemed literary lovers are effortlessly elevated or pulled down (by now, the two are indistiguishable) onto the dance floor of American teen culture.

But the poetic speed of consumption also mutates into its opposite, a state of tranquil suspension, underwater slow motion. The noisy jingle metamorphoses into a silently timeless still life, a "quiet poetical afternoon of fastidious shopping" (114):

> There is a touch of the mythological and the enchanted in those large stores where according to ads a career girl can get a complete desk-to-desk wardrobe, and where little sister can dream of the day when her wool jersey will make the boys in the back row of the classroom drool. Lifesize plastic figures of snubbed-nosed children with dun-colored, greenish, brown-dotted, faunish faces floated around me. I realized I was the only shopper in that rather eerie place where I moved about fish-like, in a glaucous aquarium. I sensed strange thoughts form in the minds of the languid ladies that escorted me from counter to counter, from rock ledge to seaweed, and the belts and the bracelets I chose seemed to fall from siren hands into transparent water. (114)

There is a distant resurfacing here of Proust's dining room in the hotel at Balbec, seen by the outsiders peering in through the windows as an aquarium of slow, magical consumption. Here, on the inside, the "eerie" atmosphere derives partly from the narrator's being out of place as a man in the women's department, but also from the literal fulfillment of the fantasy that the appeals of consumption constantly promote: this is just for you, you are the only shopper in the world, and far from you having to do anything to obtain them, the goods will simply float effortlessly into your hands.

Elsewhere the language of consumption is focused more directly on the figure of Lolita herself, an appreciatively responsive reader:

> A great user of roadside facilities, my unfastidious Lo would be charmed by toilet signs—Guys-Gals, John-Jane, Jack-Jill and even Buck's-Doe's; while lost in an artist's dream, I would stare at the honest brightness of the gasoline paraphernalia against the splendid green of oaks, or at a distant hill scrambling out—scarred but still untamed—from the wilderness of agriculture that was trying to swallow it. (161)

Here the parody of the poet *manqué* is open, as he turns away from modern necessities to find tired clichés of romanticism in the surrounding landscape, while Lo can be "charmed" by the appurtenances of words that cover the functionally basic, the very lowest of needs, with all the variants of a cutesy kitsch.

The culmination of this ambivalent celebration of Lolita as the poetic consumer occurs at the end of another sequence of the verbal offers to which she so perfectly responds:

> She believed, with a kind of celestrial trust, any advertisement or advice that appeared in *Movie Love* or *Screen Land*—Starasil Starves Pimples, or "You better watch out if you're wearing your shirt-tails outside your jeans, gals, because Jill says you shouldn't." If a roadside sign said VISIT OUR GIFT SHOP—we *had* to visit it, *had* to buy its Indian curios, dolls, copper jewelry, cactus candy. The words "novelties and souvenirs" simply entranced her by their trochaic lilt. If some café sign proclaimed Icecold Drinks, she was automatically stirred, although all drinks everywhere were ice-cold. She it was to whom ads were dedicated: the ideal consumer, the subject and object of every foul poster. (156)

It is Lolita who is the poetic reader, indifferent to things in themselves and entranced by the words that shape them into the image of a desire that consumption then perfectly satisfies. Appearing under the sign of "novelties and souvenirs," anything can be transmuted through that "trochaic lilt" into an object of interest, worth attention. It is the narrator who prosaically refuses the fascination with words in themselves or words as molding the promise of a pleasure for which a referent might then be found, as he stubbornly rejects the promise of the "Icecold" in favor of a purely informational theory of language, which suggests that words and their objects exist in an unvariable twinning of simple denomination.

This fascination with Lolita as the ideal consumer, the American girl par excellence, becomes the measure of her inaccessibility to Humbert, whose distance in this respect is signaled by his insistence on his own separation from the world that is Lolita's. The language of consumption is represented as being at once the culmination of the poetic tradition and a reprehensible attempt to imitate it. The infiltration of high and low languages goes in both directions, so that advertising interferes with the purity of poetry, but at the same time poetry acquires its modern form in the everyday aestheticization of a culture of images.

These tensions are intimately bound up with the framing narrative of the book, somewhere between a legal defense and a psychiatric case history, in which the narrator purports to be accounting for what he did to Lolita. In this text, it is not the woman but the masculine narrator whose sanity is in question, and the early period of his life is reconstructed as a conscious series of pre-Lolitas leading up to the girl herself as perverse fulfillment of the condition that must be satisfied in order for him to desire. Annabel Leigh, the first love, who dies, immobilizes his desire in the image of a pubescent beauty doomed to end, and it is she who will come to figure as the poetic ideal impossible to attain in reality. Annabel's desires are perfectly in harmony with the boy's; nothing comes between them except the normal constraints of grown-up intruders and the exceptional curtailment of her untimely disappearance.

Valeria, the temporary wife, is represented, as Charlotte Haze will be later and, to some extent, Rita too, as of no particular erotic interest, serving only as a decoy or fall-back for the continuing quest to recover and possess in Annabel/Lolita. But between Annabel and Valeria is the Paris streetwalker whose distinctive walk evokes something of "the nymphic echo" (24). Monique is poised halfway between Annabel and Lolita in other ways than biographically. Like Annabel, she is not significantly different in age from Humbert, and there is a degree of shared pleasure, so that "my last vision that night of long-lashed Monique is touched up with a gaiety that I find seldom associated with any event in my humiliating, sordid, taciturn love life" (25). But at the same time, like Lolita, Monique is a protoconsumer:

> She looked tremendously pleased with the bonus of fifty I gave her as she trotted out into the April night drizzle with Humbert Humbert lumbering in her narrow wake. Stopping before a window display she said with great gusto: *"je vais m'acheter des bas!"* and never may I forget the way her Parisian childish lips exploded on *"bas,"* pronouncing it with an appetite that all but changed the "a" into a brief buoyant bursting as in *"bot."* (25)

The frank exchange of money for love here endows Monique with the power to satisfy her "appetite" as a consumer of *"des bas"*—combining the femininity of stockings as an article of narcissistic adornment, hugging the skin, with the "low" emphasis, which descends even further in the climactic *bot* of the foot. After this, Monique loses for Humbert what she gains for herself: their next date "was less successful, she seemed to have grown less juvenile, more of a woman overnight" (25).

It is "low" consumption that both makes this girl a woman and puts her at a distance from the man by providing another source of satisfaction. In being not (yet) a woman, but absolutely a consumer, Lolita then represents for Humbert another version of this division between the purity of prewomanhood and the baseness of consumption. She herself is wholly and simply the narcissistic girl-consumer, sexually neither pure nor mature (these are not the categories that make sense from her point of view). Humbert's crime, as he recognizes, is to breach her self-containment by introducing his own, utterly incompatible terms of desire. Before the first night he sleeps with her, Humbert clearly declares that their respective scenarios are not the same:

> Since (as the psychotherapist, as well as the rapist, will tell you) the limits and rules of such girlish games are fluid, or at least too childishly subtle for the senior partner to grasp—I was dreadfully afraid I might go too far and cause her to start back in revulsion and terror. (119)

The acknowledgment is pragmatic rather than principled: it does not detract from his being "agonizingly anxious to smuggle her into the hermetic seclusion of The Enchanted Hunter" (119).

In the explicit separation it invokes, this scene replays and extends the one in which Humbert masturbates on the sofa in her mother's house with an oblivious Lolita: "What I had madly possessed was not she but my own creation, another, fanciful Lolita; . . . The child knew nothing" (66). The difference between the "senior partner" and the "child" is that one is aware of the difference, of the double perspective, and the other has no access to it. There is fantasy on each side—on Humbert's, for his poetic nymphet embodied in the modern American image of the girl; on Lolita's, for the movie-star hero resembling Humbert whose picture she pins to her bedroom wall—but Lolita's has none of the insistence and exclusiveness of his. The problem is not that such a discrepancy should exist at all (to imagine that it might not, that fantasies are normally or even ideally complementary, would be to accept, on the model of Lolita's high-school training, that human communication is normally faultless). Humbert's crime is to force his version on Lolita in a way that deprives her irrevocably of her "girlish games" (119) and their ordinary sequels, happy or not.

It is only after this violation that Lolita starts to bargain, as though in acknowledgment that only money can serve provisionally as a regulating standard between the otherwise incommensurable positions in which she and her "father" are situated. If he can have her, she can have whatever she wants that money can buy. This is the forced contract that is instigated by the array of goods that Humbert buys Lolita on the "quiet poetical afternoon of fastidious shopping" (114) before he goes to fetch her from the camp; the bribe is followed, the next day, by the compensation, the first of Humbert's numerous lists of commodities:

I bought her four books of comics, a box of candy, a box of sanitary pads, two cokes, a manicure set, a travel clock with a luminous dial, a ring with a real topaz, a tennis racket, roller skates with white high shoes, field glasses, a portable radio set, chewing gum, a transparent raincoat, sunglasses, some more garments—swooners, shorts, all kinds of summer frocks. At the hotel we had separate rooms, but in the middle of the night she came sobbing into mine, and we made it up very gently. You see, she had absolutely nowhere else to go. (149)

Here the bare list of things almost unadorned by adjectives or amplifications, just the necessary equipment for the motoring tour to come, is already some way from the dreamy strangeness of the previous afternoon, "a touch of the mythological and the enchanted in those large stores" (114).

*Lolita* demonstrates—more enchantingly perhaps than any other novel—that advertising has its poetry, that far from being incompatible, advertising language and literary language share an assumption that objects of all kinds acquire their desirability through the words and the implied stores in which they are represented. There is no separation of form between Humbert's literary world and Lolita's consumerly world; the gap is rather in the incompatibility of the particular wishes and dreams that make them up. Lolita, "as glad as an ad" (170), is the modern attraction for the literary seeker after the latest embodiment of youthful female perfection, but by depriving her prematurely of her "girlish games," he turns her story into something never shown in the happy world of advertisements.

### Notes

1. Vladimir Nabokov, *Lolita* (1955; rpt. London: Corgi, 1969), 342, 341. All further references will appear in the text.

2. Because it had failed to secure an American publisher, *Lolita* was initially published by the Olympia Press; it came out in the United States in 1958 and in Britain in 1959 (it was reprinted by Weidenfeld four times in the first year). The comparison with the fate of *Lady Chatterley's Lover* is direct, since both were considered as possible test cases in the light of the new Obscene Publications Act. In *Offensive Literature: Decensorship in Britain 1960–1982* (London: Junction, 1982) 28–29, John Sutherland suggests that there were two reasons that Lawrence's novel, rather than Nabokov's, was prosecuted: the "four-letter words" and the proposed cheap publication by Penguin (the Corgi paperback of *Lolita* appeared later, in 1961).

3. See Claude Lévi-Strauss, *Structure élémentaires de la parenté* (1949), trans. James

Harle Bell, John Richard von Strumer, and Rodney Needham as *Elementary Structures of Kinship* (Boston: Beacon, 1961).

4. Lionel Trilling, review of *Lolita* in *Encounter* (Oct. 1958), cited in Norman Page, ed., *Nabokov: The Critical Heritage* (London: Routledge and Kegan Paul, 1982), 92–102. Denis de Rougemont, *L'Amour et l'occident* (1939), trans. Montgomery Belgion as *Love in the Western World* (1956; rpt. Princeton, N.J.: Princeton University Press, 1983); and *Les Mythes de l'amour* (1961; rpt. Paris: Gallimard, 1978), 53–64.

5. "Omne fulit punctum qui miscuit utile dulci / lectorem delectando pariterque monendo" (He who mixes what is useful with what is pleasurable gains the whole vote, /By delighting the reader as much as advising him) (Horace *Ars Poetica* 11. 343). Interestingly, the next lines say that this is the kind of book that makes money and gets exported.

6. Gabriel Josipovici, "*Lolita:* Parody and the Pursuit of Beauty," in Josipovici's *The World and the Book: A Study of Modern Fiction* (London: Macmillan, 1971), 214–15.

7. David Packman, *Vladimir Nabokov: The Structure of Literary Desire* (Columbia: University of Missouri Press, 1982), 53.

8. Rodney Giblett, "Writing Sexuality, Reading Pleasure," *Paragraph* 12, no. 3 (1989): 233.

9. Ibid., 236.

10. Elizabeth Dipple, *The Unresolvable Plot: Reading Contemporary Fiction* (New York: Routledge, 1988), 74.

11. Ibid., 82.

12. Ibid.

13. Linda Kauffman, "Framing *Lolita:* Is There a Woman in the Text?" in Patricia Jaeger and Beth Kowaleski-Wallace, eds., *Refiguring the Father: New Feminist Readings of Patriarchy* (Carbondale: University of Illinois Press, 1989), 131–52.

14. Ibid., 133.

15. Ibid., 148.

16. Ibid., 141.

17. Dana Brand, "The Interaction of Aestheticism and American Consumer Culture in Nabokov's *Lolita*," *Modern Language Studies* 17, no. 2 (Spring 1987): 14–21.

18. Ibid., 14.

19. Ibid., 16–17.

20. On theories of the way that advertisements are supposed to operate on their readers or viewers, see chap. 7, "Make Up Your Mind," in Rachel Bowlby, *Shopping with Freud* (London: Routledge, 1993), 94–119.

21. For more on the figure of the *passante,* see "Walking, Women and Writing" and "P/S," chaps. 1 and 3 of Rachel Bowlby, *Still Crazy after All These Years* (London: Routledge, 1992).

22. See ibid., chap. 9, on Freud's rereading of this story.

23. Roland Barthes, *Camera Lucida: Reflections on Photography,* trans. Richard Howard (London: Jonathan Cape, 1982), 34.

24. At the beginning of Don DeLillo's novel *White Noise* (1984; rpt. New York: Penguin, 1986), 12, this process is further parodied in the fascination with "the most photographed barn in America." The barn could be any barn or anything; the point is simply to take pictures of it.

# Revisiting *Lolita*

MICHAEL WOOD

◆ ◆ ◆

PEOPLE READING NABOKOV'S *Lolita* for the first time are often baffled by their own reactions. Those who haven't read it for a while approach it again nervously, as if afraid of what they will learn about their old attitudes or their old selves. It's not just that the book, the story of the loves, travels, and undoing of Humbert Humbert and Dolores Haze, a middle-aged European man and a twelve-year-old American girl, is funnier than it ought to be and more cruel than we want it to be. Or that Humbert's tacky charm stretches much further than it has any right to. It's that we really don't know where we are, why we are laughing, or what to do with our discomfort. There's also the sense that Lolita, the girl rather than the book, has become part of our language, the name of a condition. But do we know what that condition is?

Nabokov's *Lolita* appeared in Paris (in English, published by Olympia Press) in 1955 but then was banned in France the following year, apparently because of complaints from the British embassy that too many susceptible tourists were buying it and smuggling it home. The ban was lifted three years later. Excerpts from *Lolita* were printed in the *Anchor Review* in 1957, but the book was not published in full in the United States until 1958 and in the United Kingdom until 1959. It instantly became a bestseller, remaining at the top of the American list for six months "until displaced," as

Norman Page puts it in *Nabokov: The Critical Heritage,* from which I take most of these details, "by Pasternak's *Dr. Zhivago.*"

Meanwhile the book had been much read in its Paris edition and much discussed. Graham Greene told the readers of the London *Sunday Times* that it was one of the best books of 1955, while John Gordon of the London *Sunday Express* found it to be "sheer unrestrained pornography." When the book finally appeared in the United States, Orville Prescott in the *New York Times* occupied the cultural high ground by craftily placing literary taste before morality, or perhaps by confusing the two:

> *Lolita,* then, is undeniably news in the world of books. Unfortunately, it is bad news. There are two equally serious reasons why it isn't worth any adult reader's attention. The first is that it is dull, dull, dull in a pretentious, florid and archly fatuous fashion. The second is that it is repulsive.

Another kind of high ground was occupied by the twenty-one signers of a 1959 letter to the London *Times,*[1] who were

> disturbed by the suggestion that it may yet prove impossible to have an English edition of Vladimir Nabokov's *Lolita.* Our opinions of the merit of the book differ widely, but we think it would be deplorable if a book of considerable literary interest, which has been favourably received by critics and widely praised in serious and respectable periodicals, were to be denied an appearance in this country.

This is pretty stuffy too in its way—not much hope for great books that are unfavorably received and don't have respectable folks on their side—and Dorothy Parker's militant exuberance is more cheering. Writing in *Esquire,* she said she couldn't regard *Lolita* as pornography, "either sheer, unrestrained, or any other kind." It was

> an anguished book, but sometimes wildly funny. . . . [Nabokov's] command of the language is absolute, and his *Lolita* is a fine book, a distinguished book—alright then—a great book. And how are you, John Gordon Esq., of the London *Sunday Express*?

THEN THINGS CALMED down a bit, as *Lolita* became respectable, even a classic, much translated, reprinted many times, taught in literature courses all over the world, made into a funny but quite unscandalous film by Stanley Kubrick. Now there is a new stir, caused by the non-arrival on American screens of Adrian Lyne's film of *Lolita* and by the eagerness of certain conservative columnists in the United Kingdom to get the film banned there. The work, completed in 1997, was released in Italy, Germany, and France, and is scheduled for release in Britain in May, but as yet no American distributor has taken it on or currently seems likely to. Various none-too-convincing reasons are given for this lack of interest: the film is too long, too expensive, not good enough. Could the subject have something to do with it? [Ed. note: Lyne's movie premiered at a film festival in Spain in September 1997. After its release in the United Kingdom in 1998, it still had not found a movie distributor in the United States. Instead, the cable network Showtime bought the American rights to the film and broadcast it to U.S. television audiences in August 1998.]

Celestine Bohlen, writing in the *New York Times*, suggested that the difficulty was not pedophilia in itself, which is quite widely discussed, but the film's "multidimensional portrait of a pedophile." "What people find troubling in America," Adrian Lyne says, quoted by Bohlen, "is that they like Humbert Humbert and they don't want to." "Like" may be putting it a bit strongly, but certainly the complication of our feelings about Humbert is an important feature of any response to the novel and to both of the movies made from it. Lyne also insists that Humbert, along with Lolita and Clare Quilty, the man who steals Lolita from Humbert, gets his comeuppance. "No one comes well out if it," Lyne told Richard Covington of the *Los Angeles Times.* "They all die, for chrissake."

I saw the film in Paris, in a small but fairly fancy movie theater on the Left Bank (14 Juillet-Odéon, seats you can sink into, screen high on the wall in front of you), but it was showing all over the city, in both French- and English-language versions. The theater was not full, and the audience seemed neither excited nor outraged: it was just a movie. The reviewers' reaction in France has been similar, although some critics, *cinéastes* to the core, have seen the film as an offense not against morality but against Stanley Kubrick.

In general, European reactions to the film have been quiet, although there was some real enthusiasm in Italy, putting Nabokov's novel back on the bestseller lists; and there was a move to boycott the film in Munich, on the grounds that it makes pedophilia socially acceptable, *salonfähig*, the equivalent of a criminal you wouldn't mind inviting to dinner. One in every four girls in Bavaria, a leaflet distributed outside cinemas said, has been sexually abused before she is sixteen. And of course Europeans were shaken by pedophilic murders in Belgium and by a huge child pornography ring in France. A few years back there were so many accusations of child abuse in England that the very idea of childhood began to look like a sexual temptation.

Lyne's film, the Munich leaflet added, shows the seducer as a victim and the victim as a seducer. This is true. It invites us to sympathize, fairly intensely, with the sorrows of a pedophile. But it doesn't condone his acts, and it doesn't make him into anything resembling a good guy. It also shows the victim as a victim, although in a slightly remote, conventionalized way. The main problem for Lolita, if we believe the images on the screen rather than the film's faint verbal gestures toward her plight, is not that Humbert mistreated her, but that she became a frump after she left him. She used to be fun and now she's a housewife. We might regret this emphasis, and I do, but you have to see the film to arrive at this view, and there is no reason at all for it not to be shown in this country.

Distributors and moviegoers may well have thought they had reason to expect the worst from Adrian Lyne—the difference being that the worst, if by that we mean the scabrous, the sensational, was what they used to want. The very titles of a couple of Lyne's earlier films—*Fatal Attraction, Indecent Proposal*—look like previews for a new offense, if not alternative titles for *Lolita*; and his $9\frac{1}{2}$ *Weeks*, all about sex as risk and risk as sexy, was described by an unkind English critic as "bump and grind for the Porsche owner." Lyne's *Lolita*, by comparison, is downright demure; deeply, almost debilitatingly loyal to Nabokov's novel; shot in lovely pale colors for art's sake; and accompanied by a score from Ennio Morricone that swamps everything in wistful, lyrical melancholy. You can imagine what Jeremy Irons's pained presence as Humbert does to this. Dmitri Nabokov, the novelist's son, finds the film "superb," its only fault a slight excess of fidelity to his father's text.

The difficulties of making a movie from a novel are never quite what they seem—or not only what they seem. It's not just a matter of getting story and characters to come across in a new format, adapted for different time frames and modes of representation. It's a matter of losing words as a medium, the very texture of a language. There are words in films, of course, and you can quote whole chunks of a novel verbatim, as Stephen Schiff's script for Lyne's *Lolita* does. But words are not a medium in film, only a piece of a medium: members of an orchestra, not soloists. This matters more for some novels than for others, and there are all kinds of ways of setting about the problem—directors from Hitchcock to Scorsese have devised brilliant solutions. But Humbert Humbert's language, self-delighting, self-betraying, funny, sickening, and above all endlessly intricate and fluent, is the life of *Lolita*. Without it, we have only a plodding, if fairly powerful melodrama, and paradoxically the less we have of Humbert's language the more we have of his angle: there's only the story line, and the story is his. Lyne's movie, in particular, is Humbert's movie.

Kubrick didn't use very much of the screenplay that Nabokov spent months writing—Nabokov still receives total screen credit—but he quoted generously from the novel, as Lyne does. Mainly, though, Kubrick decided to complicate and send up the melodrama through his actors. He let James Mason as Humbert do his dark, sinister stuff, along with some fine sardonic touches of comedy; he got Shelley Winters, as Charlotte Haze, Lolita's mother, to play up her helpless lack of charm for all it was worth; and he gave Peter Sellers, as Quilty, free rein to turn his whole portion of the movie into a farce with funny accents. Sellers/Quilty also appeared in several other guises in the film, so that the novel's paranoid pattern (Humbert the pervert dogged by another, even more perverted pervert) was nicely duplicated. Sue Lyon as Lolita was the amiable object of desire, lively at times but a little too successful at looking bored.

The total effect was of rather slow-moving black comedy. Nabokov was disappointed to see so much of his labor vanish, but he liked the macabre ping-pong match between Quilty and Humbert and the sight of Mason floating his Scotch in the bathtub, his mouth against the moving glass's edge, happily thinking of Winters's untimely death and his long future with Lolita. Another wonderful moment is Mason reading to himself Winters's declaration of love for him. His amusement is slow in coming, but when it comes, it knows no bounds. It's worth saying that the jokes against Charlotte, in both movies, although often funny, are broad and familiar in their attack, old jokes about lonely and pretentious aging women, and they form an insidious, misogynous part of the pedophile's case for his vice: little girls are not just little girls, they are *not adult females.*

Lyne, however, decided he wanted the melodrama. His film is far from immoral, even apart from the fact that everyone dies. It is a kind of parable against passion, rather like his *Fatal Attraction,* although far more subdued. Humbert as a child loved a girl who died. There is no suggestion here, as there is in the novel, that their passion was unconsummated and that Humbert's problem therefore is a certain kind of incompletion. It's the girl's death that matters, and Jeremy Irons looks suitably haunted from the start. Humbert then moves to America and meets Lolita—weirdly fudged and unmagical, this scene is scarcely intelligible if you don't know the book—and his travails begin. At first tantalizingly unavailable, she becomes his mistress, and he loses her again in the sheer repetitiousness and banality of their sexual life. I've said the film is demure compared with Lyne's other work but it has its share of suggestive gestures—Lolita unties the drawstring on Humbert's pajama trousers, grins, takes out her tooth-brace, grins some more. But what's really shocking in the film is the deterioration of their relationship rather than the sight of their sex acts.

Lolita prostitutes herself with Humbert, vamping him for more pocket money or permission to act in a play, her hand creeping lasciviously up his trouser leg. He hits her violently on two occasions. He grovels, she escapes. The steamiest scene—Lolita sits on Humbert's knee, wearing only his pajama top, her back to him as she reads a comic, both start to move slightly, she sweats, swoons, has an orgasm—seems relatively healthy, since it's only sex, and both are enjoying themselves. I know it isn't healthy, and I don't think it is once I remember her age. But I have to make myself remember this. Her age seems curiously abstract, an idea only. Perhaps this is a fault in the film—or something film can't do. When Lolita's age is mentioned—only once, I think, by the headmistress of her school—she is said to be fourteen. At another point we are shown a hotel sign, which says children under fourteen stay free. I'm sure there are many such signs in the world at large, but in the movie it doesn't have any point unless Lolita is under fourteen.

Dominique Swain as Lolita is appropriately sulky and gawky, and she has a sudden, delayed smile that lights up the whole film whenever it appears. There is a wonderful scene, far better than its equivalent in Kubrick, where she is about to set off for camp with her mother, remembers she hasn't said goodbye to Humbert, and rushes back into the house and up the stairs to do that. She leaps to embrace him, wraps her legs around him—this is before their affair starts, before he imagines there is any chance of an affair—kisses him enthusiastically, and is gone, clattering down the stairs in slow motion, as if she had to be slowed down to be believed. But Lyne has chosen to costume Swain as a very young child, in checks and flounces and ribbons, as if she were scarcely out of the nursery, and to show her most often in plaits and other old-fashioned hair-dos. The effect, curiously, is to make her look like an older girl—Swain was fifteen when the film was shot—disguised as a much younger one, something like Judy Garland as Dorothy in *The Wizard of Oz*, only sexier and sunnier and faster. This does something very strange to the idea of her age.

Jeremy Irons offers a rather low-key, unfreaky Humbert, but he is much more convincing here than he is, say, in Louis Malle's *Damage*, another story of an older man sliding to disaster through sex. The attraction of Irons as an actor is that you can see him suffering, see him thinking, but he's also opaque—he could be thinking about anything, and maybe he's not suffering what we would suffer in his place. His wrecked, bleached looks at the end of the film leave you certain only of the finality of his distress. Frank Langella as Quilty is gross and imposing, although perhaps not quite as sinister as one could wish.

But the real joy of the film's acting is Melanie Griffith as Charlotte. I thought at first, unworthily, that one couldn't go wrong in this role, since Shelley Winters is so memorable too. Then I thought how different Griffith is from Winters, so there's no reason why both shouldn't take full credit for what they do. If Winters is sadly pushy, Griffith is a touch more glamorous, in a tasteless way, but also tougher, and she expresses herself in a flat, all-leveling voice, which is itself a cultural commentary. You can't argue with her because she's not talking to you: she's not talking to anybody, she's simply on the air, broadcasting without a radio. Griffith, even more than Winters, is Nabokov's Charlotte as evoked by F. W. Dupee in the *Anchor Review*: "the immoral moralist, the loveless romantic, the laughless comic—whatever it is that spoils the party and dampens the honeymoon all across America."

All ends badly, of course. Humbert loves Lolita in his abject and clinging way; she loves Quilty ("the only man I was ever really crazy about"), but Quilty throws her out. She is married and pregnant when we and Humbert see her for the last time. Humbert kills Quilty messily. Most European critics have objected to the Grand Guignol quality of this scene—Quilty's piano playing Rachmaninoff even after he's left it, blood sparkling on the keys, Quilty blubbering, wounded, refusing to die—but the real problem is Quilty's irrelevance. This is Humbert's movie; he can suffer enough without Quilty, as long as he loses Lolita one way or another; and Quilty seems to have staggered in from the novel merely to die. Humbert drives away from Quilty's place, drunk and desolate, his old station wagon weaving all over the country road, Morricone's music and a washed-out landscape a perfect complement to his mood. He has oil on his hands from the gun he used, Quilty's blood splattered on his face, one of Lolita's hairpins in his hand.

Police can start to chase him, but he is oblivious. A roadblock looms ahead. He calmly turns off into a field of cows, stops the car, leaves it, still ignoring the cops. He looks down at a town in the valley and imagines he hears (that is, we hear, but see the town is too far away for the sound to come from there) the sound of children playing, and he says to himself, mournfully, these words from the close of the novel: "I knew that the hopelessly poignant thing was not Lolita's absence from my side, but the absence of her voice from that concord." We seem to be beyond guilt here but not beyond misery. This is where passion always ends, the story seems to say: waste and ruin, no one gets what he wants.

At this point Lyne, for all of his fidelity to the novel, makes a move that is its perfect opposite. Nabokov's Humbert claims to love the latest Lolita, the pregnant and married one, to have understood that one must love a person and not just a member of a generic set of little girls. We may not believe him, but this is what he says. Lyne's Humbert, forlorn and still on the edge of the valley, the blood now dry on his face, has a memory flash of the original Lolita, the one he first slept with after her mother died, the one who made the first move, scarcely knowing what she was doing. The Lolita he loves is the one he lost not recently but long ago, maybe in the same moment he possessed her.

LOLITA HAS ESTABLISHED HERSELF in the language but has also suffered a sea change in her shift from novel to general usage. Here is what the current Webster's tells us: "Lolita. *n.* [from *Lolita* (1955) by Vladimir Nabokov] a precociously seductive girl." When *Spy Magazine* in 1999 sought to describe what some people wanted Chelsea Clinton to be, the phrase that presented itself was "a seductress, a Lolita." The context was a set of articles about "the new Lolitocracy," meaning the recent fame and open desirability of some very young girls, especially in sports and in the movies. "In the last five years or so," Damon Trent wrote, "our own civilization has developed a bit of a thing for teenage girls." Alicia Silverstone and Liv Tyler started the trend, according to Trent, but they were a little old, they were women really, and we need to think, he said, about Anna Paquin (ten), Anna Chlumsky (eleven), Christina Ricci (eleven), and Natalie Portman (twelve), who have all had leading roles in recent movies. Portman, it is rumored, turned down the title role in Lyne's *Lolita*. In the same issue of the magazine, Will Self went on at some length about the delights of watching young girl gymnasts and figure skaters.

This was all meant to be (and was) a little naughty and shocking. It seems likely, Trent says, that "every man, woman, and child among us has become a vile, pustulating pedophile." Well, not likely. But in the midst of the malarkey, several interesting things were being said. These girls are not entirely Lolita's in the dictionary's sense: precocious perhaps, but not seductresses. And they are not victims, they are stars. But they are (not quite) sexual objects, which is to say that sexuality, theirs and ours, has become thinkable in relation to these children. Trent has a fine and dangerous comment on what he calls Nabokov's art: "He did more than *investigate* the idea that pubescent girls can be sexually attractive, he proved it." This, it seems to me, could be a stronger reason for American distributors worrying about the movie: not the "multidimensional portrait" of Humbert nor the fact that we may like him, but the possibility that we may understand his desire far better than we want to.

In one sense, we always did. This was what Lionel Trilling meant when he said that Lolita was "not about sex, but about love." F. W. Dupee meant the same thing, I believe, when he suggested that reviewers of the book failed "to see how much of everyone's reality lurks in its shadow play." But this is to say that love is scandalous and to take Humbert's pedophilia as a lurid caricature of passion, an emblem for whatever forms of scandal are closest to us. To say we might begin to understand his pedophilia as pedophilia is a very different thing. Those who won't show or who want to boycott the movie are not right, in my view. But they are not mere stooges of moral correctness either, and they are not talking about nothing.

Of course Humbert is not an ordinary pedophile, and Nabokov's Lolita is not a Lolita. But are there ordinary pedophiles? Isn't this a dangerous notion in itself, and doesn't Humbert, in spite of himself, do us a bit of good by giving the notion such a hard time? He is not interested in little girls, only in some little girls, not even the most beautiful, and certainly not the most seductive ones. The girls who enchant him are hidden among their generation and then magically self-revealing. This definition occurs in the novel and in both movies:

> Between the age limits of nine and fourteen there occur maidens who, to certain bewitched travelers, twice or many times older than they, reveal their true nature which is not human, but nymphic (that is, demoniac); and these chosen creatures I propose to designate as "nymphets." . . . Within the same age limits the number of true nymphets is strikingly inferior to that of provisionally plain, or just nice, or "cute," or even "sweet" and "attractive," ordinary, plumpish, formless, cold-skinned, essentially human little girls, with tummies and pigtails, who may or may not turn into adults of great beauty.

The age of the beholder is important too, as well as his eye: "There must be a gap of several years, never less than ten I should say, generally thirty or forty, and as many as ninety in a few known cases, between maiden and man to enable the latter to come under a nymphet's spell." "As many as ninety" is either Humbert teasing us or Nabokov pulling the rug from under Humbert, but for the rest we have to take Humbert's lyrical pedantry quite seriously. He is inviting us to pick out the nymphets among the other girls, and it is disturbing to find we half-believe we can. I start to think, for instance, that neither Sue Lyon in Kubrick's film nor Dominique

Swain in Lyne's is really a nymphet, that both are "essentially human," that their considerable attractions are too "normal," not secret or demonic enough. But how could I be thinking this? How do I know what a nymphet is? Would Humbert and I agree on a set of sample cases? It is, I think, because we imagine Lolita as special and demonic in our own terms, an unearthly creature masked by her American ordinariness, with an eerie identity far more fetching than mere beauty, that the book is more shocking than either of the movies, or than a movie could be. This is the girl Humbert violates, not someone else's image on a screen.

BUT WHY IS LOLITA not a "Lolita"? This is the moral crux of the novel. I think, and neither film manages to get a focus on it. It's not encouraging either that usage and the dictionary take Humbert's word for what is happening and that "abused child" does not seem to be among the current meanings of "Lolita." You will remember that Humbert claims not to have seduced his stepdaughter (although he certainly planned to) but to have been seduced by her: "Sensitive gentlewomen of the jury, I was not even her first lover." Humbert's pompous disapproval of the very sexual act he has so enjoyed is a masterpiece of hypocrisy and surely forms part of the case for the prosecution rather than the defense. Lolita, in bed with Humbert, suggests they play a game involving the activities she has learned at summer camp. "I shall not," Humbert says:

> bore my learned readers with a detailed account of Lolita's presumption. Suffice it to say that not a trace of modesty did I perceive in this beautiful hardly formed young girl whom modern co-education, juvenile mores, the campfire racket and so forth had utterly and hopelessly depraved.

"Naive as only a pervert can be" is the way Humbert has previously described himself, but this is the pervert as traditionalist, shocked to discover that the girl is not the picture of innocence he was so looking forward to corrupting. If there is any depraving going on, he wants to do it. This is one of the side effects of liberal modern ways: they spoil the pleasures of old-fashioned vice. Humbert, like the pedophile in A. M. Homes's novel *The End of Alice*, is a "classicist" in these and other matters.

THE DIFFICULTY WITH *Lolita* is not that it is an immoral book, but that it is soaked in Humbert's morality, that it leaves us scarcely anywhere else to go. Humbert plays with the idea that the distaste for pedophilia is mere local cultural prejudice, invoking Dante, Petrarch, and Poe as his noble predecessors. Mainly, though, he believes pedophilia is a heinous sin—at one point he speaks of "a world of total evil"—and that's why he likes it. He knows his Baudelaire, is fond of quoting "L'Invitation au voyage," and has almost certainly read the extraordinary passage in the notebooks where Baudelaire asserts that the only pleasure, *l'unique volupté*, lies in the certainty of doing evil. "The only pleasure" must be something of an exaggeration, but you'd have to be really perverted not to know what Baudelaire and Humbert are talking about.

On the face of it there appear to be only three ways of thinking about the moral question in Nabokov's *Lolita*, all of them unattractive. There is, chiefly and most noisily, Humbert's view, that of the Dostoevskyan sinner who finds repentance, if anything, even more fun than the original sinning—especially since he has lost the girl and has only his repentance left, along with some three hundred pages of lip-smacking memories. The second way is set up only to be laughed at.

We do laugh, although maybe a little uneasily. The book, ostensibly Humbert's memoir, is introduced by one John Ray, Jr., Ph.D., a psychologist with a smooth line in platitudes and a taste for semicolons. Here is how Ray's foreword ends:

> As a case history, "Lolita" will become, no doubt, a classic in psychiatric circles. As a work of art, it transcends its expiatory aspects; and still more important to us than scientific significance and literary worth, is the ethical impact the book should have on the serious reader; for in this poignant personal study there lurks a general lesson; the wayward child, the egotistic mother, the panting maniac—these are not only vivid characters in a unique story: they warn us of dangerous trends; they point out potent evils. "Lolita" should make all of us—parents, social workers, educators—apply ourselves with still greater vigilance and vision to the task of bringing up a better generation in a safer world.

You would think this would have put an end to moralizing readings of the book, although of course many of us have heard ourselves talking like John Ray, Jr., on too many occasions. Nabokov would have been outraged to think we needed telling that pedophilia was not a good thing—probably was outraged when it turned out we *did* need telling.

But what else is there if Dostoevsky and the educators are set aside? There is the flight into pure aesthetics, which Nabokov himself seems to recommend. No, does recommend:

For me a work of fiction exists only insofar as it affords me what I shall bluntly call aesthetic bliss, that is a sense of being somehow, somewhere, connected with other states of being where art (curiosity, tenderness, kindness, ecstasy) is the norm. There are not many such books. All the rest is either topical trash or what some call the Literature of Ideas, which very often is topical trash coming in huge blocks of plaster.

Many readers of Nabokov have taken this as their gospel, and of course the words in parentheses after "art" are alluring. But there is still the question of what emotions the work of art affords the reader, as distinct from the writer, and there is also the more urgent question of the writer's choosing to find his aesthetic bliss in a scandalous subject.

Earnest critics, Martin Amis has suggested, have often "feared for Nabokov's moral hygiene—wasn't there a bit too much brio in his empathy with the racked paedophile of *Lolita*?" Well, was there? Somewhere between the brio, too much or just right, and Nabokov's mischievously professed indifference to other people's morality lies the clue to whatever entertains us most and troubles us most in *Lolita*. When Nabokov says in a letter that an "unpleasant" quality that an editor has found in *Pnin* "is a special trait of my work in general"—he goes on to talk of "nastiness" and a "disgusting" couple —he is not, I think, embracing vice nor licensing immorality. He is saying that curiosity, tenderness, and the rest can take you to strange places and make sense only in a world that constantly threatens them.

Nabokov's irony often works by a kind of doubling. His comic characters, and indeed he himself, disguise and mangle what he means, but they don't say the opposite. What's wrong with the idea of "ethical impact" is not the suggestion that a work of art could have some sort of moral effect but the preachy directness of the claim. The trick is to understand the moral obliquity of good books and the entanglement of instruction in pleasures that aren't at all instructive. It's important to remember that Humbert is not only a moral monster but a great comic hero. He is phenomenally funny about the world he lives in but also a figure of fun, disastrously prone to the unlucky coincidence. He trips over his own feet in the midst of his most stylish or impassioned moments. Sleepless beside the sleeping Lolita, he not only evokes his "burning life" and her vulnerability, he lets us know about trucks in the night and a nearby toilet in the hotel. ("It was a manly, energetic, deep-throated toilet, and it was used many times. Its gurgle and gush and long afterflow shook the wall behind me.") When he tells us he was "burning with desire and dyspepsia," we might think the alliterative sequence does enough to spoil the pathos, but Humbert goes onto tell us what he usually does for his digestive troubles: goes to the bathroom and takes a drink of water, "which is the best medicine I know in my case, except perhaps milk with radishes." How are we supposed to concentrate on his crime, as we want to, or on his longing, as he wants us to?

But of course we can think as well as laugh, and at the risk of sounding like a chastened John Ray, Jr., I would suggest that one of the important things Nabokov's novel does is help us understand better just what an offense against a child is and understand this morally, not merely technically. But it does this only by getting everything slightly wrong and leaving the rest to us. This is where we need to understand why Lolita is not a "Lolita."

Humbert's final repentance is so awful not only because he wallows in it, but because he comes so close to understanding what he has done. He has slept with a minor, abducted her, and is guilty of rape in a sense only slightly more complicated than it looks. He is in jail for the murder of Clare Quilty, but murder, of course, doesn't frighten distributors away. Humbert says that, if he were the judge, he would give himself thirty-five years for rape and dismiss the rest of the charges. He also makes clear that his real crime, and the real sadness in Lolita's story, lies not in his theft of her virtue but in his theft of her childhood. This is when he hears the children playing in the valley and thinks "that the hopelessly poignant thing was not Lolita's absence from my side, but the absence of her voice from that concord."

What's wrong with this? He has stolen her childhood, taken from her the years when she should still have been a child. But Humbert thinks, as I'm afraid many of us think when we are not children, of childhood as an idyll. His crime is to have deprived Lolita not of an idyll but of whatever childhood she might have had, and the terrible thing about the ruin of children is not the ruin of innocence but the wreck of possibility, even malign possibility.

There is more. The English writer Ros Coward, discussing pedophilia a couple of years ago, seemed to have Humbert in mind when she said that pedophiles are difficult to catch because they are often "extremely plausible and devious people." Coward also says that we still underrate the damage that adult sexual attention does to children, and we could think of childhood not only as the realm of possibility but as the name of a condition where the idea of consent cannot be in play, whether the children seem to consent or not. Of course many adults, under duress, also find themselves in this condition, but this should help us to understand the subtler forms of damage to children.

The most intimately horrible moment in the novel, ostensibly composed of a sample list of midcentury objects and a bit of narration, occurs at the end of part 1. Nabokov's art here is at its most oblique and at its most scrupulously, morally focused. Humbert has slept with Lolita and has brutally, impatiently, told her that her mother is dead. They reach the town of Lepingville, its name a tiny allusion to the "moral leprosy" of which John Ray, Jr., says Humbert is "a shining example":

> In the gay town of Lepingville I bought her four books of comics, a box of candy, a box of sanitary pads, two cokes, a manicure set, a travel clock with a luminous dial, a ring with a real topaz, a tennis racket, roller skates with white high shoes, field glasses, a portable radio set, chewing gum, a transparent raincoat, sunglasses, some more garments—swooners, shorts, all kinds of summer frocks. At the hotel we had separate rooms, but in the middle of the night she came sobbing into mine, and we made it up very gently. You see, she had absolutely nowhere else to go.

Plenty of horror in the sleek "you see" and the tyrannical satisfaction of the word "absolutely." But Humbert is not just the villain here, playing out some pedophile melodrama. There is, I'm sorry to say, a tenderness in his voice too, a sort of protectiveness, as if he were after all the right person to be looking after this little girl. If you were sickened before, you are even more sickened as you think this, and you realize that a double confusion reigns in this scene, in Humbert and Lolita, and that it centers on the unnamed notion of consent. This confusion is precisely Nabokov's point. Both characters know, or soon will, all about force and bribery and subjection and helplessness. Neither of them knows anything about consent. Humbert doesn't know that Lolita can't have consented, even when she seemed to, even when she came sobbing into his room. She doesn't know that the very chance of her consent has been destroyed for good.

### Note

1. The signers were J. R. Ackerley, Walter Allen, A. Alvarez, Isaiah Berlin, C. M. Bowra, Storm Jameson, Frank Kermode, Allen Lane, Margaret Lane, Rosamund Lehmann, Compton Mackenzie, Iris Murdoch, William Plomer, V. S. Pritchett, Alan Pryce-Jones, Peter Quennell, Herbert Read, Stephen Spender, Philip Toynbee, Bernard Wall, and Angus Wilson.

# Interview with Vladimir Nabokov

## HERBERT GOLD

◆　◆　◆

VLADIMIR NABOKOV LIVES with his wife, Véra, in the Montreux-Palace Hotel in Montreux, Switzerland, a resort city on Lake
Geneva, which was a favorite of Russian aristocrats of the last century.
They dwell in a connected series of hotel rooms that, like their houses and
apartments in the United States, seem impermanent, places of exile. Their
rooms include one used for visits by their son, Dmitri, and the *chambre de de-
barras*, where various items are deposited—Turkish and Japanese editions of
*Lolita*, other books, sporting equipment, an American flag.

Nabokov arises early in the morning and works. He does his writing on
filing cards, which are gradually copied, expanded, and rearranged until
they become his novels. During the warm season in Montreux he likes to
take the sun and swim at a pool in a garden near the hotel. His appearance
at sixty-eight is heavy, slow, and powerful. He is easily turned to both
amusement and annoyance, but prefers the former. His wife, an unequivocally devoted collaborator, is vigilant over him, writing his letters, taking
care of business, occasionally even interrupting him when she feels he
is saying the wrong thing. She is an exceptionally good-looking, trim,
and sober-eyed woman. The Nabokovs still go off on frequent butterfly-
hunting trips, though the distances they travel are limited by the fact that
they dislike flying.

The interviewer had sent ahead a number of questions. When he arrived at the Montreux-Palace, he found an envelope waiting for him—the questions had been shaken up and transformed into an interview. A few questions and answers were added later, before the interview's appearance in the 1967 Summer/Fall issue of the *Paris Review*. In accordance with Nabokov's wishes, all answers are given as he wrote them down. He claims that he needs to write his responses because of his unfamiliarity with English; this is a constant, seriocomic form of teasing. He speaks with a dramatic Cambridge accent, very slightly nuanced by an occasional Russian pronunciation. Spoken English is, in fact, no hazard to him. Misquotation, however, is a menace. There is no doubt that Nabokov feels as a tragic loss the conspiracy of history that deprived him of his native Russia and that brought him in middle life to doing his life's work in a language that is not that of his first dreams. However, his frequent apologies for his grasp of English clearly belong in the context of Nabokov's special mournful joking: he means it, he does not mean it, he is grieving for his loss, he is outraged if anyone criticizes his style, he pretends to be just a poor lonely foreigner, he is as American "as April in Arizona."

Nabokov is now at work on a long novel, *Ada* (1969), that explores the mysteries and ambiguities of time. When he speaks of this book, his voice and gaze are those of a delighted and bemused young poet eager to get to the task.

INTERVIEWER: Good morning. Let me ask forty-odd questions.

NABOKOV: Good morning. I am ready.

INTERVIEWER: Your sense of the immorality of the relationship between Humbert Humbert and Lolita is very strong. In Hollywood and New York, however, relationships are frequent between men of forty and girls very little older than Lolita. They marry—to no particular public outrage; rather, public cooing.

NABOKOV: No, it is not *my* sense of the immorality of the Humbert Humbert–Lolita relationship that is strong; it is Humbert's sense. *He* cares, I do not. *I* do not give a damn for public morals, in America or elsewhere. And, anyway, cases of men in their forties marrying girls in their teens or early twenties have no bearing on Lolita whatever. Humbert was fond of "little girls"—not simply "young girls." Nymphets are girl-children, not starlets and "sex kittens." Lolita was twelve, not eighteen when Humbert met her. You may remember that by the time she is fourteen, he refers to her as his "aging mistress."

INTERVIEWER: One critic (Alan Pryce-Jones) has said about you that "his feelings are like no one else's." Does this make sense to you? Or does it mean that you know your feelings better than others know theirs? Or that you have discovered yourself at other levels? Or simply that your history is unique?

NABOKOV: I do not recall that article; but if a critic makes such a statement, it must surely mean that he has explored the feelings of literally millions of people, in at least three countries, before reaching his conclusion. If so, I am a rare fowl indeed. If, on the other hand, he has merely limited himself to quizzing members of his family or club, his statement cannot be discussed seriously.

INTERVIEWER: Another critic has written that your "worlds are static. They may become tense with obsession, but they do not break apart like the worlds of everyday reality." Do you agree? Is there a static quality in your view of things?

NABOKOV: Whose "reality"? "Everyday" where? Let me suggest that the very term "everyday reality" is utterly static since it presupposes a situation that is permanently observable, essentially objective, and universally known. I suspect you have invented that expert on "everyday reality." Neither exists.

INTERVIEWER: *He* does (*names him*). A third critic has said that you "diminish" your characters "to the point where they become ciphers in a cosmic farce." I disagree; Humbert, while comic, retains a touching and insistent quality—that of the spoiled artist.

NABOKOV: I would put it differently: Humbert Humbert is a vain and cruel wretch who manages to appear "touching." That epithet, in its true, tear-iridized sense, can only apply to my poor little girl. Besides, how can I "diminish" to the level of ciphers, et cetera, characters that I have invented myself? One can "diminish" a biographee, but not an eidolon.

INTERVIEWER: E. M. Forster speaks of his major characters sometimes taking over and dictating the course of his novels. Has this ever been a problem for you, or are you in complete command?

NABOKOV: My knowledge of Mr. Forster's works is limited to one novel, which I dislike; and anyway, it was not he who fathered that trite little whimsy about characters getting out of hand; it is as old as the quills, although of course one sympathizes with *his* people if they try to wiggle out of that trip to India or wherever he takes them. My characters are galley slaves.

INTERVIEWER: Clarence Brown of Princeton has pointed out striking similarities in your work. He refers to you as "extremely repetitious" and that in wildly different ways you are in essence saying the same thing. He speaks of fate being the "muse of Nabokov." Are you consciously aware of "repeating yourself" or, to put it another way, that you strive for conscious unity to your shelf of books?

NABOKOV: I do not think I have seen Clarence Brown's essay, but he may have something there. Derivative writers seem versatile because they imitate many others, past and present. Artistic originality has only its own self to copy.

INTERVIEWER: Do you think literary criticism is at all purposeful? Either in general, or specifically about your own books? Is it ever instructive?

NABOKOV: The purpose of a critique is to say something about a book the critic has or has not read. Criticism can be instructive in the sense that it gives readers, including the author of the book, some information about the critic's intelligence, or honesty, or both.

INTERVIEWER: And the function of the editor? Has one ever had literary advice to offer?

NABOKOV: By "editor" I suppose you mean proofreader. Among these I have known limpid creatures of limitless tact and tenderness who would discuss with me a semicolon as if it were a point of honor—which, indeed, a point of art often is. But I have also come across a few pompous avuncular brutes who would attempt to "make suggestions" which I countered with a thunderous "stet"!

INTERVIEWER: Are you a lepidopterist, stalking your victims? If so, doesn't your laughter startle them?

NABOKOV: On the contrary, it lulls them into the state of torpid security which an insect experiences when mimicking a dead leaf. Though by no means an avid reader of reviews dealing with my own stuff, I happen to remember the essay by a young lady who attempted to find entomological symbols in my fiction. The essay might have been amusing had she known something about Lepidoptera. Alas, she revealed complete ignorance, and the muddle of terms she employed proved to be only jarring and absurd.

INTERVIEWER: How would you define your alienation from the so-called White Russian refugees?

NABOKOV: Well, historically I am a "White Russian" myself since all Russians who left Russia as my family did in the first years of the Bolshevist tyranny because of their opposition to it were and remained White Russians in the large sense. But these refugees were split into as many social fractions and political factions as was the entire nation before the Bolshevist coup. I do not mix with "black-hundred" White Russians and do not mix with the so-called "bolshevizans," that is "pinks." On the other hand, I have friends among intellectual constitutional monarchists as well as among intellectual social revolutionaries. My father was an old-fashioned liberal, and I do not mind being labeled an old-fashioned liberal, too.

INTERVIEWER: How would you define your alienation from present-day Russia?

NABOKOV: As a deep distrust of the phony thaw now advertised. As a constant awareness of unredeemable iniquities. As a complete indifference to all that moves a patriotic Sovetski man of today. As the keen satisfaction of having discerned as early as 1918 the *meshchantsvo* (petty bourgeois smugness, philistine essence) of Leninism.

INTERVIEWER: How do you now regard the poets Blok and Mandelshtam and others who were writing in the days before you left Russia?

NABOKOV: I read them in my boyhood, more than a half century ago. Ever since that time I have remained passionately fond of Blok's lyrics. His long pieces are weak, and the famous *The Twelve* is dreadful, self-consciously couched in a phony "primitive" tone, with a pink cardboard Jesus Christ glued on at the end. As to Mandelshtam, I also knew him by heart, but he gave me a less fervent pleasure. Today, through the prism of a tragic fate, his poetry seems greater than it actually is. I note incidentally that professors of literature still assign these two poets to different schools. There is only one school: that of talent.

INTERVIEWER: I know your work has been read and is attacked in the Soviet Union. How would you feel about a Soviet edition of your work?

NABOKOV: Oh, they are welcome to my work. As a matter of fact, the Editions Victor are bringing out my *Invitation to a Beheading* in a reprint of the original Russian of 1935, and a New York publisher (Phaedra) is printing my Russian translation of *Lolita*. I am sure the Soviet government will be happy to admit officially a novel that seems to contain a prophecy of Hitler's regime and a novel that condemns bitterly the American system of motels.

INTERVIEWER: Have you ever had contact with Soviet citizens? Of what sort?

NABOKOV: I have practically no contact with them, though I did once agree, in the early thirties or late twenties, to meet—out of sheer curiosity—an agent from Bolshevist Russia who was trying hard to get émigré writers and artists to return to the fold. He had a double name, Lebedev something, and had written a novelette entitled *Chocolate*, and I thought I might have some sport with him. I asked him would I be permitted to write freely and would I be able to leave Russia if I did not like it there. He said that I would be so busy liking it there, that I would have no time to dream of going abroad again. I would, he said, be perfectly free to choose any of the many themes Soviet Russia bountifully allows a writer to use, such as farms, factories, forests in Fakistan—oh, lots of fascinating subjects? I said farms, et cetera, bored me, and my wretched seducer soon gave up. He had better luck with the composer Prokofiev.

INTERVIEWER: Do you consider yourself an American?

NABOKOV: Yes, I do. I am as American as April in Arizona. The flora, the fauna, the air of the Western states, are my links with Asiatic and Arctic Russia. Of course, I owe too much to the Russian language and landscape to be emotionally involved in, say, American regional literature, or Indian dances, or pumpkin pie on a spiritual plane; but I do feel a suffusion of warm, lighthearted pride when I show my green U.S.A. passport at European frontiers. Crude criticism of American affairs offends and distresses me. In home politics I am strongly antisegregationist. In foreign policy, I am definitely on the government's side. And when in doubt, I always follow the simple method of choosing that line of conduct which may be the most displeasing to the Reds and the Russells.

INTERVIEWER: Is there a community of which you consider yourself a part?

NABOKOV: Not really. I can mentally collect quite a large number of individuals whom I am fond of, but they would form a very disparate and discordant group if gathered in real life, on a real island. Otherwise, I would say that I am fairly comfortable in the company of American intellectuals who have read my books.

INTERVIEWER: What is your opinion of the academic world as a milieu for the creative writer? Could you speak specifically of the value or detriment of your teaching at Cornell?

NABOKOV: A first-rate college library with a comfortable campus around it is a fine milieu for a writer. There is, of course, the problem of educating the young. I remember how once, between terms, not at Cornell, a student brought a transistor set with him into the reading room. He managed to state that (1) he was playing "classical" music; that (2) he was doing it "softly"; and that (3) "there were not many readers around in summer." I was there, a one-man multitude.

INTERVIEWER: Would you describe your relationship with the contemporary literary community? With Edmund Wilson, Mary McCarthy, your magazine editors, and book publishers?

NABOKOV: The only time I ever collaborated with any writer was when I translated with Edmund Wilson Pushkin's *Mozart and Salieri* for the *New Republic* twenty-five years ago, a rather paradoxical recollection in view of his making such a fool of himself last year when he had the audacity of questioning my understanding of *Eugene Onegin*. Mary McCarthy, on the other hand, has been very kind to me recently in the same *New Republic*, although I do think she added quite a bit of her own angelica to the pale fire of Kinbote's plum pudding. I prefer not to mention here my relationship with Girodias, but I have answered in *Evergreen* his scurvy article in the Olympia anthology. Otherwise, I am on excellent terms with all my publishers. My warm friendship with Katharine White and Bill Maxwell of the *New Yorker* is something the most arrogant author cannot evoke without gratitude and delight.

INTERVIEWER: Could you say something of your work habits? Do you write to a preplanned chart? Do you jump from one section to another, or do you move from the beginning through to the end?

NABOKOV: The pattern of the thing precedes the thing. I fill in the gaps of the crossword at any spot I happen to choose. These bits I write on index cards until the novel is done. My schedule is flexible, but I am rather particular about my instruments: lined Bristol cards and well sharpened, not too hard, pencils capped with erasers.

INTERVIEWER: Is there a particular picture of the world which you wish to develop? The past is very present for you, even in a novel of the "future," such as *Bend Sinister*. Are you a "nostalgist"? In what time would you prefer to live?

NABOKOV: In the coming days of silent planes and graceful aircycles, and cloudless silvery skies, and a universal system of padded underground roads to which trucks shall be relegated like Morlocks. As to the past, I would not mind retrieving from various corners of spacetime certain lost comforts, such as baggy trousers and long, deep bathtubs.

INTERVIEWER: You know, you do not have to answer *all* my Kinbote-like questions.

NABOKOV: It would never do to start skipping the tricky ones. Let us continue.

INTERVIEWER: Besides writing novels, what do you, or would you, like most to do?

NABOKOV: Oh, hunting butterflies, of course, and studying them. The pleasures and rewards of literary inspiration are nothing beside the rapture of discovering a new organ under the microscope or an undescribed species on a mountainside in Iran or Peru. It is not improbable that had there been no revolution in Russia, I would have devoted myself entirely to lepidopterology and never written any novels at all.

INTERVIEWER: What is most characteristic of poshlust in contemporary writing? Are there temptations for you in the sin of poshlust? Have you ever fallen?

NABOKOV: "Poshlust," or in a better transliteration *poshlost*, has many nuances, and evidently I have not described them clearly enough in my little book on Gogol, if you think one can ask anybody if he is tempted by *poshlost*. Corny trash, vulgar clichés, philistinism in all its phases, imitations of imitations, bogus profundities, crude, moronic, and dishonest pseudo-literature—these are obvious examples. Now, if we want to pin down *poshlost* in contemporary writing, we must look for it in Freudian symbolism, moth-eaten mythologies, social comment, humanistic messages, political allegories, overconcern with class or race, and the journalistic generalities we all know. *Poshlost* speaks in such concepts as "America is no better than Russia" or "We all share in Germany's guilt." The flowers of *poshlost* bloom in such phrases and terms as "the moment of truth," "charisma," "existential" (used seriously), "dialogue" (as applied to political talks between nations), and "vocabulary" (as applied to a dauber). Listing in one breath Auschwitz, Hiroshima, and Vietnam is seditious *poshlost*. Belonging to a very select club (which sports *one* Jewish name—that of the treasurer) is genteel *poshlost*. Hack reviews are frequently *poshlost*, but it also lurks in certain highbrow essays. *Poshlost* calls Mr. Blank a great poet and Mr. Bluff a great novelist. One of *poshlost's* favorite breeding places has always been the Art Exhibition; there it is produced by so-called sculptors working with the tools of wreckers, building crankshaft cretins of stainless steel, zen stereos, polystyrene stinkbirds, objects *trouvés* in latrines, cannon balls, canned balls. There we admire the *gabinetti* wall patterns of so-called abstract artists, Freudian surrealism, roric smudges, and Rorschach blots— all of it as corny in its own right as the academic "September Morns" and "Florentine Flowergirls" of half a century ago. The list is long, and, of course, everybody has his *bête noire*, his black pet, in the series. Mine is that airline ad: the snack served by an obsequious wench to a young couple— she eyeing ecstatically the cucumber canapé, he admiring wistfully the hostess. And, of course, *Death in Venice*. You see the range.

INTERVIEWER: Are there contemporary writers you follow with great pleasure?

NABOKOV: There are several such writers, but I shall not name them. Anonymous pleasure hurts nobody.

INTERVIEWER: Do you follow some with great pain?

NABOKOV: No. Many accepted authors simply do not exist for me. Their names are engraved on empty graves, their books are dummies, they are complete nonentities insofar as my taste in reading is concerned. Brecht, Faulkner, Camus, many others, mean absolutely nothing to me, and I must fight a suspicion of conspiracy against my brain when I see blandly accepted as "great literature" by critics and fellow authors Lady Chatterley's copulations or the pretentious nonsense of Mr. Pound, that total fake. I note he has replaced Dr. Schweitzer in some homes.

INTERVIEWER: As an admirer of Borges and Joyce you seem to share their pleasure in teasing the reader with tricks and puns and puzzles. What do you think the relationship should be between reader and author?

NABOKOV: I do not recollect any puns in Borges, but then I read him only in translation. Anyway, his delicate little tales and miniature Minotaurs have nothing in common with Joyce's great machines. Nor do I find many puzzles in that most lucid of novels, *Ulysses*. On the other hand, I detest *Punningans Wake* in which a cancerous growth of fancy word-tissue hardly redeems the dreadful joviality of the folklore and the easy, too easy, allegory.

INTERVIEWER: What have you learned from Joyce?

NABOKOV: Nothing.

INTERVIEWER: Oh, come.

NABOKOV: James Joyce has not influenced me in any manner whatsoever. My first brief contact with *Ulysses* was around 1920 at Cambridge University, when a friend, Peter Mrozovski, who had brought a copy from Paris, chanced to read to me, as he stomped up and down my digs, one or two spicy passages from Molly's monologue, which, *entre nous soit dit*, is the weakest chapter in the book. Only fifteen years later, when I was already well formed as a writer and reluctant to learn or unlearn anything, I read *Ulysses* and liked it enormously. I am indifferent to *Finnegans Wake* as I am to all regional literature written in dialect—even if it be the dialect of genius.

INTERVIEWER: Aren't you doing a book about James Joyce?

NABOKOV: But not only about him. What I intend to do is publish a number of twenty-page essays on several works—*Ulysses*, *Madame Bovary*, Kafka's *Transformation*, *Don Quixote*, and others—all based on my Cornell and Harvard lectures. I remember with delight tearing apart *Don Quixote*, a cruel and crude old book, before six hundred students in Memorial Hall, much to the horror and embarrassment of some of my more conservative colleagues.

INTERVIEWER: What about other influences? Pushkin?

NABOKOV: In a way—no more than, say, Tolstoy or Turgenev were influenced by the pride and purity of Pushkin's art.

INTERVIEWER: Gogol?

NABOKOV: I was careful *not* to learn anything from him. As a teacher, he is dubious and dangerous. At his worst, as in his Ukrainian stuff, he is a worthless writer; at his best, he is incomparable and inimitable.

INTERVIEWER: Anyone else?

NABOKOV: H. G. Wells, a great artist, was my favorite writer when I was a boy. *The Passionate Friends, Ann Veronica, The Time Machine, The Country of the Blind,* all these stories are far better than anything Bennett, or Conrad or, in fact, any of Wells's contemporaries could produce. His sociological cogitations can be safely ignored, of course, but his romances and fantasies are superb. There was an awful moment at dinner in our St. Petersburg house one night when Zinaïda Vengerov, his translator, informed Wells, with a toss of her head: "You know, *my* favorite work of yours is *The Lost World.*" "She means the war the Martians lost," said my father quickly.

INTERVIEWER: Did you learn from your students at Cornell? Was the experience purely a financial one? Did teaching teach you anything valuable?

NABOKOV: My method of teaching precluded genuine contact with my students. At best, they regurgitated a few bits of my brain during examinations. Every lecture I delivered had been carefully, lovingly handwritten and typed out, and I leisurely read it out in class, sometimes stopping to rewrite a sentence and sometimes repeating a paragraph—a mnemonic prod which, however, seldom provoked any change in the rhythm of wrists taking it down. I welcomed the few shorthand experts in my audience, hoping they would communicate the information they stored to their less fortunate comrades. Vainly I tried to replace my appearances at the lectern by taped records to be played over the college radio. On the other hand, I deeply enjoyed the chuckle of appreciation in this or that warm spot of the lecture hall at this or that point of my lecture. My best reward comes from those former students of mine who, ten or fifteen years later, write to me to say that they now understand what I wanted of them when I taught them to visualize Emma Bovary's mistranslated hair-do or the arrangement of rooms in the Samsa household or the two homosexuals in *Anna Karenina.* I do not know if I learned anything from teaching, but I know I amassed an invaluable amount of exciting information in analyzing a dozen novels for my students. My salary, as you happen to know, was not exactly a princely one.

INTERVIEWER: Is there anything you would care to say about the collaboration your wife has given you?

NABOKOV: She presided as advisor and judge over the making of my first fiction in the early twenties. I have read to her all my stories and novels at least twice, and she has reread them all when typing them and correcting proofs and checking translations into several languages. One day in 1950, at Ithaca, New York, she was responsible for stopping me and urging delay and second thoughts as, beset with technical difficulties and doubts, I was carrying the first chapters of *Lolita* to the garden incinerator.

INTERVIEWER: What is your relation to the translations of your books?

NABOKOV: In the case of languages my wife and I know or can read—English, Russian, French, and to a certain extent German and Italian—the system is a strict checking of every sentence. In the case of Japanese or Turkish versions, I try not to imagine the disasters that probably bespatter every page.

INTERVIEWER: What are your plans for future work?

NABOKOV: I am writing a new novel, but of this I cannot speak. Another project I have been nursing for some time is the publication of the complete screenplay of *Lolita* that I made for Kubrick. Although there are just enough borrowings from it in his version to justify my legal position as author of the script, the film is only a blurred skimpy glimpse of the marvelous picture I imagined and set down scene by scene during the six months I worked in a Los Angeles villa. I do not wish to imply that Kubrick's film is mediocre; in its own right, it is first-rate, but it is not what I wrote. A tinge of *poshlost* is often given by the cinema to the novel it distorts and coarsens in its crooked glass. Kubrick, I think, avoided this fault in his version, but I shall never understand why he did not follow my directions and dreams. It is a great pity; but at least I shall be able to have people read my *Lolita* play in its original form.

INTERVIEWER: If you had the choice of one and only one book by which you would be remembered, which one would it be?

NABOKOV: The one I am writing or rather dreaming of writing. Actually, I shall be remembered by *Lolita* and my work on *Eugene Onegin*.

INTERVIEWER: Do you feel you have any conspicuous or secret flaw as a writer?

NABOKOV: The absence of a natural vocabulary. An odd thing to confess, but true. Of the two instruments in my possession, one—my native tongue—I can no longer use, and this not only because I lack a Russian audience, but also because the excitement of verbal adventure in the Russian medium faded away gradually after I turned to English in 1940. My English, this second instrument I have always had, is however a stiffish, artificial thing, which may be all right for describing a sunset or an insect, but which cannot conceal poverty of syntax and paucity of domestic diction when I need the shortest road between warehouse and shop. An old Rolls Royce is not always preferable to a plain jeep.

INTERVIEWER: What do you think about the contemporary competitive ranking of writers?

NABOKOV: Yes, I have noticed that in this respect our professional book reviewers are veritable bookmakers. Who's in, who's out, and where are the snows of yesteryear. All very amusing. I am a little sorry to be left out. Nobody can decide if I am a middle-aged American writer or an old Russian writer—or an ageless international freak.

INTERVIEWER: What is your great regret in your career?

NABOKOV: That I did not come earlier to America. I would have liked to have lived in New York in the thirties. Had my Russian novels been translated then, they might have provided a shock and a lesson for pro-Soviet enthusiasts.

INTERVIEWER: Are there significant disadvantages to your present fame?

NABOKOV: *Lolita* is famous, not I. I am an obscure, doubly obscure, novelist with an unpronounceable name.

# Suggested Reading

Alexandrov, Vladimir E. *Nabokov's Otherworld*. Princeton, N.J.: Princeton University Press, 1991.

———, ed. *The Garland Companion to Vladimir Nabokov*. New York: Garland, 1995.

Amis, Martin, "*Lolita* Reconsidered." *Atlantic Monthly*, Sept. 1992, 109–20.

Appel, Alfred, Jr., ed. *The Annotated Lolita*. Rev. ed. New York: Vintage, 1991.

———. *Nabokov's Dark Cinema*. New York: Oxford University Press, 1974.

Boyd, Brian. *Vladimir Nabokov: The American Years*. Princeton, N.J.: Princeton University Press, 1991.

———. *Vladimir Nabokov: The Russian Years*. Princeton, N.J.: Princeton University Press, 1990.

Clegg, Christine, ed. *Vladimir Nabokov*. Lolita: *A Reader's Guide to Essential Criticism*. Cambridge: Icon, 2000.

Clifton, Gladys M. "Humbert Humbert and the Limits of Artistic License." In Rivers and Nicol, *Nabokov's Fifth Arc*, 153–69.

Connolly, Julian W., ed. *Nabokov and His Fiction: New Perspectives*. Cambridge: Cambridge University Press, 1999.

Cornwell, Neil. *Vladimir Nabokov*. Jackson: University Press of Mississippi, 1999.

Couturier, Maurice. "Nabokov's Performative Writing." In *Les Américanistes: New French Criticism on Modern American Fiction*, 157–81, 225–26. Ed. Ira D. Johnson and Christiane Johnson. Port Washington, N.Y.: Kennikat, 1978.

Dolinin, Alexander. "*Lolita* in Russian." In Alexandrov, *Garland Companion to Vladimir Nabokov,* 321–30.

Dupee, F. W. "A Preface to *Lolita.*" *Anchor Review* (June 1957): 1–14. Rpt. in Dupee, "*The King of the Cats" and Other Remarks on Writers and Writing,* 117–31. New York: Noonday, 1965.

Ermarth, Elizabeth Deeds. "Conspicuous Construction; or, Kristeva, Nabokov, and the Anti-Realist Critique." *Novel* no. 21, 2–3 (Winter–Spring 1988): 330–39.

Field, Andrew. *Nabokov: His Life in Art.* Boston: Little, Brown, 1967.

Grayson, Jane, Arnold McMillin, and Priscilla Meyer, eds. *Nabokov's World,* vol. 1: *The Shape of Nabokov's World* and vol. 2: *Reading Nabokov.* Basingstoke, U.K., and New York: Palgrave, 2002.

Johnson, Kurt, and Steve Coates. *Nabokov's Blues: The Scientific Odyssey of a Literary Genius.* Cambridge, Mass.: Zoland, 1999.

Josipovici, Gabriel. "*Lolita*: Parody and the Pursuit of Beauty." In Josipovici, *The World and the Book: A Study of Modern Fiction,* 201–20. London: Macmillan, 1971.

Juliar, Michael. *Vladimir Nabokov: A Descriptive Bibliography.* New York: Garland, 1986.

Kauffman, Linda. "Framing Lolita: Is There a Woman in the Text?" In Kauffman, *Special Delivery: Epistolary Modes in Modern Fiction,* 53–79. Chicago: University of Chicago Press, 1992.

Levine, Robert T. "'My Ultraviolet Darling': The Loss of Lolita's Childhood." *Modern Fiction Studies* 25, no. 3 (1979): 471–79.

Nabokov, Vladimir. *The Enchanter.* Trans. Dmitri Nabokov. New York: Putnam, 1986.

———. *Lectures on Literature.* Ed. Fredson Bowers. New York: Harcourt Brace, 1980.

———. *Lolita: A Screenplay.* New York: McGraw-Hill, 1974.

———. *Speak, Memory: An Autobiography Revisited.* New York: Putnam, 1966.

———. *Strong Opinions.* New York: McGraw-Hill, 1973.

Page, Norman, ed. *Nabokov: The Critical Heritage.* London: Routledge, 1982.

Pifer, Ellen. "Her Monster, His Nymphet: Nabokov and Mary Shelley." In Connolly, *Nabokov and His Fiction,* 158–76.

———. "*Lolita.*" In Alexandrov, *Garland Companion to Vladimir Nabokov,* 305–21.

———. *Nabokov and the Novel.* Cambridge, Mass.: Harvard University Press, 1980.

Raguet-Bouvart, Christine. "That Intangible Island of Entranced Time: Vladimir Nabokov's *Lolita.*" In *Sounding the Depths: Water as Metaphor in North American Literatures,* 205–18. Ed. Gayle Wurst and Christine Raguet-Bouvart. Liège, Belgium: Liège Language and Literature, 1998.

Rampton, David. *Nabokov: A Critical Study of the Novels.* Cambridge: Cambridge University Press, 1984.

Rivers, J. E., and Charles Nicol, eds. *Nabokov's Fifth Arc: Nabokov and Others on His Life's Work.* Austin: University of Texas Press, 1982.

Roth, Phyllis A., ed. *Critical Essays on Vladimir Nabokov.* Boston: Hall, 1984.

Schiff, Stephen. *Lolita: The Book of the Film.* New York: Applause, 1998.

Shapiro, Gavriel, ed. *Nabokov at Cornell.* Ithaca, N.Y.: Cornell University Press, in press.

Toker, Leona. *Nabokov: The Mystery of Literary Structures.* Ithaca, N.Y.: Cornell University Press, 1989.

Trilling, Lionel. "The Last Lover: Vladimir Nabokov's *Lolita*." *Griffin* 7 (Aug. 1958): 4–21. Rpt. in *Encounter* 11 (Oct. 1958): 9–19.

Walter, Brian. "Romantic Parody and the Ironic Muse in *Lolita*." *Essays in Literature* 22, no. 1 (Spring 1995): 123–43.

White, Edmund. "Nabokov: Beyond Parody." In *The Achievements of Vladimir Nabokov,* 5–27. Ed. George Gibian and Stephen Jan Parker. Ithaca, N.Y.: Cornell Center for International Studies, 1984.

Whiting, Frederick. "'The Strange Particularity of the Lover's Preference': Pedophilia, Pornography, and the Anatomy of Monstrosity in *Lolita*." *American Literature* 70, no. 4 (Dec. 1998): 833–62.

Wood, Michael. *The Magician's Doubts: Nabokov and the Risks of Fiction.* London: Chatto and Windus, 1994.